RESTRUCTURING F
CONVERGENCES A.

Social policies in many liberal welfare states have undergone significant change in recent years; this is especially true in regard to programs for families with children. Increasingly, governments are making family policy trade-offs, reducing support for some families but improving it for others. Why are such trade-offs occurring, and how do governments differ in their approach to family social policy? This study addresses these questions by examining the political, demographic, and socio-economic factors influencing the restructuring of family-related programs in countries belonging to the Organisation for Economic Co-operation and Development (OECD).

Adopting a feminist political economy approach, Maureen Baker shows that while some governments encourage their citizens to see children as 'future resources,' and promote strong support for reproductive health programs, child welfare services, women's refuges, subsidized childcare, and pay equity, others make such claims while simultaneously reducing family incomes through the deregulation of labour markets and restrictions on income support. Ultimately, Baker demonstrates that nation states with the best outcomes for families offer a variety of social supports, which are increasingly important as global markets reduce economic security for some families while improving the financial situation of others. This study also explores strategies employed by states to absorb or resist international pressures, and the reasons why some states tenaciously defend their family policy traditions while others restructure according to international guidelines.

Drawing from nation-based research, cross-national studies, and international databases, *Restructuring Family Policies* successfully integrates mainstream academic debates about restructuring welfare states with feminist research findings and current policy concerns.

MAUREEN BAKER is a professor in the Department of Sociology at the University of Auckland.

MAUREEN BAKER

Restructuring Family Policies

Convergences and Divergences

UNIVERSITY OF TORONTO PRESS
Toronto Buffalo London

© University of Toronto Press Incorporated 2006
Toronto Buffalo London
Printed in Canada

ISBN-13: 978-0-8020-8783-6 (cloth)
ISBN-10: 0-8020-8783-3 (cloth)

ISBN-13: 978-0-8020-8571-9 (paper)
ISBN-10: 0-8020-8571-7 (paper)

∞

Printed on acid-free paper

Library and Archives Canada Cataloguing in Publication

Baker, Maureen
Restructuring family policies / Maureen Baker.

Includes index.
ISBN-13: 978-0-8020-8783-6 (bound)
ISBN-13: 978-0-8020-8571-9 (pbk.)
ISBN-10: 0-8020-8783-3 (bound)
ISBN-10: 0-8020-8571-7 (pbk.)
1. Family policy.   I. Title.
HQ518.B343 2006   362.82'561   C2006-903353-6

University of Toronto Press acknowledges the financial assistance to its publishing program of the Canada Council for the Arts and the Ontario Arts Council.

University of Toronto Press acknowledges the financial support for its publishing activities of the Government of Canada through the Book Publishing Industry Development Program (BPIDP).

Contents

List of Tables ix

Preface xi

1 Restructuring Family Policies 3

The Focus of This Book 5
Methodology 7
Chapter Outline 9
Defining Key Terms 13
   Defining 'Families' 13
   Defining 'Family Policy' 15
   Defining 'Restructuring' 16
   Globalization and Restructuring 18
Conclusion 22

2 Socio-demographic Changes and Family Policy Restructuring 23

Rising Cohabitation Rates 24
   Gay and Lesbian Cohabitation 26
Declining Fertility but More Births outside Marriage 29
Influences on Family Demography 34
   Work Patterns Influence Family Patterns and Practices 34
   Changing Technology Influences Family Patterns 37
   Changing Ideas Influence Family Patterns and Practices 38
Conclusion 40

vi Contents

3 Welfare Regimes, National Politics, and Family Policies 41

Conceptualizing Welfare Regimes 42
  Liberal or Residual Welfare Regimes 43
  Corporatist or Conservative Regimes 44
  Social Democratic Welfare Regimes 45
  Welfare Regimes as Ideal Types 46
Debates about Welfare Regimes 47
  Feminist Critiques of Welfare Regimes 48
Alternative Welfare Regimes Focusing on Caring and Family 51
Comparing State Support for Women as Mothers and Workers 54
Comparing State Support for Families in General 56
The Influence of National Politics on Policy Debates 59
Conclusion 62

4 Growing Internationalization and Family Policies 65

The Growing Internationalization of Labour Markets and Trade 65
Increased International Migration, Travel, and Communication 70
Pressure from International Organizations to Reform Family
    Policies 75
Freer Trade, Neoliberal Restructuring, and Families 79
Conclusion 81

5 Reproductive Health and Childbirth 84

Basic Indicators of Well-being 85
Reproductive Health Policies and Services 87
  Contraception Programs and Sexuality 87
  Access to Abortion 91
Fertility and the State 95
  Maternity Care Policies and Practices 97
  The 'Medicalization' of Childbirth 99
  Breastfeeding Policies and Practices 104
  Medically Assisted Conception 106
Conclusion 109

6 Work, Gender, and Parenthood 113

Parenthood and Paid Work 113
Concerns about Maternal Employment 117

Contents vii

Making Adaptations for Earning and Caring   119
Policy Approaches to Working Parents   122
Differing Models of Maternity/Parental Benefits   126
  Targeting Benefits to Mothers   128
  Targeting Benefits to Parents   129
  The Laissez-Faire Model   130
Whose Interests Are Protected by Various Leave Policies?   131
Reforming Parental Leave Policies   133
The Gendered Division of Domestic Work   136
Conclusion   140

7 The Care and Welfare of Children   143

Childcare Policies for Employed Mothers   144
  Funding and Regulating Childcare   144
  Cross-national Variations in Childcare Programs   147
  The Growing Demand for High-Quality Childcare   149
State Support for Childcare at Home   153
'Legitimacy' and Adoption   155
From Foster Care to Kin Care   158
Children's Rights and Programs to Counter Abuse   160
Conclusion   164

8 Social Housing and Income Support   168

Recent Arguments about Family Income Support   169
  The Need to Reduce 'Child Poverty'   169
  Preventing 'Social Exclusion' Is More Important Than
    Reducing Poverty   174
  Benefit Recipients Should Become More Employable   177
  Investing in Children   179
Social Housing and Family Well-being   180
State Income Support   184
  Restructuring Family Income Support in Canada   185
  Restructuring Income Support for Australian Families   196
  Comparing Canadian and Australian Reforms   202
Conclusion   207

9 Divorce, Child Support, and International Migration   209

Changing Attitudes to Divorce   209

Comparative Divorce Rates 211
Separation, Divorce, and Children 213
Lone Parenthood and Re-partnering 215
Legal and Policy Issues 217
  The Division of Family Assets and Spousal Support 217
  Guardianship, Custody, and Access to Children 218
  Awarding and Enforcing Child Support 221
International Agreements on the Enforcement of Child Support 223
  Child Custody, Domestic Violence, and the Hague Convention 224
  Child Custody, Domestic Violence, and Border Crossings in
    Specific Countries 226
    United States 227
    Canada 228
    Australia 229
    New Zealand 231
    England and Wales 231
    European Countries 232
Conclusion 233

10 Strengthening and Reducing Family Support 235

Which Family Programs Have Been Strengthened? 236
  The Expansion of Paid Parental Leave 236
  The Expansion of Childcare Services 238
  Child Benefits and Child Support 240
  Improvements to Child Welfare Practices 242
  New Ways of Dealing with Violence against Women 243
  Relationship Rights for Same-Sex Couples 243
  Better Pay for Part-time Workers in Some Jurisdictions 244
Which Family Benefits Have Been Eroded? 244
  Cuts to Income Support 244
  Reproductive Services 246
  Waiting Lists for Family Services 247
  Changing Employment Protections 248
Which Governments Best Protect Family Benefits? 249
Family Policy and Future Convergence 252

Works Cited 257

Index 289

Tables

2.1: Total Fertility Rate, 1970–5 and 1995–2000 (Births per Woman)   30
2.2: Teen Birth Rate, 1998 (Per 1,000 Women Aged 15–19 Years)   32
2.3: Extramarital Birth Rate as a Percentage of All Births   33
3.1: Countries Ranked Levels of General Family Support and Dual-Earner Support, 1985–90   58
4.1: Incidence of Part-time Employment in OECD Countries as a Percentage of All Female and Male Employment, 1990 and 2000   67
4.2: Youth Unemployment and Total Unemployment in Selected OECD Countries, 2001   69
4.3: Incidence of Low-Paid Employment in OECD Countries, by Gender, Mid-1990s   70
4.4: Foreign and Foreign-Born Populations, Change between 1990 and 2000 and Percentage of Total Population in 2000   72
4.5: International Rulings or Agreements on Specific Family Policy Areas   76
5.1: Percentage of Population under 15 Years and 60 Years and Older for Selected Countries, 2000   86
5.2: Fertility and Contraception Statistics for Selected Countries, 1995–2002   88
5.3: Induced Abortion Rates in Selected Countries   92
5.4: Birth Statistics in Selected Countries, Late 1990s–2002   100
6.1: Economically Active Mothers and Fathers with a Child Aged 0–10 Years, 1985–93   114
6.2: Hourly Earnings of Women vs. Men, 1998–2001 (Gender Wage Ratio)   115
6.3: Maternity/Parental Leave Benefits in Selected OECD Countries   127

- 7.1: Child Maltreatment Deaths for Selected Countries, 2000   163
- 8.1: Child Poverty in Lone-Parent Families and Other Families   171
- 8.2: The Development of Income Support Programs in Selected Countries   186
- 9.1: Crude Divorce Rates in Selected OECD Countries, 1973–98 (Per 1,000 Mid-year Population)   212
- 10.1: Overview of the Erosion and Strengthening of Family Policies   245
- 10.2: Right/Left Views on Selected Family Policies   250

Preface

Numerous books and articles have been written about restructuring 'the welfare state,' but generalizations can be misleading. Policies and programs relating to different social issues (such as employment, child welfare, or health care) vary even within the same jurisdiction. If a country offers generous retirement benefits, it does not necessarily provide generous childcare to employed parents. This book focuses on the restructuring of 'family policy' in countries belonging to the Organisation for Economic Co-operation and Development (OECD). It acknowledges the increasing pressures on governments to restructure policies related to families with children, and questions which factors have the greatest impact, including new family patterns, globalizing labour markets, multi-country agreements, ideas about relationships, national politics, and existing structures for social provision.

As an expatriate Canadian living in New Zealand, I have found that the realities of global labour markets and new forms of communication certainly touch my own life. I work and live in New Zealand, publish and give presentations in Canada and other countries, and conduct my academic collaboration now almost exclusively through email. Employment takes more of us farther from 'home,' altering our relationships with kin, yet many of us are still able to maintain close contact with colleagues and family wherever they may live.

I want to express my sincere thanks to Virgil Duff at the University of Toronto Press for his continued support for my scholarly research in preparing this book. I also want to convey my appreciation to the anonymous reviewers, especially the second reviewer, who provided insightful and constructive comments on the initial draft. The University of Auckland provided several research and travel grants that enabled me to complete this book while teaching and doing administrative work. I especially appreciate the work of two former graduate students from the Sociology Department of the University of Auckland, Lucy Husbands and Magdalena Harris, who helped locate statistics and specific studies and provided some of the research data for this book. As always, I am indebted to David Tippin for providing valuable comments on the final draft and sharing my enthusiasm for life in the 'winterless north' of New Zealand.

Maureen Baker
Auckland, New Zealand
January 2006

RESTRUCTURING FAMILY POLICIES:
CONVERGENCES AND DIVERGENCES

1 Restructuring Family Policies

In 2004, Pope John Paul II initiated a report asking governments to help women attend to 'their family duties' when they enter the labour market ('Pope has Warning' 2004). The Vatican rejected feminist ideologies that men and women are essentially the same, and appealed to governments to assist women to cope with their 'maternal vocation,' suggesting that the recent decline in fertility, especially in southern Europe, is symptomatic of a 'breakdown in values.' Greater selfishness among couples that are 'more interested in consumer goods than creating life' was targeted as the cause of fertility decline. This papal warning is only one example of the growing pressure on welfare states to counteract current demographic trends by reforming family policies, as women's employment increases and birth rates fall throughout the world.

A second example of pressure on national governments comes from the European Union (EU). Although the legislative framework for the European Community was originally designed to govern trade relations, current EU legislation as well as cases brought before the European Court of Justice illustrate that a number of family issues underlie the field of social security (Hantrais 2000). Recently, the EU has developed equality directives on part-time and temporary work, and the concept of the parent-worker is becoming embedded in directives relating to the regulation of working time. The EU has also legislated against employment discrimination based on sexual preference, advocated the extension of abortion services, and promoted policies to reduce violence against women (Walby 2004). Even though EU institutions have little treaty power over family policy, they nevertheless carry out a fair amount of 'soft' politicking in the form of informing and urging member states (Ross 2001).

A third example of pressure on national government relates to policy debates about same-sex relationships, which debates are occurring in most OECD countries. Since 2001, several jurisdictions have passed legislation offering some measure of legal protection for lasting same-sex relationships. For example, in July 2004, after years of public pressure, the New Zealand Labour government introduced a bill into Parliament to legalize 'civil unions,' and this bill became law in April 2005. The government did not call this new legal relationship 'marriage' because the conservative political parties and many religious organizations had already signalled that the word held specific meaning for them. In early parliamentary debates, conservative opponents argued that although this bill would ostensibly create two classes of marriage – one between men and women that is sanctified by the church and another between same-sex or cohabiting heterosexual couples who would gain some legal rights and responsibilities – it would in effect grant the latter the status of marriage.

Left-wing critics of civil unions also noted that the New Zealand bill would make significant amendments to welfare legislation because individual income-support benefits would be denied to people living together if their relationship was deemed to be 'in the nature of marriage' (McIvor 2004). Welfare groups expressed concern over how this would be determined and whether people deemed 'married' would be expected to pay back social benefits already received. This third example shows the contradictory pressures from local advocacy groups that oppose the same attempted reform for different reasons, in order to protect their beliefs and vested interests.

These three examples illustrate the range of pressures on national governments to reform family policy, pressures often based on different 'models' of family and different interpretations of the meaning and consequences of current socio-demographic trends. Decades ago, national and state governments in most industrialized countries developed social policies and programs to encourage heterosexual marriage, promote reproduction within marriage, bolster family income, protect vulnerable family members, and help parents combine employment and childcare. Most of these programs were initiated from the 1940s to the 1970s, often borrowing policy solutions from other countries with similar cultural backgrounds.

Since the initial creation of these programs, most governments have restructured their family policies after considerable political pressure from outside as well as within their national boundaries. International pressure on governments to restructure family policies seems to be increasing as more states sign multilateral trade agreements, labour markets become international, and investors and employers' groups promote neoliberal ideas and practices. International organizations such as the United Nations also continue to press governments to sign social policy agreements with new ideas about human rights and equity, while national advocacy groups join up with like-minded lobbies around the world. At the same time, new forms of technology now permit the separation of sex and reproduction, medically assisted conception, Internet sex, rapid international communication, and more global travel. All of the above trends have changed patterns of intimacy, altered ideas about the role of the state in family life, and encouraged family policy reform.

Within nation states, a variety of opinions prevail about the role of the state in family and personal life. Some groups focus on keeping the state out of issues relating to sexuality, cohabitation, or reproduction, while others argue for a return to 'family values' or privileging the rights of heterosexual married couples with children. Some want to maintain the status quo, while others attempt to restructure family policies to coincide with current ways of living. However, family policy is only one part of social policy, and programs for families with children are only one segment of family policy. Any reforms to family policies for children must consider the consequences for funding and delivering other forms of social provision (including programs for seniors). In addition, national or regional politics influences policy agendas and enables or prevents the implementation of particular policy options. In summary, this book deals with both external and internal political pressures on governments to reform family policy.

The Focus of This Book

The central focus of this book is an examination of the external and internal pressures on governments to restructure or amend social policies, programs, and services designed for families with children. In terms of external pressures, it investigates the ways that factors such as the internationalization of labour markets, increased transnational cooperation, more global communication and travel, and technological changes alter family life and affect policy reform. Do multilateral trade agreements encourage member states to 'harmonize' their family-related programs, or do these organizations merely focus on economic and employment policies? If international organizations push for the harmonization of family-related programs, which programs are included, what strategies do they use, and how successful are their efforts? Do these international pressures alter the power of national governments to control their own family policy agendas?

Socio-demographic patterns seem to be converging in OECD countries: declining legal marriage and fertility rates, more cohabitation and intermarriage, more dual-earner families, less stable relationships, and aging populations (Lewis 2003). I argue that this apparent convergence in family patterns is influenced by similar socio-economic conditions and prevailing ideas about personal choice and individual rights. Do these socio-demographic trends motivate national governments to restructure their family-related programs in similar ways? In this book, I ask if demographic changes have more impact on the restructuring of family policy than globalizing economies, neoliberal ideas, or national political pressures.

Within countries, I argue that political parties conceptualize family life in particular ways that offer more or less support for specific family configurations or 'models of family.' Conservative parties have tended to favour the male-breadwinner family in which wives are primarily viewed as the main care providers even when they earn household income. In contrast, centre-left political parties have typically offered more social and economic support to the 'parent-worker,' to mother-led households, and to alternatives to the nuclear family. I also note, as did Leira (2002), that a correlation is apparent between the 'welfare regime' favoured by countries over many years and the model of family they typically support. In chapter 2 the concept of welfare regimes is discussed in more detail, as well as the family benefits such regimes typically offer. Throughout the book, my research demonstrates that national and local politics, prevailing ideas about family, and existing institutional structures help shape family policy restructuring.

In this work I analyse ideas about the role of the state in family life, the public and political 'discourse' about family reform, and actual policy changes. I investigate what policy makers hope to gain by talking about 'parental responsibility' for child care and support, and why they have toughened their campaigns against 'deadbeat dads,' vilified 'welfare moms,' and cut social services. Some family services and benefits have always been controversial and were the culmination of long and difficult political struggles. The investigation extends to which programs have been eroded and which have been strengthened in recent years.

This book also explores the strategies states employ to incorporate or resist international pressures, and reasons why some states tenaciously defend their social policy traditions while others restructure their family laws and programs according to prevailing ideas or international guidelines. I examine the various justifications countries use when they assist the 'dual-earner family' or continue to support the 'male breadwinner/female caregiver model.' This book also questions whether governments of particular political orientations respond to external pressures in similar ways.

Some lobby groups and governments encourage their citizens to see children as a 'future resource' and promote strong public support for reproductive health programs, child welfare services, women's refuges, subsidized childcare, and pay equity. Others say that they are enhancing child benefits in order 'to fight child poverty' while engaging in neoliberal restructuring, such as deregulating the labour market and tightening eligibility for income support. I show that most states have made significant policy trade-offs in recent years, reducing public support in certain areas but improving it in others. Furthermore, I argue that neoliberal economic reforms have actually augmented family poverty and required governments to enhance social benefits for children and parents.

Methodology

This book focuses on the restructuring of family policies and programs since the 1980s, but it is sometimes necessary to refer to earlier developments in order to understand the controversies relating to restructuring. Consequently, I have occasionally gone farther back in history to elucidate the extent of change in family patterns, social provisions, or public discourse. My focus is also on countries belonging to the Organisation of Economic Co-operation and Development because comparative statistics and policy reports are readily available from this organization, and because family policies are well developed within most of these countries, as compared to those of developing nations. I place particular emphasis on European Union countries because several recent studies have examined family policy debates within the European Parliament and Court, discussing the impact of these debates on ideologies of family and the policy agendas of member states (Hantrais 2000; Weiss 2000; McGlynn 2001; Hantrais 2004; Stratigaki 2004; Walby 2004).

This study synthesizes an extensive body of research and theorizing about socio-demographic trends in families, social policy restructuring, social care work, gender and work, family law reform, and family-related programs and services. The analysis uses international and national statistics, comparative studies of family trends and policies, and national and international policy documents. It also includes my own empirical and policy research on family trends and comparative family policies. Consequently, the book says more about the 'liberal' welfare states, including Canada, the United States, the United Kingdom, Australia, and New Zealand, than any others countries. The reason for this focus is that relevant documents and studies are available in English, the book is published in Canada, and much of my accumulated knowledge has been directed towards family trends and policies in these countries (Baker 1995; Baker and Tippin 1999; Baker 2001b).

In a broad study such as this it is not possible to make equivalent and detailed policy comparisons among all OECD countries within the space of one book. A discussion of the context of policy differences for each country would require several volumes of details that would not necessarily enable theoretical statements to be made about factors influencing restructuring. Furthermore, comparative studies and statistics are available for some of these countries and for certain policy issues but not for others. The intent of including so many countries is to highlight the range of policy options and to enable some tentative conclusions to be made about the importance of the socio-economic, cultural, and political contexts of family policy restructuring.

One problem with comparative research is that family laws, policies, and programs sometimes differ among the jurisdictions within as well as between countries. Especially in federations such as Canada and the United States, provincial and state governments retain jurisdiction over some policy issues but not others (Vosko 2002; Bernard and Saint-Arnaud 2004). When discussing federal states with internal variations, I have tried to focus on national averages or trends, although atypical policies in specific states or provinces may be highlighted.

Comparing family policies is further complicated because laws and social programs are always in a state of reform; comparative databases often take years to compile but rapidly become outdated. Consequently, I have relied on documents and articles from the Internet, newspapers items, unpublished articles, and conference papers as well as published books, academic articles, and reports from governments and international organizations. In addition, I have tried to note changes anticipated in the near future. I have used research and statistics from international databases when available because they usually contain comparable measurements and definitions or note when these differ.

Cultural understandings about family, gender, and parenting vary cross-nationally, but these differences must become part of the analysis. The focus of social provision and eligibility rules also varies, partly because these programs have been negotiated and modified over the years with input from different governments and lobby groups with varying agendas. Despite these challenges, I still believe that this kind of comparative project is worth pursuing because policy makers often look to other jurisdictions for answers to similar problems. However, they usually focus on one or two countries rather than examining policies from many jurisdictions. I believe that comparing family programs in a wider range of countries can highlight new policy options and enhance theoretical understandings about the nature of policy reform and the contingency of policy discourse.

Chapter Outline

Considerable background material is needed before we can begin to answer in any comprehensive way the complex questions underpinning this book. In the rest of this chapter, I define some key terms relating to the study, including 'family,' 'family policy,' 'neoliberal restructuring,' and 'globalization.' The next three chapters outline what I see as the main pressures on national governments to reform family policies: socio-demographic changes in family patterns, existing patterns of social provision and national politics, and globalizing labour markets and pressures from international organizations. Chapters 5 to 9 deal with substantive policy issues, including reproductive health and childbirth, integrating earning and caring, childcare and child welfare issues, social housing and income support, and the 'post-divorce' family. Chapter 10 provides my conclusions about the most significant pressures on governments to reform family policies and how much policy convergence or divergence is apparent.

Chapter 2 argues that socio-demographic patterns have changed considerably in the past three decades and that many elements of convergence are apparent in OECD countries. However, reform advocates use these trends to recommend quite different policy solutions even within the same country, because their arguments are based on values and beliefs about the ideal family as well as the appropriate state intervention. Therefore, effective political advocacy is more important than demography in shaping policy. Chapter 3 begins with a discussion of the concept of 'welfare regimes,' arguing that patterns of social provision for families can be quite enduring over time because they represent cultural ideas about family as well as the appropriate role of the state in family life. New policy ideas that do not fit well with existing institutions, traditions, and ideologies are either resisted by the electorate or modified by policy makers. Chapter 4 discusses the impact of internationalizing labour markets, more migration, freer trade, and multilateral social policy agreements on the restructuring of family policies. The chapter argues that many transnational agreements cannot force national governments to alter their social policy even though they may place pressure on them. Some governments have refused to sign agreements (or portions of them) that they believe will interfere with their national autonomy. Others have signed but neglected to make certain policy changes expected by supranational organizations. In other words, such countries agree in principle but fail to put these ideas into practice.

Turning to substantive family policy issues, Chapter 5 explores trends in programs and policies relating to reproductive health and childbirth, noting increased contraceptive use, more medicalization in conception and childbirth, and reductions in both state-provided maternity services and access to abortion with neoliberal restructuring. Mindful of international guidelines on childbirth issues as well as rising medical costs, states have urged health care institutions to encourage safe childbirth but shorten hospital stays and limit unnecessary technology. However, this chapter shows that childbirth and breastfeeding practices are also influenced by factors other than international agreements and national government policies. These factors include new technologies, changing labour markets, medical and corporate profits, and the politics of choice.

Chapter 6 discusses the integration of employment and parenting, noting the gendered patterns of paid and unpaid work. This chapter argues that attempts to create more international and 'flexible' labour markets tend to disadvantage certain kinds of family configurations, especially lone mothers with low education and several children. Two 'liberal' welfare states (Canada and Australia) are used as examples of the politics of restructuring family programs, to show how that restructuring is influenced by other political agendas. While Canadian policies now encourage full-time employment for both parents, Australian policies have continued to support mothering at home. (However, recent political announcements move Australia in the same policy direction as Canada.)

Chapter 7 examines childcare and child welfare issues, which are both areas where liberal welfare states have been reactive rather than proactive. Governments in these countries often focus on low-income and mother-led households, with visible-minority families continually over-represented in child welfare systems. Unlike in the northern European countries, few state programs in the liberal welfare states encourage fathers to become more involved in child rearing. As well, few programs focus on eliminating poverty or reducing stress, anger and racial/cultural discrimination; yet these issues lie behind a considerable amount of family strain and conflict.

Chapter 8 compares social housing and family income support, noting variations in the type of family that receives the most attention (i.e., one-parent families, two-earner families, large families, or all families with children). Higher levels of social spending and universal programs are shown to be related to several measures of family well-being. Chapter 9 discusses policies relating to the 'post-divorce family' living in a socio-economic context that involves new patterns of work and more international migration. It indicates that policy makers from many countries continue to struggle with solutions to the specific policy problems related to child custody, child support, and the poverty and poor health prevalent in so many mother-led households.

The concluding chapter argues that a number of family policies have been strengthened in OECD countries in recent years, including parental benefits, services and benefits for children, ways of dealing with violence within households, legal rights of same-sex couples, and improvements to wages and benefits for part-time workers in some jurisdictions. At the same time, other policies have been eroded, such as eligibility for income support for mothers with older children, reproductive services in certain countries, some family services, and labour market protections (especially in liberal welfare states). Chapter 10 also summarizes the lobby groups and political parties that support specific family policies. I argue that conservative and religious-based parties generally focus on the two-parent heterosexual family with children, and often promote the male breadwinner family as well as increased fertility rates. Centre-left governments tend to support two-earner families, via such measures as pay equity for women, more generous childcare arrangements, and enhanced maternity benefits. They are also more likely to offer statutory protections to same-sex couples.

Conservative governments operating within global market conditions frequently send the nation mixed messages about the importance of family and children. They usually encourage couples to enter and remain in stable relationships, buy a home, and raise children. They publicly talk about children as 'social capital' and a future national resource but at the same time emphasize parental rather than social responsibility for children's well-being and behaviour. Neoliberal governments also elevate the importance of paid work, often without ensuring affordable housing, childcare services, employment leave for family responsibilities, or income security. Yet working long hours or for low wages can easily leave one little time or energy for developing lasting relationships, creating families, and nurturing children.

Throughout this book, I show that the impact on family policy of external forces, such as the neoliberal restructuring of labour markets and social programs or the creation of multi-country social policy agreements, has been uneven and inconsistent. International organizations such as the European Union, the World Health Organisation, the International Labour Organisation, and the United Nations continue to place considerable pressure on national governments to harmonize their social programs and legislation relating to family life. Some national policy debates are actually framed by the very fact that these organizations put specific issues on their agendas, but governments respond differently because they are faced with different internal pressures.

Widespread demographic, social, political, and economic changes strengthen arguments to reform family policies, but similar pressures do not lead to the same policy solutions. I show in this book that national and local politics always intervene to alter policy outcomes. Policy restructuring remains heavily influenced by the activities of strong and effective lobby groups as well as political alliances created between these groups and governments in power. In addition, governments operate within institutional constraints, such as existing patterns of social provision and public expectations. These institutional arrangements encourage policy makers to favour certain ideas and policy options while ruling out others that require major reform or alter the basic assumptions behind existing social programs.

This does not mean that family policy change is impossible, but only that reformers operate within a complex mixture of cultural and political constraints. In many OECD countries, policy reform is typically incremental, building on existing laws and regulations that contain assumptions about acceptable levels of taxation and program funding. Lobby groups and political advisors often attempt to persuade politicians to make specific reforms, sometimes fighting for years on particular agendas. Individual politicians may try to push new ideas on their political colleagues or constituents, but politicians are usually expected to abide by the policies already agreed upon by their party. Democratic governments also need to ensure that the electorate are convinced of the need for specific policy changes, or risk losing the next election.

The increasing internationalization of labour markets since the 1980s has encouraged governments to reform employment policies, contributed to the reduced effectiveness of trade unions in some places, and influenced the work and living arrangements of many individuals and their families. However, I argue that 'economic globalization' has not led to the harmonization of social programs predicted by some researchers or advocated by certain transnational organizations. Throughout this book, I emphasize that national and regional influences as well as international ones affect family policy restructuring, highlighting the inconsistencies and contradictions involved. Finally, I argue that strong social programs are increasingly important as global markets reduce economic security for some families while improving it for others.

Defining Key Terms

Defining 'Families'

Sociologists and anthropologists have argued for years over what constitutes a family. They used to talk about 'the family' as a social group joined by blood, marriage, or adoption and characterized by common residence, economic cooperation, and reproduction (Murdock 1949; Parsons and Bales 1955; Goode 1963). For more than a century, anthropologists have highlighted the cultural variations in family structure, marriage patterns, living arrangements, and systems of authority, descent, and inheritance. Yet the family is still being discussed in some circles as though it were a single institution meaning the same thing to all people.

In North America, both the academic and policy portrayals of families have been ethnocentric, conservative, and sexist, focusing on the experiences of white middle-class American families in which two heterosexual parents and their biological children share a household with no other relatives present (Eichler 1997; 2005). Opponents of same-sex marriage still promote this image as the typical family even though the majority of people in OECD countries no longer live in these kinds of households (Lewis 2003). Although social science research now emphasizes the multidimensional nature of family life, this fact is not always incorporated into public discourse or social policy.

Most policy definitions of family focus on its structure, including how many adults share a household and the legal status of their relationship to each other as well as to any children involved. Increasingly, researchers and advocacy groups argue that definitions should be broadened to encompass caring and enduring intimate relationships regardless of their legal or blood ties (Eichler 1997; Jamieson 1998; Smart and Neale 1999). As more couples cohabit, separate, and reconfigure their families through re-partnering, the two-parent heterosexual 'nuclear' family with its own biological children sharing a residence becomes less prevalent. In Canada in 2001, only 41.4 per cent of families consisted of legally married couples living with the children they created together or from previous relationships (Vanier Institute of the Family 2004; 40).

The structure and legal status of the family unit are becoming less important to family members themselves than the services they provide for each other or how they feel about their relationship. However, in comparative policy analysis it is not really feasible to define 'family' in such a subjective way. Governments establish specific definitions and are usually unwilling to allow people to create their own family definitions when making decisions about eligibility for partnership rights, immigration access, or social benefits (although states are now being pressed to become more inclusive in their definitions). This book focuses on policies for families with dependent children, but I am using an inclusive definition of 'families,' one shared by Canada's Vanier Institute of the Family (2004). This definition includes lone parents and their dependent children and both legally married and cohabiting couples living together with or without children. Gay/lesbian couples sharing a residence and resources also fall within my definition, as well as couples and their children sharing a household with their adult siblings or parents (or 'extended' families). In other words, my discussion includes both nuclear and extended families as well as long-term cohabiting couples.

When referring to official statistics, however, it is necessary to abide by the specific definition used by the government or organization involved. In most cases, a 'family with children' refers to a heterosexual couple or lone parent sharing a dwelling with never-married children under the age of sixteen or eighteen years. A lone-parent or sole-parent family usually refers to one parent who shares a household with his or her never-married children under eighteen years old, without another adult present. To bridge this divide I will, when necessary, raise issues of definition or use hyphenated words to clarify the concept or argument.

Defining 'Family Policy'

This book focuses on 'family policy' rather than social policy in general. This narrower focus makes more manageable the analysis of the vast amount of research and the extensive and controversial academic debates about factors relating to the development and restructuring of the welfare state in general. It also avoids some of the problems encountered by other scholars, discussed in Chapter 3, who have over-generalized about the origins of 'the welfare state' and about countries with similar social programs. I argue that many of these researchers assumed more consistency than is apparent among different types of social programs within the same country, as well as among countries categorized as similar. For example, if a country provides generous employment-related programs for full-time workers, this does not necessarily mean that its childcare provisions are also generous.

My definition of 'family policy' is relatively broad. In this book, I am referring to official decisions to implement certain state-sponsored social programs, services, regulations, and laws relating to families. These might relate to reproductive health, family well-being, or the maintenance of family income. They could reinforce financial support or caring obligations among family members, protect vulnerable family members from harm or neglect, or enable the integration of earning and caring work. Family programs do not have to be delivered directly by the state, but they would need to be mandated or regulated by the state in order to be discussed in this study.

Programs contracted out to voluntary agencies or subsidized by the state would be included in this definition of family policies and programs. Examples of the former are child protection services contracted to child welfare agencies, and an example of the latter might be formal childcare services provided by a church group but given a capital grant and regulated by the government. Employer-sponsored programs for parental leave or family responsibilities are also discussed in this book because they are often required by individual states or included in the declarations or conventions of transnational organizations that are ratified by national governments.

Family members, friends, and voluntary associations provide a considerable amount of 'welfare' in the form of emotional support, counselling, financial loans, assistance with housework and childcare, and offers of food and housing. Policy makers often assume the existence of this form of welfare, especially caring work provided by wives and mothers, when they design or restructure social programs. However, these assumptions are not always accurate or seen as equitable, issues which are discussed throughout this book. Adult children often move far away from their parents, and women's increased involvement in paid labour means that many are no longer available to sustain the caring or volunteer activities to which they contributed in the past. New forms of communication do permit relatives to maintain closer contact and even to perform some caring work from afar. However, public expectations on families and especially on women are increasingly out of sync with the complex social realities of their daily lives, as well as with ideas implicit within some social programs.

The politics of family policy restructuring have been intensely controversial. Throughout the following chapters, I demonstrate that cross-national variations in such policies reflect different views about the role of the state in family life, and different models of family accepted by policy makers and the electorate. The final chapter contains a more comprehensive summary of the particular types of family policy supported by various political parties, but the entire book emphasizes the political nature of family discourse and especially discussions of parental obligations. Of course, discourse changes over the years, but in recent decades much debate has been motivated by neoliberal ideas about restructuring the state and the forms of governance that often follow.

Defining 'Restructuring'

The concept of 'restructuring' is used to describe the process of initiating broad changes to the private or public sectors, such as merging companies or government departments, altering governing structures, contracting out services or production, and adding new regulations or procedures for service providers, suppliers, or producers. When applied to family policy, the concept suggests deliberate changes to legislation or policy directives that alter eligibility or entitlement rules, levels of income support or subsidies, the services available to families, or the departments or agencies that implement social programs. These changes could raise the level of services and benefits for some families while cutting them back for others, but would seldom have the same impact on all family configurations.

Governments usually introduce family policy changes in an upbeat way by using the word 'reforms,' which implies positive improvements for individuals, families, and society in general. However, I note throughout the book that many family policy changes, although accompanied by the discourse of helping families, involve downsizing benefit levels and reducing eligibility. Governments sometimes restructure social programs in order to improve services, but they also strive to become more effective and efficient at catching incidents of 'welfare fraud' and reducing public expenditures. Consequently, some policy changes improve well-being for a specific sector of the population while reducing it for others.

Policy restructuring is usually preceded by extensive lobbying from powerful groups demanding change to accommodate their particular interests. This may include concern about human rights violations, unsupervised children, or the long-term costs of children living in poverty. Business groups also pressure governments to reduce payroll deductions for work-related benefits, to give employers more flexibility in hiring or firing staff, and to reduce 'compliance costs.' Restructuring is often motivated by concern over increased international business competition, declining profits, and the high cost of labour, research and development, and service delivery.

A major influence on recent restructuring is neoliberalism, also called 'market liberalism' or 'the new right perspective,' which reflects a system of ideas and governing principles that give priority to economic markets in public policy. Neoliberals generally argue that the Keynesian welfare state involved too much state intervention and unwarranted interference with the freedom of individuals to organize their own affairs.[1] Instead of maintaining expensive income-support programs,

---

1 The post–World War II welfare state, the concept of which was introduced by English economist John Maynard Keynes, was characterized by deficit financing by governments, state programs to support the growth of public-sector jobs, and state income-support programs to cover lost earnings in times of unemployment, sickness, and disability (McGilly 1998; 13).

the state should deregulate the labour market, become less involved in economic activities, and reduce income taxes. Neoliberals often assume that families are autonomous economic units responsible for their own survival, that jobs provide the best income security, and that individuals make rational decisions to maximize their earnings. They also believe that many social services can be provided more effectively by the private sector than by the state, and consequently refer to people as 'customers' or 'consumers' rather than citizens with social rights (Pusey 1993; Kelsey 1995; Brodie 1996).

If government 'interference' in the labour market was decreased and income taxes and payroll taxes were reduced, neoliberals argue, then employment rates would rise because corporate profits would be higher and employers would be able to hire additional staff and pay them more. Higher take-home pay would enable employees to make rational choices about which services to purchase on the open market (Hayek 1948; Friedman 1962). Most neoliberals agree that state income support should be available, but only as a last resort for those in absolute need and unable to work. In addition, income support should be transitional and time-limited assistance rather than a universal entitlement.

Globalization and Restructuring

Academics have long debated the driving forces behind welfare state restructuring. Research on this topic arises from several different disciplines that do not always agree on basic definitions, the unit of analysis, what initiates policy change, how rapidly it can occur, and the importance of economic changes, political interests, or ideas. The concept of 'globalization' has been widely discussed in academic circles since the 1970s, prompting considerable debate and controversy about its nature, scope, and impact. Entire books have been written about globalization and its national variations, including major arguments about its extent and impact on social and economic policies. In this section, I can provide only a brief overview of a few of the debates that relate specifically to family policies.

Researchers who combine the concept of globalization with the study of social policy all argue that the concept has been used so generally and so often that its meaning has become unclear (Mishra 1999; Gough 2000; Yeates 2001; Held and McGrew 2002). The concept is defined in various ways but generally includes the growing internationalization of many facets of life: finances and capital ownership, markets, technology, consumption patterns and culture, governance, political unification, perception, and consciousness (Petrella 1996). 'Globalization' denotes the expanding scale, growing magnitude, increasing speed, and deepening impact of transcontinental flows and patterns of social interaction. It refers to a transformation in the scale of human organization that links distant communities and expands the reach of power relations across the world's regions and continents (Held and McGrew 2002; 1). The concept holds varying emotional connotations, as some welcome the increasing international flow of capital, people, and information while others see it as a 'sinister shadow' (Yeates 2001).

One debate in the globalization literature relates to the nature and pace of social change. Many social scientists argue that the transitions brought about by globalization are revolutionary and transformative, while others contest both the extent and impact of recent change. These latter argue that global exploration and colonization go back centuries: in the nineteenth century, they encouraged massive waves of international migration, the spread of European culture and ideas about the role of the state in family life, and the eventual development of similar social programs in the colonies. Furthermore, national governments always have been constrained by international flows of trade and finance. What is now so different? In response, other researchers argue that the process has been accelerated, involves more people, and encompasses more aspects of everyday life.

Several researchers note that economic globalization involves spreading neoliberal ideas and governing practices around the world (Teeple 1995; Mishra 1999; Peck 2001, Kingfisher 2002; Peck 2004). Global markets are created to enhance corporate profits by expanding markets, finding cheaper areas for production, locating new consumers, and becoming more competitive internationally. This means that business interests and producers often need governments to sign free trade agreements with other countries. They also want governments to help them search for new markets, to subsidize local production when cheaper goods are imported, and to help make their ventures more profitable. Global trade often depends on international agreements about financial transactions, trade, employment practices, immigration, and governance.

Of particular importance to the theme of this book is the argument that economic globalization and its accompanying agenda of neoliberalism are reducing the power of national governments to make policy decisions in the national interest. If national governments attempt to enforce strict employment laws or raise minimum wages to assist employees, then employers might suffer if they are trading in countries without these requirements. Employers with international connections could always search for less costly labour conditions in another jurisdiction if trade agreements permit. Corporate threats to relocate worry politicians because such moves could diminish their country's economic prosperity, raise unemployment rates, and possibly cause strikes and social unrest.

Mishra (1999) analysed the impact on 'the welfare state' of economic globalization (or the openness of national economies to trade and financial flows). He first asked if economic openness deprives national governments of their autonomy, and if so, how does this affects social protection. Secondly, he asked if globalization necessarily entails a 'race to the bottom' as nations vie with one another to compete in the international marketplace (ix). He argued that globalization shifts the balance of power away from labour and the state and in favour of capital. This constrains policy options by virtually excluding left-of-centre approaches and 'spells the end of ideology' as far as welfare state policies are concerned (102). Globalization makes national economies more open to transnational economic activities in search of profits and higher returns, 'making the whole world into a giant market' where national boundaries are downplayed (105). Globalizing trends come into conflict with the logic of national communities and democratic politics. In order to ensure that social standards increase with economic growth, he recommended a transnational approach to social policy.

Mishra argued that the ascendancy of a global market economy, combined with the demise of communism, have 'handed neoliberalism a powerful new weapon with which to contain and neutralize the counter-pressure of domestic politics' (3). Globalization increasingly pressures national governments to reduce social protection. Opening up the economy particularly curtails policy autonomy in the realm of macroeconomic programs for full employment and economic growth, worsens wages and working conditions, and increases the gap between the rich and the poor. Ideologies stemming from neoliberalism and globalization (including the prioritizing of deficit and debt reduction, lowering of taxation, and legitimizing of inequality of rewards) also encourage national governments to reduce social spending and diminish the generosity of social programs.

As it relates to family policy, the key feature of globalization is neoliberal forms of governance, including a shift towards increasing 'marketization,' a redrawing of the public/private distinction, valorization of possessive individualism, and shifts in state expenditure (often accompanied by increasing interference) in social arenas (Kingfisher 2002; 4). Many researchers argue that neoliberal ideas and practices involve a qualitative reordering of state/economy relations, and a privileging of market distribution over social redistribution and elite interests over mass interests. Peck (2004) noted that 'neoliberalization' is a changing process. The 'roll back' period of the 1980s was dominated by deregulation and cutbacks, but the more recent period of 'roll out' involved experimental re-regulation, fiscal responsibility, and new forms of state governance.

Globalization does not necessarily lead to a harmonious world society; it can create new animosities and conflicts and 'fuel reactionary politics and deep-seated xenophobia' (Held and McGrew 2002). Some researchers argue that most of the world's population is excluded from the so-called global market, with a growing gap between the OECD economies and others (R.J.B. Jones 1995; Hoogvelt 2001). Rugman (2001) suggested that the world economy is increasingly fragmenting into various regional zones dominated by powerful forces, economic competition, and rivalry. In addition, numerous researchers argue that the negative impact of globalization and neoliberalism has been more apparent in the English-speaking countries than in Europe or Japan (Mishra 1999; Jenson and Sineau 2001b; Swank 2002). In other words, governments develop economic and social policy to fit in with national politics and cultural values rather than as a result of economic necessity.

Yeates (2001) critiqued the 'strong' globalization thesis by emphasizing the continued importance of political agency, social conflict, and struggle in determining the pace, course, timing, and impact of globalization. Focusing on the social politics of globalization, she counterbalanced the emphasis in other studies of globalizations' impact on social policy. She highlighted which 'actors' or organizations have been involved in supporting globalization, the interests they represent, and the strategies they adopt. Yeates argued that the degree to which globalization gives rise to systematic changes in funding, regulation, and provision of welfare has been overestimated. Instead, she showed that national and domestic forces remain decisive in understanding the development of social policy. In short, she argued that politics matters now as much as it ever did, which is one of the arguments I make in this book with respect to family policies.

Conclusion

This book deals with the restructuring of family policies in OECD countries, with a focus on the liberal welfare states. Throughout the chapters, I show that arguments for policy reform are always discussed, interpreted, and negotiated within 'welfare regimes' consisting of institutional structures, vested interests, and prevailing ideologies about women, family, and the role of the state in personal life. I argue that existing welfare systems establish the baseline for further restructuring, which often involves amendments to existing legislation or programs. This means that it would be very difficult to transplant quite different social programs from one place to another unless the two shared similar political cultures, institutional structures, ideologies about work and family, or socio-demographic changes in family patterns.

The impetus for policy restructuring and change is continual and originates from new ideas, changes in lifestyle and technology, and transformations in the economy. However, policy outcomes involve considerable planning, political negotiations, and strategizing. Stakeholder groups and politicians must negotiate over various policy solutions, including the need for reform; the structure of new programs; their eligibility requirements, delivery mechanisms, and levels of funding; and the specific wording of new legislation. In addition, politicians have to be able to justify or 'sell' new policy ideas to the citizens and taxpayers, or risk being voted out of office. In other words, the restructuring of family policy is often a complex political process. It involves financial planning, knowledge of support or opposition groups, and carefully constructed political discourse that portrays new family programs as improvements over the status quo.

In the next three chapters, I discuss the main sources of pressure that encourage national governments to restructure family policy, including changes in family demography, political forces from within welfare regimes, and pressures from international labour markets and supranational organizations. These three factors form the basic theoretical argument of the book, while the remaining chapters provide the data to substantiate the arguments.

2 Socio-demographic Changes and Family Policy Restructuring

Socio-demographic changes in family patterns are the first of three major influences on governments considering the restructuring of family policies. Governments are pressured to modify social programs when people's daily lives seem out of step with the assumptions underlying those programs. Over the past few decades, family demography has changed substantially in most OECD countries, with lower rates of legal marriage, more cohabitation, declining fertility, higher rates of separation and divorce, more mothers in the workforce, more repartnering, and aging populations. Although many of the trends are in a similar direction, the pace of change, the starting point, the timing, and the intensity vary (McRae 1999; Lewis 2003; Hantrais 2004).

Throughout this book, I demonstrate that the same socio-demographic changes are used to make quite different political arguments about the need for policy reform, because projected 'problems' and policy solutions are based on different values and assumptions. Both politicians and lobby groups have argued that social policies need to be 'modernized' to better conform with new family patterns, considering that people are living longer, more mothers are employed, and families are smaller and less likely to comprise two legally married parents who stay together for life. They also note that most social programs were designed during an era of post-war prosperity and in a time of near full employment when most families consisted of a male breadwinner, a wife who was a mother and caregiver at home, and at least two or three children. There is widespread agreement that social programs need to be restructured to accommodate modern family life, but conflicting ideas about why and how.

In the political sphere, there are pressures to shape family patterns or force people to conform to certain standards of behaviour. For example, some governments have encouraged recipients of state income support to produce fewer children by advocating contraception or sterilization. Other policy advocates strive to make abortion illegal or difficult to obtain, expecting women to give birth and have their babies adopted or marry the father and live as a family unit. Some policies, based on concern about declining fertility, offer financial incentives for (married) couples to produce more children. However, attempts to modify family patterns have often failed because these patterns are influenced by so many factors. Because the major demographic trends are discussed throughout the book, I will focus on only two issues in this chapter to illustrate the complexity of concerns, the variety of publicly expressed factors and proposed policy initiatives. The first demographic trend deals with rising cohabitation rates, including the formation of gay and lesbian families, while the second focuses on declining fertility but more births outside marriage.

Rising Cohabitation Rates

More couples now live together without legally marrying, especially the young, the poor, the previously married, and the childless. Jane Lewis (2003) noted that 70 per cent of 'marriages' among sixteen to twenty-nine year olds in Sweden and Denmark are consensual, as well as half of Canadian 'marriages' among people twenty to twenty-four years. Changes in Quebec are more dramatic than in the rest of Canada, as 70 per cent of women in that province begin their 'conjugal lives' through 'common-law relationships' or cohabitation, compared to 34 per cent in the rest of Canada. Although younger people are now more likely to start their conjugal life with cohabitation, most eventually marry. Three-quarters of Canadians aged thirty to thirty-nine in 2001 are expected to marry at some point in their lives, but this is much lower than the 90 per cent of men and women aged 50 to 69 who have already married (Statistics Canada 2002b). These predictions clearly signal a decline in the popularity of legal marriage.

While social conservatives often oppose consensual unions, sociologists ask whether cohabitation is really any different from legal marriage. Statistically, the answer appears to be 'yes.' Couples who cohabit tend to experience shorter relationships and are less likely to reproduce than those who legally marry. Those who cohabit before they marry also experience higher divorce rates than those who did not first cohabit

(Wu 2000). These trends have been explained in two ways. Firstly, cohabiters differ from legal marriage partners: they are somewhat less conventional and less religious people who are more likely to see separation as an acceptable alternative to relationship unhappiness. Secondly, living together is often seen as a form of 'trial marriage.' If things work out, cohabitation leads to a legal relationship and possibly childbearing, if the arrangement is unsuccessful, the couple breaks up. Whichever approach one takes to cohabitation, separation rates are higher than for legal marriage (Wu 2000, 120).

A number of policy concerns emanate from the rise in cohabitation. Firstly, the state must decide whether cohabitation should be considered similar to or different from legal marriage in terms of spousal entitlements and obligations during the relationship. One concern relates to the entitlement to employment benefits (such as relocation expenses or health benefits for the employee's partner and children) and immigration entitlements (such as the partner's right to be accepted as an immigrant).

Secondly, if cohabiting couples separate and ask the courts to decide about financial support or the division of family assets, should the state treat their relationship the same as it does legal marriage? Some cohabiting partners want to maintain a social and legal distinction between their living arrangements and legal marriage. They may see cohabitation as less permanent, based more on shared earning and caring, as an opportunity to remain childless and/or accept fewer obligations to the partner's kin, and as involving fewer expectations of financial support or shared property (Barber and Axinn 1998; Elizabeth 2000). Others may see long-term cohabitation and marriage as very similar. Some governments have resolved these concerns by assuming that after a certain period (one to three years) cohabiting couples are deemed to be 'married,' at least for the division of assets. If partners, in the event of separation, do not want to divide their property equally, or the same as married couples, they must sign a legal contract within a specified period after moving in together. However, most OECD countries expect parents to support their children whether or not they are legally married or living with these children.

Goldscheider and Kaufman (1996) argued that cohabitation generally represents a lower level of commitment to relationships but that for men it also means a lower level of commitment to children. Cohabiting fathers are more likely than married fathers to separate from their partners and lose contact with their children, although men who are

26   Restructuring Family Policies

more involved with their children are less likely to separate. A non-residential father can have a positive influence on the children if he is involved with them, but the tenuous relationship with the mother on issues of parenting can also bring conflict into the children's lives. This kind of research finding heightens opposition to cohabitation, but especially to childbearing by cohabitating partners.

Gay and Lesbian Cohabitation

The rise in cohabitation also includes an increase in gay and lesbian couples living together. While heterosexual couples sometimes argue that the state has no right to interfere with their living arrangements, some same-sex couples have been fighting for years for legal recognition of their relationships. This could include partnership rights and same-sex marriage, as well as equal access to assisted reproduction services, fostering, and adoption (Weeks, Donovan, and Heaphy 1998, 84; McNair et al. 2002). Some jurisdictions have recently granted legal rights to same-sex partnerships, including Belgium, the Netherlands, Denmark, France, Germany, and the Canadian provinces of Ontario, British Columbia, and Quebec (Luxton 2005). These relationships are sometimes called 'civil unions' to differentiate them from (heterosexual) legal marriage, and using this terminology has sometimes dampened opposition from those who continue to view marriage as a sacred bond between a man and a woman. However, the wisdom of creating two kinds of 'marriage' and the legality of these unions have been disputed, including by the president of the United States and within the Supreme Court of Canada (Moore 2003).

Gay marriages have been legal in Belgium and the Netherlands since 2001. However, when these couples travelled or worked in other parts of Europe, the rights that accompany marriage (to be considered a 'spouse,' to joint ownership of property, to next-of-kin entitlement to pensions, and to inheritance) were not always recognized (Arie 2003). Denmark, France, and Germany allow 'civil unions' that provide many of the same rights as marriage but are easier to dissolve, but same-sex marriages are unacceptable in Italy and Greece. In September 2003, European Union ministers endorsed a proposed set of rules ensuring that same-sex married couples from the Netherlands and Belgium are recognized as married across the EU, but this measure was strongly opposed by the Vatican, with Pope John Paul II affirming that the official position of the Catholic Church is that marriage is a sacred union between a man and a woman (Arie 2003; Winfield 2003).

In 2004, several jurisdictions debated the issue of civil unions. As we saw in chapter 1, civil unions became legal in New Zealand in April 2005. As of that time, individual income support benefits are denied to people living together if their relationship is deemed to be 'in the nature of marriage.' Each relationship will have to be examined to see if there was evidence of emotional commitment, financial interdependence, sharing of household duties, provision of domestic services, sharing of a sexual relationship, and sharing of companionship (McIvor 2004). Some beneficiaries of state income support in heterosexual and same-sex relationships might be expected to pay back monies already received if they are deemed to have been 'married'. This legislation will encourage even more state scrutiny of the domestic lives of the poor.

Official statistics of gay or lesbian couples living as families were available only recently, and for this reason are probably vastly under-represented. In Canada and New Zealand, census figures report that same-sex couples form less than 1 per cent of all couples (Statistics New Zealand 1998, 39; Statistics Canada 2002a). In other research, less than three per cent of Canadian adults described their current family situation as a same-sex relationship (Bibby 2004–5). About 10 per cent of same-sex couples in New Zealand have been previously married (Statistics New Zealand 1998, 39), and 20 per cent of Australian lesbians, gay men, and bisexuals reported that they have children even though many do not live with them (Mikhailovich, Martin, and Lawton 2001). The number of lesbian-headed families in Australia appears to be increasing (Millbank 2002). While many of the children of lesbian mothers were conceived in previous heterosexual relationships (before these women 'came out'), more lesbian couples are having children through self-insemination, clinically assisted donor insemination, and other assisted reproduction procedures, as well as through sexual intercourse (McNair et al. 2002).

Public opposition to viewing same-sex families as similar or equal to heterosexual families remains strong in some segments of the population in most OECD countries. This is especially the case among social conservatives and the 'Christian right' in the United States (Moore 2003), where President Bush endorsed an unsuccessful proposal in 2004 to change the American Constitution to prohibit same-sex marriages (Hulse 2004). However, part of the opposition to this prohibition was that marriage should remain under state rather than federal control. Opposition to same-sex marriage has also been apparent in Australia (Skene 2002) and New Zealand (Baker 2004), where these couples have been excluded from state-funded fertility treatments.

In Canada, 38 per cent of those surveyed said that they neither approve of nor are willing to accept homosexual behaviour (Bibby 2004–5). Opponents of same-sex marriage sometimes assume that these relationships are 'abnormal' or 'sinful' and suggest that children would suffer unless two heterosexual parents raised them. However, research comparing lesbian families with heterosexual ones finds few differences in parenting style or ability to parent effectively. Children with lesbian parents show consistent evidence of good adjustment, with no notable differences in sexual identity (Allen and Burrell 1996; Patterson 2000). Nevertheless, there is widespread belief that heterosexual families are the best structure for raising children.

As cohabitation rates rise in many jurisdictions, we can assume that separation rates will also increase because, as mentioned above, these relationships have higher rates of dissolution than legal marriage. Whether or not cohabitation is an attempt to reduce the risk of divorce, financial entanglements, or overly 'gendered' relationships by avoiding a legal commitment, its prevalence creates fewer permanent relationships in the general population (Beck-Gernsheim 2002). Without legal protections similar to those of marriage, widespread cohabitation could also lead to more disputes about the division of property, child custody, and financial support after separation.

Although legal and heterosexual marriage rates are declining in many OECD countries, most young middle-aged adults (those aged thirty-five to forty-four) are either legally married or living as a couple. For example, in Italy and Spain, only about 15 per cent of women aged 35 to 44 do not live with a partner, although this percentage is higher in Canada (22 per cent) and the United States (28 per cent) (González-López 2002). Researchers are also beginning to discuss a new kind of relationship, called 'living apart together' (LAT), in which couples maintain separate residences but share sex and some of their resources. About 6 per cent of 35- to 44-year-old women in France and 10 per cent of 25- to 34-year-old women in Austria report being in such a relationship (Gonzalez-López 2002, 31). These relationships indicate that living arrangements are becoming more varied, but also suggest that employment opportunities have a strong and growing influence on family life. LAT relationships are usually justified by the location of job prospects for young dual-career couples who have not yet reproduced.

Declining Fertility but More Births outside Marriage

Fertility decline is one of the most controversial trends in family demography because it leads to concerns about how to finance future services for an aging population with fewer working-age taxpayers. 'Below replacement' fertility rates also lead to projections of long-term population decline and future labour shortages. These economic implications encourage some social conservatives to see child-free couples (especially women) as selfish and even unpatriotic. At the same time, social reformers on the left suggest that more people would reproduce if governments and employers provided more generous childbirth leave, flexible work arrangements, and affordable childcare services. Others simply argue that not everyone should reproduce because some people make poor parents or have other worthwhile ambitions. Also, fewer children per family could raise the quality of parental childcare and reduce the need for state income support.

Many people assume that fertility decline has been caused by the widespread use of contraceptives since the 1960s, but fertility rates have been falling since industrialization in the late nineteenth century (Beaujot 2000; 241). After the Second World War, a 'baby boom' was apparent in North America, Australia, and New Zealand, but less so in Europe. This period of population growth was actually an exception to a long-term decline in fertility, which then accelerated after the 1960s when the contraceptive pill went on the market.

From 1970 to 2000, the total fertility rate (or average number of children per women) fell in most OECD countries (Table 2.1). Few countries now replace deaths with new births, as the 'replacement rate' is calculated to be about 2.1 children per woman (OECD 2001, 24). Particularly the southern European countries of Greece, Portugal, and Spain experience low total fertility rates, with an average of 1.3 children per woman in 1998. This is surprising because a few generations ago these Catholic countries had high birth rates. The recent OECD statistics undermine any previous statistical association between high fertility, low employment rates for women, Catholicism, and traditional family values (Castles 2002). In 2000, the Canadian total fertility rate reached a low of 1.49 before rising slightly to 1.51 in 2001 (Lawlor 2003).

Reasons for fertility decline are many and complex (Weston and Parker 2002). Lower infant mortality has permitted couples to produce fewer children because more are expected to reach maturity (Chesnais 1992). Unlike a century ago, parents in OECD countries now seldom rely on their children for financial support or old age security because

Table 2.1
Total fertility rate, 1970–5 and 1995–2000 (births per woman)

Country	1970–5	1995–2000
Australia	2.53	1.79
Canada	1.97	1.55
Denmark	1.97	1.72
Finland	1.62	1.73
France	2.31	1.71
Germany	1.64	1.30
Ireland	3.82	1.90
Italy	2.28	1.20
Netherlands	1.97	1.50
New Zealand	2.40	1.95
Portugal	2.75	1.37
Spain	2.89	1.15
Sweden	1.89	1.57
United Kingdom	2.04	1.72
United States	2.02	1.99

Source: Extracted from Lewis 2003, 18; Statistics New Zealand 1998, 15

compulsory education laws keep children in school and governments or employers provide retirement benefits. The cost of raising children has increased while the benefits of a large number of children per family have declined. The financial cost is now calculated in terms of women's lost earnings and the need for more spacious accommodation in better school zones or safer areas as well as the direct costs of food, clothing, care, and education. Declining fertility is also related to improvements in contraception, access to legal abortion, women's and men's personal choices to have smaller families, and the difficulty mothers experience in combining paid work with child rearing (Hakim 2000; McDonald 2000).

Castles (2002) argued that social programs *can* influence fertility rates, as jurisdictions with formal care provisions for children under three years old and flexible workplace arrangements tend to have moderately high fertility rates. Women generally have fewer children when they must struggle to earn a living, such as through job discrimination, low wages, few childcare facilities, or public discourse that makes them feel guilty about neglecting their children. Current employment trends in OECD countries suggest that most women cannot afford or no longer wish to refrain from paid work in order to raise large families.

Policy makers are concerned about low fertility because they assume that an aging population will produce a diminished tax base if fewer people are working. However, there are a number of ways to augment the tax base besides encouraging couples to have more children. Governments could accept more tax-paying immigrants who already have children or are likely to produce them. But this would be insufficient to counteract the shortfall of children, because immigrants typically bear *fewer* children than native-born populations. Furthermore, high rates of (non-white) immigration have already caused a political backlash in many countries (such as Britain and Australia).

Governments could increase tax revenue by encouraging more people to work and pay income taxes. Many states are already doing this by encouraging mothers to return to paid work earlier, by developing welfare-to-work programs for recipients of social assistance, and by promoting 'active aging' policies for seniors. Urging more mothers to remain in the labour force throughout their childbearing years would increase income tax revenue but would also require more childcare services and flexible workplaces. Governments could also increase payroll taxes or income taxes in order to support an aging population, although this may not be feasible politically. However, if taxes were indirect or increased gradually, or a special tax was created for a specific and well-explained purpose, this policy option might become politically acceptable.

One reason why women now produce fewer children is that they are bearing their first child later in life, now around twenty-eight to thirty years old (OECD 2001, 25). However, there is little chance that policy makers can successfully encourage earlier reproduction. The growing tendency to postpone childbirth has some advantages for women, who are able to complete their education and find paid work before giving birth. A period of continuous full-time employment is often required before women become eligible for maternity benefits. However, postponing motherhood until later in life can also make conception more difficult and pregnancy riskier.

One non-controversial fertility trend is the decline in teenage birth rates in most countries. The fertility rate for first births for Canadian women aged fifteen to nineteen years declined from 45.6 in 1957 to 17.56 in 1998 (Ram 1990, 83; Bélanger, Carrière, and Gilbert 2001, 96), but cross-national differences are apparent. In 1998, teen birth rates (births per thousand women aged fifteen to nineteen years old) varied

Table 2.2
Teen birth rate, 1998 (per 1,000 women aged 15–19 years)

Country	Teenage birth rates	Country	Teenage birth rates
Korea	2.9	Germany	13.1
Japan	4.6	Austria	14.0
Switzerland	5.5	Czech Republic	16.4
Netherlands	6.2	Australia	18.4
Sweden	6.5	Ireland	18.7
Italy	6.6	Poland	18.7
Spain	7.9	Canada	20.2
Denmark	8.1	Portugal	21.2
Finland	9.2	Iceland	24.7
France	9.3	Hungary	26.5
Luxembourg	9.7	Slovak Republic	26.9
Belgium	9.9	New Zealand	29.8
Greece	11.8	United Kingdom	30.8
Norway	12.4	United States	52.1

Source: Extracted from OECD 2003b, 81.

from a high of 52.1 in the United States to a low of 2.9 in Korea, as Table 2.2 indicates (OECD 2003b, 81). This suggests that there are cultural, social, and policy factors affecting these rates.

National birth rates are influenced by variations in sexual practices, access to contraception, cultural ideas about women's roles, poverty rates, and the ethnic, age, and gender composition of the population. Teen fertility rates remain relatively high in countries such as New Zealand and the United States, which contain large percentages of 'visible minorities' with low household incomes and few employment opportunities (such as Maori, Pacific Islanders, indigenous peoples, and Afro-American and Hispanic people). These groups tend to cohabit and marry at younger ages, and place a high value on parenthood as an indicator of adult status and love between partners (Mink 1998; Baker 2001b, 19; Edin 2003). Family poverty is certainly related to early pregnancy, which in turn contributes to the perpetuation of low income throughout adult life. Many studies have found a strong correlation between teenage pregnancy, early family formation, and poor life chances for both parents (especially mothers) and their children (Hobcraft and Kiernan 2001).

Births outside marriage have also increased in many OECD nations, as Table 2.3 indicates, but most are to cohabiting couples in which the woman is between twenty-five and thirty-five years old. Lewis (2003;

Table 2.3
Extramarital birth rate as a percentage of all births

Country	1988 (%)	1998 (%)
Australia	17	29
Canada	22	31
Denmark	45	45
Finland	21	37
France	26	40
Germany	16	20
Ireland	12	28
Italy	6	9
Netherlands	10	21
Portugal	14	20
Spain	9	15
Sweden	51	55
United Kingdom	25	38
United States	26	33

Source: Lewis 2003.

29) noted that the extramarital birth rate in the United Kingdom increased from 5.9 per thousand single, divorced, and widowed women (aged fifteen to forty-four years) in 1940 to 39.6 in 1995. As a percentage of all births, extra-nuptial birth rates in 1997–8 were the highest in nations such as Sweden (55 per cent) and Denmark (45 per cent), which both have high rates of non-marital cohabitation (Lewis 2003, 28). In Australia, 31 per cent of babies were born outside marriage in 2001, compared to 10 per cent in 1976 (Australian Bureau of Statistics 1995, 2002); but again, most of these births occur within cohabiting relationships. We have already noted that cohabitation tends to produce less relationship stability than legal marriage. Therefore, we might assume that many of these children will experience the separation of their parents during childhood, and, should they decide to cohabit when they become adults, will themselves have a higher chance of separating.

Declining fertility definitely requires policy responses, but it is not necessarily the recipe for national disaster often implied by journalists. Nevertheless, reforms are needed to deal with and to counteract an aging population, including adjustments to immigration quotas, employment programs, childcare services, working hours, old age pensions, health care funding, and taxation. However, we should keep in mind that declining fertility also brings advantages to individuals, families, and the larger society. Fewer teenage pregnancies and unwanted births can reduce the need for social services and state income support. Large families often require income supplements, so fewer children per family would help ensure that parents are able to support their children on their own earnings. Fewer children would also enable women to pursue their educational goals and retain paid employment, which would raise the standard of living for many families as well as provide more income tax revenue to the state. Theoretically, fewer children per family would also enable each child to receive more parental attention.

In the 1960s, the United Nations encouraged member states to support zero population growth and to provide reproductive services such as abortion and contraception. Now, more governments are expressing concern about the national economic consequences of declining fertility. This highlights the significance of the political interpretation of demographic trends rather than the actual trends themselves. However, when politicians attempt to modify family patterns, they find that they are influenced by many different factors, noted in the next section.

Influences on Family Demography

Political attempts to shape family demography have not always been successful because family life is influenced by so many factors. Three factors, which are recurring themes throughout this book, include changing patterns of work and remuneration, technological innovations, and new ideas about entitlements, lifestyles, and state obligations to family. These are outlined below.

Work Patterns Influence Family Patterns and Practices

Current labour market trends create an insecure environment for family formation, child rearing, home ownership, and marital stability. Patterns of work in particular are changing as more companies export internationally, create branch plants in countries with cheaper production costs, and advertise globally for higher-level positions. In a competitive environment, 'flexible staffing' helps corporate managers maximize profits and cushion their companies against economic downturns. Hiring staff on temporary contracts permits employers to make these workers redundant when their services are no longer needed. In some jurisdictions, employers are also permitted to pay lower wages and fewer benefits to temporary and part-time staff. Although some workers use this kind of work to manage studying or caring work, many find that current labour practices reduce income security and make future planning difficult.

Some employers permit staff to work from home, from satellite offices, or from their vehicles, reducing the need for expensive office space and promoting employee loyalty by allowing some choice in work arrangements. The opportunity to 'telework' may reduce time and expenses and help some workers combine earning with household responsibilities. However, if more people worked from home on a regular basis, changes would be required in home design, the domestic division of labour, and the maintenance of work/family boundaries.

With more competitive conditions, employees and the self-employed in the liberal welfare states are working longer hours, and higher percentages are working during evenings and weekends (Bittman 2004; Crompton 2004). Family practices such as eating the evening meal together are becoming less prevalent because more family members are employed and more work in 'non-standard hours.' Mobile telephones and laptop computers enable people to 'work anywhere,' as the advertising slogans tell us. However, this blurs the distinction between work time and family/leisure time. Business matters can now intrude in our lives at any moment – while we are driving our children to school or trying to cook dinner. The twenty-four-hour economy requires special initiatives to maintain a work/life balance, as working long hours is stressful, imposes on couple time, and requires the other partner to manage the childcare or housework.

Working conditions are changing as national governments enter into free trade agreements. More executives now travel abroad to locate new trading partners, establish and maintain export markets, or develop branch plants. Employees and consultants are travelling farther from home for work purposes, with implications for family relationships but especially for caring responsibilities. Dual-earner parents with several children are disadvantaged under such conditions unless they can afford to hire domestic help. Workplace stress often encourages one parent to opt out of full-time employment, and mothers are more likely than fathers to accept this alternative. At the same time, a greater number of educated women avoid potential conflicts by having fewer or no children.

Changes in the structure of work gradually shape preferences about what and where to study, how long to remain in school, which employment skills to develop, and which occupations are considered desirable.

Employers urge schools to promote entrepreneurial skills, business knowledge, and work incentives. International labour markets encourage achieving students to aspire to foreign study and encourage others to seek employment abroad. Young people learn to anticipate the need for computer skills, tertiary education, and national and international mobility in order to secure work experience. Some plan accordingly, but others feel that they cannot for financial or family reasons.

Young people are increasingly subjected to advertising telling them to look fashionable in order to find friends or sexual partners, to indulge themselves with consumer goods, and to create comfortable material lives. However, they need secure incomes and few dependants to afford this lifestyle. With readily available credit cards and insecure jobs, young people are accruing higher levels of personal debt and therefore experiencing difficulty building family assets throughout their lives. Increasingly, young couples respond to these pressures by delaying marriage, childbirth, and home ownership.

Legal marriage is still seen as a long-term commitment, and raising children is more often viewed as expensive and time consuming, especially if mothers are expected to make employment sacrifices to provide care. Many middle-class youth live with their parents longer, and cohabiting couples now delay buying a home and having a child while they establish a career and strengthen their financial security. At the same time, their relationships become more vulnerable to separation given the pressures of more residential mobility, precarious income security, the need to accommodate two careers, high levels of student and personal debt, and larger mortgages. Personal life is altered in many ways by these new educational requirements, labour market demands, material aspirations, and debts.

Women born in the same period in different countries have had very different experiences in terms of the number and pace of family events (González-López 2002). However, a woman's age is still a better predictor of her family circumstances than where she lives (Carling 2002). Cohort differences are apparent: younger women are more likely to be educated, to work for pay, to be childless, or to have fewer children than their mothers' generation. Social class differences also remain relevant, as family income and a woman's education are important correlates with many family patterns. Latten and de Graaf (1997) have argued that highly educated women can be seen as trendsetters for the way that family life will be organized in the future.

Changing Technology Influences Family Patterns

The second influence on family demography is technological innovation, which has reduced fertility, enabled the separation of sex and marriage, and encouraged more residential mobility and travel. Early in the twentieth century, life expectancies increased with the invention of antibiotics and inoculations, as well as improvements in nutrition, sanitation, and health care. Declining infant mortality, with greater certainty that babies would survive to adulthood, reduced the need for couples to produce more children than they wanted. After the 1960s, improvements in birth control encouraged more people to engage in sexual intercourse outside marriage by reducing the risk of pregnancy. These improvements also enable more women and couples to remain childless or to ensure that family size is consistent with income and preferences.

Advances in artificial insemination also assist reproduction, even though only a small percentage of babies are currently born through medically assisted conception (Ford et al. 2003). Undoubtedly, this will increase as the technology improves and will expand the potential for radical family change. The ability to freeze sperm means that conception can happen after the biological father's death, 'designer babies' are possible, post-menopausal women can have babies, and wealthy couples can commission low-income women to produce children for them (Eichler 1997).

Improvements in transportation technology also influence family life. Early in the twentieth century, the invention of automobiles allowed more privacy for 'courting' couples, altering patterns of residence and intimacy. Now, many families own more than one car, which increases household costs but enables couples to work in different locations farther from home. Technological improvements in air travel (and lower fares) make international travel more feasible for work or pleasure. More affordable international travel also enables people to flee from family conflict or abusive partners and to find a safe haven in other jurisdictions. However, new computerized surveillance technologies and multilateral agreements between governments assist officials to apprehend those who cross borders to shirk their family responsibilities, as we will see in chapter 9.

Current migration trends show that more families are spread throughout the world and immigrants are arriving from a larger range of countries with different family practices (OECD 2005). However, research suggests that especially young migrants and the second generation modify their family demography to make it more consistent with patterns in their adopted country (Albanese 2005). Some immigrants gravitate to ethnic enclaves to gain cultural services, such as satellite television from their home country. However, many maintain regular contact with relatives through email, electronic financial transfers, and regular air travel. Some parents earn money in one place and raise children in another, and small percentages become 'transnational citizens' who are equally comfortable living in several countries.

New computer technology permits people to earn money while living in remote areas. Cell phones and electronic mail enable family members and friends to keep in touch and parents to 'supervise' their children from a distance, even while working. Television and the Internet bring international ideas, sexual encounters, and advertising into our homes, introducing us to new forms of consumerism and different ways of living, raising our material aspirations, and spreading a more cosmopolitan outlook.

Concern is also increasing about the impact of technology on children, including the consequences of spending long hours watching television, playing computer games, or 'surfing' the Internet. These practices can reduce sociability and physical exercise, and promote inadequate social skills and childhood obesity. Many parents also worry about the violent and sexual images on television and video games, as well as the rays that are emitted from cell phones and computer screens.

The Internet enables global marketing, the rapid spread of news, international lobbying, chat groups, and new dating practices, but also the dissemination of pornography and stalking. In general, technology increasingly permeates our sexual practices, childrearing, the maintenance of relationships, the design of our homes, and patterns of work and leisure. However, it is not just the new technology that is of concern, but the ideas it brings into our homes.

Changing Ideas Influence Family Patterns and Practices

The third influence on socio-demographic patterns is the growing internationalization of Western ideas about personal choice and consumerism, which alter aspirations and expected lifestyles. Increasingly, people around the world watch the same television programs and films, read the same books and material on the Internet, and view the same images and advertisements. Subtitles, translations, international marketing, and the globalization of the English language through videos and the Internet permit similar ideas to reach people worldwide.

The 'globalization of culture' consists largely of Western ideas from the United States, the United Kingdom, and Europe circulating to parts of the rest of the world. Especially young people in remote or less developed areas can be enticed by these images and ideas, and may try to simulate the fashions and lifestyles of the West. Although cultural and national differences remain, more people expect to choose where they live and with whom, what they buy, how they will earn a living, and how they spend their leisure time. Increasingly, young people want to improve their living standards and live stylish and exciting lives.

Although more people eat 'ethnic' foods and decorate their homes with artefacts from other cultures, young people around the world also wear similar clothes, listen to the same music, and develop similar 'world views.' Westernization encourages contraceptive use, freer choice of marriage partners, nuclear family living, a greater acceptance of divorce, and more gender equality within marriage (Giddens 1992). Western culture tends to frown on dowries, bride prices, enforcement of female virginity until marriage, arranged marriages without choice, and large numbers of children per family. With more travel and Internet usage, some cultural variations in personal life may diminish, although many endure.

New ideas about human rights, family obligations, and entitlement to social benefits also shape expectations and family patterns in subtle ways. Policy reforms first change people's expectations and then gradually influence their behaviour. For example, policy reform has altered expectations about future state support and made paid employment seem like the normal situation for mothers well as fathers. However, changing family behaviour also encourages governments to modify social programmes.

Governments in the liberal welfare states were forced to reform their divorce laws during the 1960s and 1970s when more people separated, causing a backlog of divorce applications in the courts and economic insecurity for mother-led households (Baker 2001b). After reform, divorce rates increased briefly to accommodate the backlog of applications but then levelled off in many countries. As more couples cohabited, they could separate without applying for a divorce or paying lawyers, but governments eventually changed the laws to enforce child support and the equal division of family assets after separation, regardless of marital status. In many jurisdictions, couples are now treated as married after living together for one or two years. As people change their lifestyles, politicians reform laws and policies to enforce family obligations.

Conclusion

This chapter has shown that demographic trends are always interpreted with political intentions, and the same trend can be used to argue for quite different policy options. Declining fertility, for example, could be used as an argument to increase resources for future retirement pensions by raising the contribution rates of social insurance programs. It could also persuade governments to set higher immigration targets to increase the working-age population. Declining fertility is often associated with the difficulty of combining maternity with employment, and the state could improve parental leave and benefits for employed parents, require employers to provide more generous family-related leave, and provide higher subsidies for childcare services.

This suggests that demographic trends alone seldom lead to policy changes, but instead are used by political actors, including interest groups, as a platform to advocate for reform. The most compelling arguments have related to the costs of fertility decline and subsequent population aging. These have been used across the political spectrum by those concerned with a variety of issues, including the financing of old age and retirement pensions, the building of retirement complexes, and new ways of delivering health care services for the elderly. The aging population argument has led to some redistribution of funding to chronic care and geriatric services, the use of public and private capital to build retirement villages, and attempts to increase private savings and reduce state expenditure on pensions. Yet as Gauthier (1996) argued, advocacy groups are always the intermediaries in the interplay between demographic change and government policy.

More people now expect to make their own choices about sexuality, contraception, marriage, and reproduction, without the church or the state telling them how they must behave. At the same time, more people expect the state to enforce child support after divorce, to protect children from abusive relatives, and to protect women from violent partners. Some advocacy groups continue to urge governments to assist parents who are struggling to care for children on low incomes, while others press for limitations to state income support. However, politicians 'have to carry their electorates with them if they want to remain in power,' and therefore carefully monitor public opinion before launching into policy reform (Hantrais 2004; 197). In the next chapter, this argument that 'politics matters' is expanded and further developed.

3 Welfare Regimes, National Politics, and Family Policies

In chapter 2, I acknowledged that socio-demographic changes in family patterns encourage governments to restructure family policies but argued that the various ways these issues are framed and the policy solutions offered to deal with the perceived problems differ considerably. In this chapter, a second set of influences on the nature and direction of family program reform is introduced. I argue that historical patterns of social provision and the prevalent debates in national politics can substantially alter the restructuring of family policies by excluding some policy options and giving preference to others.

Systems of social provision involve assumptions and ideologies about the typical composition of families, the expected division of labour by gender, and the appropriate role of the state in family life. These assumptions are enduring, which means that family policy development and restructuring to some extent becomes 'path dependent' within these regimes (P. Pierson 2000). These systems of social provision become institutionalized, with vested interests discouraging radical change. However, new ideas from interest groups or international organizations or stemming from changes in family circumstances can lead to policy restructuring if those who introduce the ideas can successfully justify them within the existing culture of social provision (Béland 2005).

This chapter examines some of the comparative research on social provision and institutional structures, concluding that earlier studies of welfare regimes generally under-reported activities and developments relating to caring work and family welfare. When family policies are considered in the development of welfare states, these general conceptualizations of welfare regimes need to be modified. Nevertheless, I argue that patterns of social provision are discernible for family-related programs and that new policy options are always negotiated within these parameters.

Conceptualizing Welfare Regimes

From the 1940s to the 1970s, governments in most industrialized countries developed a range of social programs designed to guarantee citizens at least a minimal level of income in the event of unemployment, accidents, sickness, pregnancy and childbirth, disability, and retirement. The development of 'the welfare state' was premised on the belief that governments as well as employers, voluntary associations, communities, families, and employees have a role to play in maintaining income security. In addition, welfare states were based on the idea that the state should assist families at certain stages of the life cycle (such as childbirth and retirement) or at times of personal or family crisis (such as illness, an incident of domestic violence, or divorce) (Baker and Tippin 1999, 4). Different nation states, however, did not always accept the same ideas about social provision. A number of major variations are apparent in the delivery and funding of social programs, based on different philosophical ideas about who deserves public support and how best to assist those in need.

In the 1970s, theorists such as Titmuss (1974) and Mishra (1977) began to construct typologies of welfare state provision and attempted to explain cross-national variations. Considerable effort was devoted to analysing and classifying welfare state development and creating 'ideal types' or models of social provision (Korpi 1983; Mishra 1984; Esping-Andersen 1990; Mishra 1990; Kangas and Palme 1992–3; Drover and Kerans 1993; and Esping-Andersen 1966b). These researchers argued that some continuity in social programs, delivery mechanisms, and funding was discernible even though welfare states were established and modified over many years with input from different political parties and interest groups.

Patterns were noted in the assumptions underpinning social program development concerning why some people are in need, how the state should assist them, and how social benefits and services are best delivered. These patterns of assumptions as well as the social programs developed from them have been called 'welfare regimes' (Esping-Andersen 1990; O'Connor, Orloff, and Shaver 1999). Specific jurisdictions have generally favoured one predominant type of welfare regime over the years, depending on the philosophy of the party governing most of the time, the political power of various interest groups, coalitions among interest groups and political parties, and prevalent social and cultural ideas.

Throughout the 1980s, theories to explain the uneven development of welfare states were based mainly on analyses of social programs designed to replace lost income from paid work, such as unemployment or retirement benefits. Explanations of cross-national variations focused on different political alliances between governments and lobby groups, such as trade unions seeking to reduce class inequality and reinforce income security for working men. One of the most well-known but often criticized categorizations was devised by Esping-Andersen (1990).

Esping-Andersen rejected the functionalist view that welfare regimes are simply products of the Industrial Revolution or rising prosperity, and concluded that politics makes a difference. He argued that the reason why some states developed more generous social programs than others relates to the history of political coalitions within those countries (Borchorst 1994). This approach, called the 'power-resource theory,' emphasizes the strategic alliances between governments and influential and well-funded interest groups (O'Connor and Olsen 1998).

Power-resource theorists argue that interest groups with political power and economic resources are able to force their governments to introduce social programs that protect their own interests. These theorists also note that the combination of strong trade unions and governments dominated by left-wing political parties has been effective in developing welfare regimes promoting greater income equality and narrowing the gap between the rich and the poor. Consequently, they categorize welfare regimes according to the underlying philosophies and trade-offs these regimes make between equity (whether services are adequate to meet needs) and efficiency (whether public resources are used for maximum effect at minimum cost). Esping-Andersen's classification is based on the quality of social rights, the pattern of stratification resulting from policies, and the nature of the state-market nexus. In the next section, I elaborate on this model but outline why it is less useful for analysing family policy development and restructuring. Several alternative models will be discussed that focus more on family-related issues.

Liberal or Residual Welfare Regimes

Esping-Andersen (1990) labelled nations such as the United Kingdom,

Canada, the United States, Australia, and New Zealand as 'liberal' welfare regimes because most social programs assume that individuals are normally responsible for their own financial support and well-being. The underlying assumption in these countries is that the state should intervene only when people are in serious financial or family difficulty and cannot obtain assistance from household members. Consequently, liberal states invest relatively low levels of public money in social programs and rely mainly on means-tested benefits targeted to those who have exhausted their private resources or clearly cannot cope.

People in need may be expected to sell or liquidate their assets before qualifying for state income support, which is relatively ungenerous, financed through general taxation, and set below the minimum wage to provide work incentives. The liberal welfare state emphasizes efficiency rather than equity and individual rather than collective responsibility. The state permits wealthier people to retain most of their income by creating relatively low personal and corporate income tax rates, tax benefits for individuals and businesses, and consumption taxes rather than wealth taxes. Political leaders sometimes assume that wealthier people will invest their extra resources in job creation activities. Liberal states often refer to citizens as 'consumers,' 'taxpayers,' or 'customers' and emphasize their personal choices to purchase services or insurance from private providers (Pusey 1993; Brodie 1996).

Neo-liberal regimes add a moral dimension by distinguishing between the 'deserving poor' (such as low-income widows with infants or persons with severe disabilities) and the 'undeserving poor' (such as youth who leave school early and sell drugs to gain income). Beneficiaries are sometimes blamed for their own misfortune because they did not search hard enough for a job or mishandled their own affairs. Examples of neo-liberal welfare states would include the United States, Thatcher's Britain, New Zealand throughout the 1990s, and the Canadian provinces of Alberta and Ontario in recent years (Pierson 1994; Kelsey 1995; Lightman 1997; Bashevkin 2002a).

Corporatist or Conservative Regimes

Esping-Andersen (1990) labelled nations such as France, Germany, or Italy as 'corporatist' welfare regimes because employers' groups collaborated with trade unions and governments to create social insurance programs. These were intended to share the risk of lost income due to an economic downturn, unemployment, sickness, or disability, and were originally designed to promote income security for those with stable jobs. Social insurance programs are usually financed through payroll deductions from employees and employers (based on a percentage of the employee's earnings and the employers' payroll) and sometimes matched with government contributions. A commission representing all three groups often administers the fund, and any surplus is invested for protection in hard times or low-employment periods where contributions are smaller.

Social insurance benefits are typically generous for employees with moderate incomes who work full time throughout their lives and contribute the maximum amount to the fund. For example, retiring employees in Italy and France have received retirement pensions representing about 80 to 90 per cent of their previous earnings. This is much more generous than liberal welfare states, which often pay less than 50 per cent (Esping-Andersen 1996b, 70). However, the contributions or payroll taxes might be quite high for employers. In addition, those outside the labour force are often excluded from social insurance. Initially, corporatist states expected them to rely on their families or charitable organizations, but later developed less generous social assistance programs with flat-rate benefits (the same amount for everyone).

Corporatist welfare regimes are also called 'conservative' because they are not designed to promote equality or redress existing income discrepancies. Instead, they were intended to maintain income stability for employees and employers and social stability for governments. These regimes are also conservative because lower earners make smaller contributions and consequently receive lower benefits. Thus, the discrepancy between the rich and the poor is maintained, as is the gap between the social security benefits of those working full time (mainly men/fathers) and those working part time or outside the labour force (many mothers with preschool children and the chronically unemployed).

Social Democratic Welfare Regimes

Esping-Andersen (1990) labelled Nordic countries such as Sweden or Denmark as 'social democratic' welfare regimes because their social programs were designed to prevent poverty and inequality by offering universal services to all citizens and by redistributing income through a progressive income tax system. These regimes have also made serious efforts to create jobs for everyone (including mothers with young children) and to establish relatively generous benefits regardless of household income or labour force attachment. Programs are designed to reduce both class-based inequality and gender inequality, and include guaranteed annual incomes, public childcare and health services, and tertiary education without or with minimal tuition fees. Social democratic programs are usually financed through general taxation or a combination of general taxation and employer payroll deductions. Citizens might be asked to pay a small user fee, but social services are usually heavily subsidized with public funds (Stephens 1996).

Esping-Andersen (1990) argued that social democratic regimes are the most generous because they are characterized by a high degree of 'de-commodification,' which means that social programs allow a decent standard of living independent of labour force participation. (We will revisit this concept when we discuss feminist critiques later in this chapter.) Official statistics verify that social democratic welfare regimes have been most successful in minimizing the gap between the rich and the poor as well as between men and women. For example, Sweden has the lowest child poverty rates for lone-parent families (mainly led by mothers) among OECD nations, with 6.7 per cent of children in these families classified as 'poor,'[1] compared to about 51.6 per cent in Canada and 55.4 per cent in the United States (UNICEF 2000, 10).

In social democratic nations citizens and corporations are expected to pay relatively high income taxes and corporations pay high payroll taxes, but this revenue is used to create generous social programs. OECD statistics indicate that Sweden has the highest rate of public social spending as a percentage of gross domestic product (about 34 per cent, compared to a 24 per cent average in OECD countries) (OECD 2001, 73). Furthermore, most adults pay income taxes because most are employed. However, employees with children are supported by public childcare services, extended parental benefits, and leave for family responsibilities (Leira 2002).

Welfare Regimes as Ideal Types

Welfare regimes are formulated as ideal types for cross-national comparisons. In reality, there is considerable variation among countries within the same category, and most now support all three categories of social programs. For example, Canadian provincial 'welfare' programs are targeted to those with very low incomes and fit into the liberal

---

[1] UNICEF uses relative poverty rates, measured by household incomes that are less than 50 per cent of median income in that jurisdiction.

model. Federal old age security, while paid at a relatively low rate, is available to all Canadians regardless of income and is more typical of the social democratic model, but the federal unemployment benefit operates as social insurance, exemplifying the corporatist model.

Canada is classified as a liberal welfare state because it usually relies on the free market for well-being rather than state support or government intervention in the economy, labour force, or family life. Many benefits are set at ungenerous levels compared to those of Nordic countries. In fact, several provincial welfare programs are considered neo-liberal with their meagre benefits and punitive attitudes towards beneficiaries. However, Quebec's childcare program is closer to the social democratic model in its intent and generosity, and recent reforms to the federal child tax benefit make Canada look more generous now than a decade ago. Most other liberal welfare states have also reformed child benefits in recent years.

No other models of social provision seem to have created as much debate as Esping-Andersen's (1990). Some of the critiques will be presented in the next section, as well as alternative models that focus on family programs and caring work.

Debates about Welfare Regimes

Numerous researchers have tested the validity of Esping-Andersen's model by comparing specific social programs in OECD countries. Some have concluded that he erroneously placed countries with quite different patterns of social provision within the same category. For example, several researchers have argued that Australia and New Zealand differed from other liberal welfare states because trade unions historically allied with governments in both countries to regulate wages, production, immigration, imports, and exports rather than to create extensive state income support programs or social insurance (Saunders 1994; Castles and Pierson 1995; Mitchell 1995; Castles and Shirley 1996). Both Australia and New Zealand have been called 'wage-earner's welfare states' because high male wages were ensured through centralized bargaining, arbitration, and limited immigration. Full (male) employment, high wages, and above-average rates of home ownership protected economic well-being more effectively than income support programs, and particularly Australians have historically enjoyed favourable living standards.

Researchers have also disputed the inclusion of southern and western European countries within the same category of corporatist welfare regimes. Some have argued that southern European countries do not really fit into this model, as they have a history of authoritarian political regimes, less-developed family policies, a heavily gendered labour market, and more reliance on the church and family members rather than government for social services (Flaquer 2000). Similarities as well as differences have been found between family institutions and policies in Spain, usually classified as corporatist, and Finland, classified as social democratic (Oinonen 2000).

Some researchers have disputed the very existent of patterns called 'welfare regimes.' A few researchers have found so many differences among social programs in countries classified as similar that they have discounted any attempts at classification (Daly and Rake 2003). However, the most important critiques for our discussion of family policies are the feminist ones.

Feminist Critiques of Welfare Regimes

Feminist scholars have argued that earlier theorists misrepresented welfare state development because they relied too much on the analysis of employment-related programs used mainly by men (Sainsbury 1994). For example, Bock and Thane (1991) concluded that women's lobbying efforts were essential to the early development of social programs in Europe, and that political alliances and ideologies explain the many different ways that women were perceived or used by welfare states.

Pedersen (1993) argued that gender and family issues were central to welfare state development but that these have been overlooked or downplayed by (male) researchers who focused on trade unions and employers' groups. She showed that social reformers and activists who shaped the early welfare policies of Britain and France were interested in fertility decline, child health, the family wage, mothers' caring responsibilities, and women and children's citizenship. McKeen (2004) also saw gender and family as central to Canadian social policies, discussing reasons why the efforts of feminists were not more successful in counteracting the 'familialist and liberal-individualist constructions' underpinning the welfare state.

Numerous scholars, including Orloff (1993) and Lister (1997), noted that Esping-Andersen's (1990) concept of 'de-commodification' has never been relevant for most women. Historically, women have had a lower attachment to paid work, and especially mothers have performed unpaid caring work at home while their male partners earned household money. Therefore, categorizing welfare states by how effectively they allow employees to maintain an income when they become unemployed or when they retire does not really apply to those normally outside the labour force. Rather than focusing on de-commodification, feminists compare welfare regimes on 'de-familialization,' or how well they enable women to live without depending unduly on the financial support of their male partners or parents.

Feminists often ask how various welfare regimes help women into paid work and how they protect or disregard their interests when they become lone mothers or widows (Orloff 1993; Lister 1997; Mahon 2001; Christoper 2002). They ask whether social programs enable or prevent women from forming autonomous households when they want to or need to, independent from both the state and their families. Most feminist scholars conclude that women living in social democratic countries are best able to form autonomous households without having to marry or depend on relatives. However, focusing on the ability to form autonomous households has enabled some feminists to privilege the employed mother over the homemaker (Shaver 2002).

Esping-Andersen's regimes become somewhat blurred when public funding for care is examined, and especially the way that states draw the line between private and public responsibility for the care of very young children and the frail elderly (Orloff 1993; Baker 1995; Millar and Warman 1995; Sainsbury 1996; Lewis 1997; Adams and Padamsee 2001; Daly and Rake 2003). Although the social democratic countries provide abundant resources for both the very young and very old, some of the so-called corporatist states (such as France and Italy) also provide ample services for young children though not for the frail elderly (Anttonen and Sipilä 1996).

The discourse and ideas implicit within social policies often form the focus of feminist analyses. The ways that politicians and journalists talk about social issues or certain groups are considered to shape policy reform, but this public discourse varies cross-nationally. For example, caring for children at home by low-income mothers has been referred to as 'dependency' in the United States but has been considered 'good mothering' in Australia.[2] In the United States, mainly black lone moth-

---

2 The discourse is rapidly changing in Australia, especially after the May 2005 budget, which placed more emphasis on the employability of mothers receiving social benefits. However, there is still considerable opposition to expecting mothers with school-age children to become earners.

ers have been vilified by negative talk about 'welfare moms,' including portraying them as unwilling to work, as 'bad mothers' who are 'poor role models' for their children, and as a 'drain on the public purse.' By using these portrayals, politicians have gained sufficient acquiescence from white middle-class Americans to cut social assistance payments well below the level of other liberal welfare states. Although American welfare cuts have increased employment rates among these mothers, they have not reduced family poverty (Polakow 1997; Mink 1998; Bashevkin 2002b).

An emphasis on discourse and ideas has led researchers to conclude that the state and family are intertwined, with the state mobilizing 'the family' for its own political ends (Wilson 1977; Bryson 1992; Ursel 1992). Furthermore, state regulation can redefine an array of familial roles and responsibilities. Haney (2003) compared policy debates and welfare practices in Hungary and the Czech Republic, showing that massive restructuring led the two states on separate family policy paths: Hungary moved towards a liberal welfare state, while the Czech Republic followed a social democratic model. In both cases, state restructuring was justified through 'narratives of the family.' The malleable discourse of 'familialism' lends itself to being appropriated by quite divergent political actors.

Feminist scholars have also argued that the concept of 'welfare dependency' makes the false assumption that all wage-earning citizens (including their home-making wives who are not earning a wage) are 'independent' whereas all those relying on state income support are 'dependent.' Feminist theorists typically argue that the power-resource theory cannot ignore (women's) unpaid caring work and needs to be refined to take into consideration the relations among states, markets, families, and voluntary organizations (Pederson 1993; Baker 1995; O'Connor; Orloff & Shaver 1999; Leira 2002). They also reinforce the idea that welfare states can be compared on different policy dimensions, and countries with similar work-related policies do not always share similar policies relating to family support or women's employment.

When discussing the development of welfare states, however, both feminist and mainstream researchers have downplayed the considerable amount of welfare work done by voluntary organizations, mutual aid societies, informal networks, and social movements (Brush 2002). The 'thin-ness' of both the concept of gender and the notion of welfare in welfare regime studies is revealed by the largely volunteer, non-governmental, and non-familial shelter movement for women battered by their partners. The original refuges for battered women relied on feminist activism, in-kind contributions, and volunteers who often had personal experience with violence against women, and did not rely on or appeal to state authorities (Brush 2002). Yet these types of organizations are largely absent from studies of the development of social welfare.

Alternative Welfare Regimes Focusing on Caring and Family

One of the first scholars to include gender in welfare state analysis was Jane Lewis (1992), who suggested that varying models of family are implicit within social policies. Comparing the United Kingdom, France, and Sweden, she identified a different emphasis on the husband/father as the main breadwinner and found variations in family-related rights and the gendered division of labour. From this analysis, she proposed a new classification of welfare states based on the prevalent model of family and the expected role of women. She distinguished among social policies that placed a strong, moderate, or weak emphasis on the male breadwinner.

Since then, several researchers have reinforced the idea that different kinds of welfare states are based on different models of family. Leira (2002) expanded on Lewis's model, noting that the 'gender-differentiated family' (in which fathers earn the household income while mothers care for the home and children) is prevalent in the United Kingdom. The family in which the mother's employment is sequential or secondary to that of the father's is widespread in France. In Sweden, the dual-earner care-sharing family has become very prevalent. The idea that different types of welfare regimes tend to emphasize particular models of family seems well supported, but I would add that these family models are resistant to change because they are typically implicit rather than openly debated. Also, social programs are often reformed incrementally rather than starting with new assumptions, which means that traditional ideas easily linger in social policy (Baker 1990).

In addition, different models of family may be apparent even within the same country or cluster of countries. For example, two models are inherent within social programs in liberal states: the male breadwinner/female caregiver model has been widespread in welfare and retirement programs, while the egalitarian model is implicit within divorce reform but is becoming prevalent in social assistance with the greater emphasis on employability (Baker and Tippin 1999). The first model assumes that men support their wives financially and women care for family members at home. The egalitarian model assumes that both men and women are potential wage earners responsible for supporting themselves and each other during cohabitation.

The egalitarian model is becoming more prevalent in Canadian and American social programs, reflecting the fact that more women have become wage earners. However, this model is also consistent with neo-liberal ideas that paid work is morally superior to 'dependency' and that taxpayers should not have to support families who are not earning money ('workless households'). The egalitarian model tends to ignore or downplay the gendered division of labour at home and in the workplace, and especially the lower earning capacity of mothers (Mink 1998; Baker and Tippin 1999). Baker and Tippin (1999) showed that low-income mothers with dependent children face quite different benefit levels and work expectations depending on where they live within liberal welfare states. These differences vary with labour markets, local politics, and ideologies of good mothering.

Gauthier (1996) traced the development of family policies from the 1900s to the 1990s in twenty-two industrialized countries. She demonstrated that state support for families has expanded considerably over the twentieth century and mapped out five different periods of 'landmarks in policy development.' She also identified four models of current state support: the pro-family/pro-natalist model (France and Quebec), pro-traditional model (Germany), pro-egalitarian model (Denmark and Sweden), and pro-family non-interventionist model (United States). Gauthier argued that demographic changes have acted as major catalysts in the call for reformed family support by the state. Changes such as fertility decline, an aging population, and increases in lone parenthood and women's employment have led to specific government interventions. However, she saw advocacy groups as intermediaries in the interplay between demographic change and government policy and emphasized the political nature of policy formation, as I do in this book.

Hantrais (2004) identified clusters of European countries with similar family policies and factors influencing their development. She focused on the generosity of social benefits, modifications to the 'gender regime' and male breadwinner models, and the extent of 'defamilialization' or the degree to which people can maintain a socially accepted standard of living without relying unduly on family support. The four categories she developed are 'Defamilialized,' 'Partially Defamilialized,' 'Familialized,' and 'Refamilialized' (Hantrais 2004, 200). In the first category she placed such countries as Sweden, Denmark, and France, where family policy is explicit, coherent, legitimized, coordinated, supportive of working parents, and universal. The United Kingdom, Ireland, Austria, and the Netherlands fell within the second category, where family policy is implicit or indirect, rhetorical, partially coordinated, and based on residence. The southern European countries were in the 'familialized' sector, where family policy is fragmented, non-institutionalized, weakly legitimized, uncoordinated, and poorly funded. In the fourth category she located countries such as Poland, Hungary, and the Czech Republic, where family provision used to be universal during the Soviet era but the regime has since undergone a shift towards a minimalist state. In these countries, family policy is implicit or indirect, rhetorical, pro-natalist, semi-legitimized, uncoordinated, institutionalized, transitional, and underfunded. Each category of family policies was further divided into two subgroups based on historical development, institutional structures, funding, and delivery.

Differences in political ideology, powerful lobby groups, and cultural values have promoted variety in national family-related programs within Europe, despite European Union policies and directives. The EU cannot devote resources to family policy as a specific domain, but they have focused on policies that enhance paid work and support family income (Hantrais 2004, 211). Similar policy concerns are evident across the European Union, but there is no universally agreed definition of family policy and no clear criteria to determine the boundaries of legitimacy and acceptability of state intervention either across or within European countries (Hantrais 2004).

The efficiency and effectiveness of family policies are difficult to assess, as outcomes may be intended or unintended, wanted or unwanted, direct or indirect. The many attempts to measure policy outcomes have shown that it is not enough to identify the presence or absence of a particular policy; it is also important to assess the level and quality of the measure, the access and take-up, and the public perception about its impact (Hantrais 2004, 198).

After exploring the configuration of care, work, and social provision within eight countries in Europe and the United States, Daly and Rake (2003) argued that attempting to classify welfare states is not a worthwhile exercise. Countries differ so much that accurate generalizations are difficult to make. Care is increasingly becoming a significant policy issue in western Europe, but childcare and elder care are seen as different. Policies are fragmented both within and among countries, and considerable controversy continues around which conditions lead to good-quality care. Increasingly, welfare states promote policies that are inconsistent with family needs. However, care is expensive, which makes it difficult for welfare states to respond to the increasing demand.

Gender used to be marginal to the analysis of comparative welfare regimes, but it has now become incorporated into mainstream scholarship. However, studies continue to be based on narrow understandings of both gender and welfare institutions, with a strong focus on employed mothers. Shaver (2002) argued that discussions of welfare regimes should make more effort to integrate the linkages among gender, agency, and power. 'Gender' refers to both men and women, and relations among women and among men need to be considered as well as relations between them. Feminists must join the mainstream debates and deal with the relations among social citizenship, social opportunity, and various forms of social difference. I believe that this is a worthwhile goal and have endeavoured to follow this approach in this work.

Comparing State Support for Women as Mothers and Workers

Studies of state support for women as mothers and workers follow from feminist critiques of welfare state research and the development of caring regimes. Sainsbury (1993) noted that many countries have created 'dual welfare states' with benefits divided roughly along gender lines. In liberal and corporatist welfare states, men are more likely to use social insurance, which is contributory, related to earnings, relatively generous, and based on individual income. Women more often use social assistance, which is designed for those unattached to the labour market, is non-contributory, and is based on need, but eligibility is related to household income rather than individual income. Because social insurance is more generous and less punitive than social assistance, men tend to benefit more from social provision in dual welfare states. Bryson (1995) presented a similar scenario for Australia.

Many researchers have discussed the gendered inconsistencies inherent in social programs. For example, McKeen (2004; viii) argued that real gender equality is impossible within Canadian social policy because the 'dual-breadwinner economic system [is] harnessed to a single-breadwinner social policy system.' Furthermore, governments continue to ignore 'social reproduction' and the fact that the majority of unpaid care work is done by women, which means that women disproportionately pay the price in high rates of poverty and stress. The second-wave women's movement advanced an alternative vision of social policy in the mid-1970s that recognized the social context of people's lives and focused on the 'social individual' as the unit of benefits rather than the household or family. However, left-liberal social policy and anti-poverty organizations helped to restructure policy in ways that were readily incorporated into the emergent neo-liberal social policy regime, with its emphasis on targeting and its reassertion of a male-centred familialist approach. Gender and women's issues slipped from view, and the focus now remains on children. Yet in current political discourse, such as the focus on 'child poverty,' children are abstracted from their family connections as well as from gender relations (McKeen 2004).

Despite the emphasis on the mother-worker, welfare states continue to support 'wifely labour' through their tax and benefit packages. Shaver and Bradshaw (1995) studied fifteen countries, showing that welfare states provide benefits for wives with and without young children, and for those who are engaged in paid as well as unpaid work. However, they concluded that levels of support vary considerably by country, although not necessarily according to the classification set out by Esping-Andersen (1990). In another study of nine countries, wives' dependency on their husband's earnings increased with the presence of young children and higher numbers of children. Dependency was reduced when employment rates and earnings were high relative to those of their husbands, and in families relying more on unearned sources of income. These factors influenced dependency regardless of welfare regimes or policy initiatives (Bianchi, Casper, and Peltola 1999).

The Luxembourg Income Study has been used to explore how tax and transfer systems and employment supports influence the poverty rates of different categories of mothers. Christopher (2002) found that the tax and transfer systems are the 'friendliest' to all mothers in Sweden and Finland, while those in Finland, the Netherlands, and the United Kingdom are the friendliest to lone mothers. However, employment supports for mothers are the most favourable in Finland, Sweden, and France. Where women are able to form non-poor autonomous households, they have greater opportunities to exit from relationships they do not find attractive or safe. This option can help prevent domestic violence and other harmful situations for women and children. Christopher concluded that mothers fare the best in countries that support *both* their employment and caring work.

Studies focusing on gender have also relied on qualitative research. For example, Rudd (2003) used an analysis of women's life histories to provide information about how privatization and the rise of market capitalism have affected family relations. Focusing on East Germany, she showed how shifts in the state's economic and social roles have led to a devaluation of familial work and the marginalization of motherhood. Orloff (2003) provided a historical overview of how the 'male breadwinner ideology' underpinned the development of the welfare state in the United States. She examined paternity regulation, child support enforcement, and the Personal Responsibility and Work Opportunity Reconciliation Act, concluding that the contemporary American welfare regime has become focused on disciplining men into becoming breadwinners rather than alleviating poverty in families with children.

The discussion in this section has shown that focusing on women, motherhood, and caring work leads to new and different ideas about the generosity of various types of welfare states. In addition, focusing on gender reinforces the link between doing unpaid caring work at home and lacking money and power in the larger society. Gendered patterns of work are influenced by perceptions of need and opportunities, but also by prevailing ideologies about gender and appropriate family patterns. The ways that policy issues are framed influence restructuring, but only some ideas can be incorporated into policy, while others are rejected.

Comparing State Support for Families in General

Comparative studies of general family support predate feminist research, and were first initiated in the late 1970s (Kamerman and Kahn 1978). Further research by Kahn and Kamerman (1983, 1988) showed widespread variations in family benefits and focused on the contextual issues and policy details within each country. Since then, numerous studies have tried to measure and explain cross-national variations in family benefits. For example, Pampel and Adams (1992) compared the level of family allowance expenditure in eighteen countries from 1959 to 1986 and found that the most decisive factors in cross-national generosity were both political and demographic. These included a high percentage of the population being over sixty-five years of age (generating public concern about declining fertility and population aging), combined with certain institutional and political conditions, such as corporatism, class-based interest groups, and leftist party rule.

Wennemo (1994) studied the family policies of eighteen OECD countries, concluding that national political trends can best explain family policy restructuring. She found that countries with strong left-wing political movements, a history of left-wing parties in government, and political parties with strong religious affiliations participating in government tend to provide higher levels of cash benefits and less support for tax reductions. Little or no association was found between fertility rates or gross domestic product and cash benefits for families with children, but countries delivering family benefits through social insurance (such as France) were found to provide higher cash benefits than other countries.

I have compared family policies in eight industrialized countries in an attempt to explain why some countries have developed extensive and comprehensive programs while others have expected families to cope with little state support (Baker 1995). I showed that the liberal welfare states typically provided lower levels of support than social democratic countries, with less emphasis on poverty prevention, child protection, and support for social care. Nevertheless, state support for mothering at home remained high in the United Kingdom and Australia, while support for dual-earner families and childcare provisions was more generous in Sweden and France. In explaining variations, I focused on different ideologies, institutional structures, and political coalitions.

Korpi (2000) examined the contribution of both gender and class to inequality by comparing the state provision for families in eighteen industrialized countries from 1985 to 1990. He created three models of family policies: state support for families in general, support for the dual-earner family, and market-oriented policies with little state intervention. General family support included the provision and generosity of child allowances, family tax benefits, and childcare services for children over three years old, and essentially served Leira's (1992) 'gender-differentiated family.' Government support for dual-earner families included the provision and generosity of childcare for children under three years, maternity/parental benefits, and home help for elderly, which served the dual-earner care-sharing family. Market-oriented policies encourage families to seek private solutions to their care service needs.

As Table 3.1 indicates, Korpi (2000) found that Belgium and Germany offer the best general family support and the Scandinavian countries provide the most support for the dual-earner family. Countries that were considered market oriented, such as the United States, New Zealand, and Australia (all 'liberal' welfare regimes) as well as Japan,

58   Restructuring Family Policies

Table 3.1
Countries ranked by levels of general family support and dual-earner support, 1985–90

General family support*	Dual-earner support**
1. Belgium	1. Sweden
2. Germany	2. Denmark
3. France	3. Finland
4. Norway	4. Norway
5. Italy	5. France
6. Austria	6. Belgium
7. Denmark	7. Germany
8. Ireland	8. Italy
9. Sweden	9. Netherlands
10. Finland	10. Austria
11. Netherlands	11. Ireland
12. Canada	12. United Kingdom
13. United Kingdom	13. Canada
14. Switzerland	14. Japan
15. Japan	15. Australia
16. Australia	16. Switzerland
17. New Zealand	17. United States
18. United States	18. New Zealand

* General family support includes cash child allowances as a percentage of net average wage of single worker, family tax benefits and percentage of public childcare spaces for children three to school age as a percentage of number of children in that age group.
** Dual-earner support includes public childcare spaces for children under three years as a percentage of age group, a measure of the value of paid maternity leave and paternity leave, and public home help for the elderly (percentage receiving services at home).
Source: Korpi 2000.

ranked at the bottom in terms of both general family support and dual-earner support. Korpi explained these variations with reference to the ideologies of prevailing political parties and the relative strength of religious and women's groups.

Bradshaw and Finch (2002) studied the child benefit packages in twenty-two countries, including tax benefits, cash payments, and social services. Using data provided by researchers living in each country, they found considerable variation in how countries evaluate 'appropriate' levels of income support and the needs of families of different sizes and types. After housing costs and services, the level of social assistance for lone-parent families was the highest in Ireland, Denmark, Norway, Austria, and the United Kingdom and the lowest in Spain and Portugal. For two-parent families with three children, social assistance was the highest in Luxembourg, Austria, and Sweden and the lowest in Spain and Italy. When Bradshaw and Finch examined the entire child benefit package, Austria, Luxembourg, and Finland appear to be the most generous, while New Zealand, Portugal, Spain, Japan, the Netherlands, and Greece were labelled as 'welfare laggards.'

The most generous countries do not target their support to low-income families, but allocate most or all benefits to all families with children (Bradshaw and Finch 2002). Furthermore, these rankings bear little resemblance to Esping-Anderson's (1990) welfare regimes. The social democratic countries generally appear in the top half of the table, but they are not the 'leaders.' Bradshaw and Finch argued that patterns of family provision cannot be explained by a nation's wealth, the character of the labour force, or level of earnings; rather, social expenditure is the determining factor, and more specifically, social expenditure on children rather than the elderly. However, they did not adequately explain why some countries are willing to spend more on children than others. Instead, they noted that the level of child benefits is 'associated with reducing market-generated levels of child poverty and it is possibly also associated with higher fertility rates' (13).

Although I have mentioned only a few cross-national studies dealing with family support, these projects clearly indicate that the scheme of ideal types of welfare regimes must be revised. Generally, these studies support the power resource theory but argue that researchers need to consider more than employment-related programs with trade unions and employer's organizations as the major lobby groups for social programs. Specific concerns about fertility, child allowances, children's welfare and their rights, family violence, and many other issues lie behind the development of welfare states.

The Influence of National Politics on Policy Debates

Throughout this book, numerous examples show that policy reforms can be explained more effectively by the political and fiscal goals of national governments, against a background of historical patterns of social provision, than by 'demographic realities' or 'economic necessity.' Governments often respond to pressure groups that consistently and persistently demand reform if the political allegiance of those groups would make a difference in future elections.

In the prosperous 1960s and early 1970s, many centre-left governments expanded entitlement and created new social programs with pressure from labour unions, anti-poverty associations, women's groups, and international organizations such as the United Nations and the World Health Organisation. These groups tended to support an expansion of human rights, equal opportunities for men and women, and a stronger role for the state in social security. Since the 1980s, advocacy groups on the political right have became more powerful, coinciding with the mid-1970s downturn in the world economy and growing concern about pressures on corporate profits, business competition, government expenditure, and public debt. By the 1990s, new trade configurations, two decades of uncertainty in the global economy, and rising public debt enabled pressure groups representing small and large business interests to effectively argue for lower taxes and cutbacks to public spending. Most liberal welfare states responded to these pressures, at least by attempting to reduce social spending, to limit eligibility for social benefits, and to privatize some social services. However, not all governments responded in the same way, nor were they equally successful in their cost-cutting agendas (Pierson 1994).

New Zealand is a prime example of a country that accepted arguments about the economic necessity to reduce tariffs, income taxes, and social spending in order to become more competitive internationally. These arguments were used mainly by conservatives[3] and supported by employers' groups who wanted to restructure large portions of the state from the mid-1980s to the late 1990s. In their attempts to reduce social spending, the conservative National government modified several social programs for families with children in the 1990s, including targeting child allowances and reducing income support to families as well as individuals. The primary reason given was 'economic necessity.' When demographic trends were acknowledged, the National-led governments typically used them to justify reductions in public expenditures rather than program expansion. For example, higher maternal employment rates meant that mothers relying on income support could be expected to find paid work when their children were younger. However, the National government did not eliminate the benefit enabling lone mothers to care for their children at home (the Domestic Purposes Benefit), which is a major cornerstone of social provision in New Zealand. This benefit continues to remain more generous than provincial welfare in Canada (Baker 2004a).

---

3 The New Zealand Labour government began to restructure the state in 1984, and its right-wing members supported major social program cuts. However, most of these were carried out by National governments throughout the 1990s.

Conservative interest groups in liberal welfare states convinced governments and taxpayers that promoting business competitiveness and reducing taxes would stimulate employment growth and increase prosperity. Several governments reduced income taxes and introduced consumption taxes that more negatively affected low-income earners. Governments in liberal welfare states restructured social programs with the justification that they were 'enforcing private responsibility,' 'decreasing dependency,' and 'making citizens more employable.' Despite these policy changes, many parents still rely on income support and some separated fathers still fail to support their children. Housing costs have become less affordable for many families, yet income support programs do not always compensate for these additional expenses. More parents work for low wages, experience childcare problems, and require the state to supplement their earnings. Income taxes were reduced for higher-income earners, but consumption taxes now add to the burden of low-income parents (Baker and Tippin 1999; Kelsey 1999).

The political right remains powerful, well funded, and well organized in most jurisdictions of the liberal welfare states. Business-oriented taxpayers continue to question whether the state needs to fund or regulate so many services, and governments are most likely to cut those programs with few defenders. Universal policies benefiting all families continue to be viewed as unnecessary by the political right, who believe that the state should intervene only when families are destitute or in serious conflict. In addition, the political right tends to believe that even some means-tested programs encourage 'dependency' and should be further targeted. However, emotional and financial dependency within family households has always been socially acceptable and encouraged by the state. Creating new forms of dependency on the labour market when so many jobs are low paid and insecure cannot by itself become an effective solution to family poverty, especially in mother-led households (Baker and Tippin 1999).

Politicians in the liberal welfare regimes have also claimed that they intend to eliminate 'child poverty' but have reduced income taxes, introduced consumption taxes, deregulated the labour market, and reduced or tried to reduce benefit levels. Many of these reforms have actually increased the poverty of households with children. The dominance of neoliberal ideas and practices has meant that alternative policy initiatives such as state job creation, wages for care, and universal daycare are often discredited as politically unfeasible and lack political sponsorship. Even political parties historically supporting the development of social security, such as the Labour Party in Britain and New

Zealand and the Liberals in Canada, have reduced the duration of social benefits and endorsed employability programs, although they have also improved parental benefits and childcare services. In contrast, conservative or centre-right governments continue to focus on the male breadwinner/female care provider model of family. They combine this with greater reliance on private care services and state partnerships with voluntary organizations.

Retrenchment advocates are not always able to achieve their full agendas, but opponents of the welfare state have been most successful when they were able to divide the supporters of social programs, compensate those negatively affected, or hide what they were doing from potential critics (Pierson 1994). Furthermore, certain institutional reforms continue to place pressure on the welfare state, including the politics that strengthen the hands of budget cutters, weaken the government's revenue base (such as tax cuts), and undermine the position of pro–welfare state interest groups (such as reductions in the power of trade unions) (Pierson 1994). These conclusions seem relevant to our discussion of the restructuring of family-related policies.

Governments are continually faced with conflicting ideas about social spending, and many people believe that politicians and bureaucrats mismanage the taxpayers' money. However, the liberal welfare states have designed policy incentives to reduce welfare dependency that are based primarily on models of rational economic motivation. Against this, parents sometimes feel that they must give priority to their children's well-being over their own employment prospects or even economic self-sufficiency. As we will see throughout this book, some welfare regimes are better able than others to help parents integrate earning and caring.

Conclusion

This chapter has outlined a set of national or cultural factors that influence family policy restructuring, including existing patterns of social provision, and political negotiations between various interest groups and past and present governments. When discussing existing patterns of social provision, I introduced the concept of 'welfare regimes,' focusing initially on the model presented by Esping-Andersen (1990) but also identifying other models more central to women and family. Like other early models, Esping-Andersen's welfare regimes emphasize state income support for (male) workers normally attached to the full-time labour force rather than family-related programs and services.

When social provision for caring work and women's employment is examined, the inclusion of specific countries within particular welfare regimes is often disputed. In addition, many feminist researchers argue that the concept of 'de-commodification' is less relevant for women. While men require state assistance when they cannot work due to unemployment, illness, injury, or retirement, women more often need to be helped into employment in order to become more independent of family support. Therefore, feminist scholars argue that the effectiveness of welfare states for women should be measured by their ability to 'de-familialize' rather than de-commodify.

Despite these criticisms, most researchers agree that Nordic or social democratic countries have provided the most generous social programs for families with children, especially when these families contain an employed mother without another breadwinner in the household. More than other welfare regimes, social democratic regimes have maintained the incomes of both two-parent and one-parent families above the poverty level, have helped mothers integrate earning and caring, and have enabled women to survive without a male breadwinner. In doing so, these countries have generally expected their citizens to pay higher income taxes and discouraged mothers from caring for their children at home without paid work. However, these regimes have enabled mothers to gain permanent employment while ensuring that their children are well cared for and supervised.

Interest groups in social democratic regimes, such as trade unions and women's groups, have argued for social citizenship rights, women's employment equity, the protection of human rights (including children's rights), social housing, and social care work, as we will see in later chapters of this book. Many governments in these countries have responded to these concerns and supported more state intervention in the economy, in labour practices, and in the protection of children. In contrast, business groups have been powerful in most liberal welfare states since the 1980s, successfully pressuring governments to curb social program costs, reduce income taxes, and deregulate labour markets.

Ideas about welfare provision and social citizenship are discussed, interpreted, and negotiated within welfare regimes consisting of existing social programs and institutional structures, and within nation states with political agendas and established vested interests. Because social policy in OECD countries is usually restructured through incremental changes rather than dramatic reforms, the existing social welfare system establishes the baseline for further restructuring. Furthermore, national and local interest groups promote certain agendas that may be less important in other countries or welfare regimes. Therefore, it would be very difficult to transplant social programs from one jurisdiction to another unless the two shared the same political culture, values, and institutional structures.

Increasingly, however, all countries and categories of welfare regimes are confronted with globalizing economies and pressures from supranational organizations to modify employment practices, income tax systems, and existing social programs. In the next chapter, I focus on some of these international pressures.

4 Growing Internationalization and Family Policies

The previous chapter showed that family policy restructuring is influenced by national politics but also by welfare regimes, or existing patterns of social provision. Welfare regimes are resistant to new agendas that threaten either cultural beliefs (about 'good mothering,' for example) or vested interests generated by existing programs and institutional structures. This chapter, which discusses the third influence on the restructuring of family policies, focuses on the increasing internationalization of work, travel, and communication. I argue that three aspects of 'globalization' influence living arrangements and family policy reform. These include the internationalization of labour markets; increased international travel, migration, and intercultural contact; and more pressure from key international organizations to harmonize social policies.

The Growing Internationalization of Labour Markets and Trade

With new trade agreements and electronic financial transactions, investors and entrepreneurs can now move their capital and business ventures more freely throughout the world. Many employers attempt to maintain international competitiveness by extending their production or service hours to allow for global time differences, to satisfy customer demands, and to reduce resources lost from 'down time' during the evenings and weekends. Many employers have also replaced certain employees with new technology and continue to keep as few permanent staff as possible on the payroll. Employing casual staff sometimes enables employers to avoid paying certain fringe benefits, to downsize their labour force during hard times, and to reduce union obligations.

Because capital moves more freely than people under the terms of many bilateral and multilateral free trade agreements, employers may be able to carry out part of their business in other countries or relocate their firms if they believe they can establish more profitable businesses elsewhere. Employees are often more restricted in their movements. Within the European Union, however, there is now free movement of labour, permitting citizens in any member state to live and work in the others. Countries such as Australia and New Zealand have also signed bilateral agreements permitting the free flow of labour as well as certain goods. The North American Free Trade Agreement does not allow the free flow of workers but regulates the movement of certain categories of workers within the United States, Canada, and Mexico (OECD 2001, 28).

Freer trade, new technologies, and international variations in labour costs have edged some industries and workers out of the market but have allowed others to prosper (Torjman and Battle 1999). Some manufacturing jobs that were previously unionized and nationally based have shifted outside the borders of Western economies and lost both their legislative and trade union protections. The service sector of the labour force has also expanded in many OECD countries, providing more new positions that are temporary and part time rather than full-time year-round jobs (Banting and Beach 1995; Edwards and Magarey 1995; Van den Berg and Smucker 1997). From 1991 to 2001, rising part-time employment offset declining full-time employment in Austria, Finland, Italy, and Japan, and accounted for over half the total employment growth in nine other countries (OECD 2003a, 49). Table 4.1 shows that part-time work increased in most OECD countries throughout the 1990s for both men and women, but that women are far more likely than men to work part time.

Increasingly, labour markets extend beyond national boundaries as more employers try to recruit top candidates in order to compete globally. Competition for high-level professional and managerial positions increases when applications arrive from other countries, which may threaten local job security because it enlarges the pool of candidates with varied and international experience. Global labour markets also require more people to develop internationally recognized qualifications as well as to gain a wider range of employment experience and develop broader networks. Some employers still prefer to hire local residents, but this is becoming more difficult as international agreements require them to hire the most-qualified candidates or risk employment appeals.

Table 4.1
Incidence of part-time employment in OECD countries as a percentage of all female and male employment, 1990 and 2000

	1990–3		2000–1	
Country	Women	Men	Women	Men
Australia	36	11	44.6	12.6
Belgium	30	5	34.4	6.9
Canada	27	9	27.0	9.8
Denmark	30	10	23.9	8.6
Finland	10	5	13.5	6.6
France	22	4	24.8	5.3
Germany	25	2	33.7	4.4
Hungary	4	2	5.1	1.6
Italy	18	4	23.4	5.5
Japan	33	9	39.4	11.8
Luxembourg	19	2	28.4	1.9
Netherlands	53	13	57.1	13.0
New Zealand	NA	NA	35.4	10.6
Norway	39	7	42.5	9.7
Portugal	12	3	12.6	3.0
Spain	NA	NA	16.4	2.5
Sweden	25	5	22.6	7.6
Switzerland	46	9	45.8	8.4
United Kingdom	40	5	40.2	7.6
United States	20	8	19.4	7.4
OECD average	NA	NA	25.8	6.5

Source: Extracted from UN 2000a, 139; OECD 2002, 69, Table 2.1

When states open their borders to international business ventures, foreign owners may take over local companies. Multinational employers often pay higher wages and more generous employment benefits than local businesses, but they also expect international work standards and use global hiring to fill top positions. This means that while some local people are able to obtain better-paid jobs, others cannot compete even in their own communities. At the same time, certain governments have restructured income support programs to urge more beneficiaries to become 'economically active.' Others also provide incentives for employers to hire former beneficiaries, but these employees are not always the kind preferred by multinational employers concerned about global competition. Although some people benefit from globalizing labour markets, paid employment is no longer a guarantee against poverty for a substantial percentage of the population, especially in the liberal welfare states (UNICEF 2000).

One family strategy to cope with these current labour market trends is to acquire multiple earners in each household. As tuition fees rise in many countries, more students are now working part time than in the 1970s and more wives are accepting regular employment in the labour force. With extended business hours, more family members work at varying schedules from each other. Nearly 40 per cent of dual-earner couples working full time in Canada work on shifts outside nine-to-five hours, including 10 per cent working at completely different times of the day (Marshall 1998). These schedules alter family meals, the household division of labour, and childcare arrangements.

Although employment patterns for men and women are beginning to converge, they still remain gendered in terms of job category, working hours, and pay differentials (Armstrong 1996; Webb, Kemp, and Millar 1996; OECD 2003a). Many mothers with young children work part time, especially in the Netherlands, Australia, Switzerland, the United Kingdom, and Norway (OECD 2002, 69). Part-time employment permits mothers to retain caring responsibilities while earning household income, but it does not pay enough to support themselves and their children. Gershuny and Sullivan (2003) showed that people who live in countries with 'liberal market regimes' work longer hours on average than those in other types of welfare regimes. However, they found little variation among welfare regimes in the gendered division of domestic labour or time spent in leisure activities.

With changes in technology and the structure of work, many workers have been forced to retrain, to become self-employed, or to take early retirement. The jobs available to new labour market entrants (young people) and those seeking re-entry (former beneficiaries and mothers with school-age children) have been the focus of labour market restructuring. New entrants are sometimes able to obtain stable and long-term jobs but often can find only part-time or temporary positions that lack union protection, regular working hours, and employment benefits (Jenson 1996; Myles 1996). Working for the same employer throughout life is now less prevalent than in the past, and more people are experiencing longer bouts of unemployment (Torjman and Battle 1999, 15). Particularly young people experience high unemployment rates, as Table 4.2 indicates, especially in eastern and southern Europe.

As labour markets become polarized into 'good jobs' and 'bad jobs,' disparities in earnings and wealth are augmented. Successive waves of

Table 4.2
Youth unemployment and total unemployment in selected OECD countries, 2001

Country	Total unemployment rate	Unemployment rate for youth (aged 15–24)
Australia	6.7	12.7
Belgium	3.5	15.3
Canada	7.3	12.8
Denmark	4.2	8.3
Finland	9.2	19.9
France	8.8	18.7
Germany (2000)	8.0	8.4
Greece	10.4	28.0
Hungary	5.7	10.8
Iceland	2.3	4.8
Italy	9.6	27.0
Japan	5.2	9.7
Luxembourg	1.9	6.7
Mexico	2.2	4.1
Netherlands (1999)	3.3	6.6
New Zealand	5.4	11.8
Poland	18.6	41.0
Slovak Republic	19.3	39.1
Spain	10.5	20.8
Sweden	5.1	11.8
Turkey	10.9	19.9
United Kingdom	4.8	10.5
United States	4.8	10.6
OECD	6.7	14.1
EU	6.2	13.5

Source: Extracted from OECD 2003b, 33.

Canadian men earned less than their elders at every stage in their work lives from the 1970s to the 1990s (Beaudry and Green 1997), but the same labour market changes have not occurred in all countries or have not happened at the same pace. The prevalence of low-paid employment and the twenty-four-hour economy (Presser 1998) varies considerably by nation, influenced by local labour market conditions, employment policies, and other social programs (OECD 2001, 67). As Table 4.3 shows, low-paid work is more characteristic of the liberal welfare states (except Australia[1]) and particularly of North America.

---

[1] In 2005, Prime Minister John Howard introduced new labour legislation that is likely to create a more 'flexible' labour force with less union intervention and lower wages in Australia in the future.

Table 4.3
Incidence of low-paid employment* in OECD countries, by gender, mid-1990s

Country	Total	Men	Women
Australia	13.8	11.8	17.7
Austria	13.2	7.0	22.8
Belgium	7.2	3.9	14.2
Canada	23.7	16.1	34.3
Finland	5.9	3.3	8.7
France	13.3	10.6	17.4
Germany	13.3	7.6	25.4
Italy	12.5	9.3	18.5
Japan	15.7	5.9	37.2
Netherlands	11.9	NA	NA
New Zealand	16.9	14.4	20.7
Sweden	5.2	3.0	8.4
Switzerland	13.0	6.8	30.4
United Kingdom	19.6	12.8	31.2
United States	25.0	19.6	32.5

* Low-paid employment receives less than two-thirds of the median wage for full-time employment.
Source: Freiler and Cerny 1998, 24

This suggests that the forces of 'economic globalization' do not need to override national policies and employment protections.

Increased International Migration, Travel, and Communication

In addition to labour market changes, international travel and global communication have become easier and more prevalent in recent years. Detailed travel information can be accessed from home, and arrangements can be booked by telephone or over the Internet. More people travel internationally when airline prices fall relative to wages, when travel times are reduced, and when international agreements permit them to live and work in foreign countries. Especially young people take advantage of new opportunities to gain work permits and additional passports.

In most OECD countries, the number of foreigners and the size of the foreign-born population have increased over the past ten years (OECD 2005, 30). Inflows of foreign workers can provide important job skills for 'nation building,' and immigration departments often invite particular categories of workers or business investors to apply for temporary or permanent residence. Immigration is also seen as a partial solution to fertility decline and population aging, bringing more young people or couples with children into the country. However, the presence of a foreign population can also lead to social strains, especially if the newcomers are culturally or racially different from the local majority.

Most migration into OECD countries comes from one of three routes: the granting of temporary or permanent residence to those with certain employment skills or business assets, family reunification, and asylum seekers. Many countries have developed a points system to qualify for permanent residence in which language skills, educational credentials, a job offer, the importing of cash, or willingness to invest in a local business accrue points towards entry. In the family reunification category, migrant residents are permitted to sponsor the immigration of a relative, such as a spouse, sibling, or parents. However, governments maintain strict definitions of 'family' that may not fully encompass the definition within the migrants' culture. Thirdly, governments also sign international agreements about the acceptance and treatment of refugees.

Regardless of the route, an increasing number of people now live as expatriates, become citizens of more than one country, and become friends and intimates with people from different nationalities and cultures. As more people intermarry, policies of biculturalism and dual citizenship become more important to them. Increased migration also means that governments need to regulate the movements and rights of migrants and to provide culturally sensitive services to ensure their integration.

The perception prevails in many high-immigration countries that governments have accepted too many immigrants who take work away from citizens, bring down local wages, change the local culture, and require social assistance for unemployment and settlement problems. Opposition in the liberal welfare states has been particularly strong against immigrants from certain Asian, African, and Middle Eastern countries, partly because these people form 'visible minorities' but also because many of them come from countries with different religions and family systems. These immigrants are often forced to accept low-paid jobs and live in depressed neighbourhoods with multiple community problems. They sometimes experience language problems and financial difficulties, and may also dress differently and maintain distinct cultural practices. All of these issues make them targets for local prejudice.

Some countries attract foreign residents more than others, depending on employment and investment opportunities, living conditions, services, and the local acceptance of foreigners. Across the OECD, Austra-

72   Restructuring Family Policies

Table 4.4
The foreign and foreign-born populations, change between 1990 and 2000 and percentage of total population in 2000

Country	Annual change between 1990 and 2000 (%)	Foreign/foreign-born population as % of total population 2000
Korea	15.6	0.4
Finland	13.2	1.8
Spain	12.4	2.2
Portugal	6.8	2.1
Italy	5.9	2.4
Slovak Republic	5.3	0.5
Austria	5.2	9.3
Denmark	4.9	4.8
Ireland	4.7	3.3
Japan	4.6	1.3
USA	3.9	10.4
Luxembourg	3.8	37.3
Switzerland	–	19.3
Germany	3.2	8.9
Canada	2.7	17.4
Australia	2.1	23.6
Sweden	–0.1	5.4
Belgium	–0.5	8.4
France	–1.1	5.6
Hungary	–1.6	1.3
Mexico	–	0.5
Poland	–	0.1

Source: Extracted from OECD 2003b, 29.

lia, Canada, Luxembourg, and Switzerland have the highest percentages of foreign-born populations, while the percentages remain low in Mexico, Korea, Poland, the Slovak Republic, and Japan (OECD 2003b, 29), as Table 4.4 indicates. The proportion of foreign and foreign-born population is particularly high in Luxembourg at 37 per cent and in Australia at almost one-quarter of the resident population (OECD 2005, 30). Although many immigrants to Australia come from Britain and Europe, a growing number are arriving from Middle Eastern and Asian countries.[2]

Considerable public debate has surrounded asylum seekers in recent

---

[2] Until 1973, the Australian government retained a policy that excluded many non-white immigrants and temporary residents.

years, but the refugee population comprises more than one per cent only in the Nordic countries and Germany, Switzerland, and Australia. Most other OECD countries accept only 150 to 400 refugees for every 100,000 population (OECD 2005, 30). This suggests that perceptions of 'too many' refugees may give rise to public discussion and policy reform even when the actual numbers are negligible.

Increased migration means that governments and supranational organizations need to ensure that their policies are inclusive and sometimes must reconsider their definitions of 'family' within immigration policies and social programs. This is particularly relevant to migrants with extended family systems but also to same-sex couples. Same-sex marriages have been legal in several European countries since 2001, but when these couples travel or work in other parts of Europe the rights that accompany marriage have not always been recognized. European Union ministers endorsed a proposed set of rules in 2003 ensuring that same-sex married couples from countries recognizing their union are recognized as married across the European Union (Arie 2003).

In addition to international travel, rapid global communication has proliferated with the World Wide Web. The Internet has enhanced 'e-commerce,' business arrangements, the publication of ideas, and policy exchanges. Social activists can also use virtual networks to promote their causes and spread new policy ideas, as Pudrovska and Ferree (2004) illustrated with the European Women's Lobby. The Internet has also enabled easier communication among friends and family, as well as 'chat groups,' on-line dating, and the dissemination of pornography.

With more people using the Internet and travelling internationally, the probability of establishing relationships with people from other social and cultural backgrounds increases. When these people become intimate couples and live together, they may need to negotiate basic issues such as where to live, which language to use, and how to combine their cultural customs at home. If these couples reproduce together, their children often become bilingual and bicultural, moving easily between cultural groups. Many people live with partners from different backgrounds, combining their cultural practices in ways that enrich their family lives and language skills and their children's opportunities. However, previous family research suggests that marriages in which partners differ in religion, culture, age, and socio-economic status are more stressful and prone to separation and divorce (Sev'er 1992, 167; McDaniel and Tepperman 2004, 401).

Potential disputes in cross-cultural marriages relate to decisions about where to live and how to deal with the differing cultural expectations or opinions about child rearing. If these marriages dissolve, disputes can arise over child custody and support, especially if there is a discrepancy between the laws of the homeland and the current place of residence. In a small number of well-publicized cases, cultural differences, personal grievances, and domestic violence could lead to children being 'abducted' and taken back to one parent's homeland, often the mother's (Coester-Waltjen 2000). This could cause anguished searching by the other parent as well as problems for police and child welfare agencies. Increasingly, governments are signing international agreements to help deal with parents attempting to cross borders to avoid paying child support, retain custody, or seek refuge, matters that are further discussed in chapter 9. Multilateral agreements also protect children and restrict families involved in international adoptions.

High-immigration countries have been forced to acknowledge that more of their residents live with dual or multiple cultural identities. Some immigrants continue for years to send money back to their villages or maintain an active interest in the politics and activities of their homeland (Macpherson 2000). Many immigrants make regular visits back to their homeland or visit family members who have migrated to other countries. Some countries now permit residents to choose multiple ethnicities on census forms or to obtain citizenship without giving up the passport of their birthplace or former country of residence. This means that more travellers are using multiple travel documents, and could use one passport to exit from a country and another to re-enter it, making it more difficult for officials to monitor their movements.

More international travel, communication, and migration introduce new challenges for both families and the state. Families with friends and relatives in different countries maintain contact through electronic mail, text messages, long-distance telephone calls, letters, and air travel, but long-distance relationships are costly and stressful. The state also struggles to adjust to more mobile populations, amending legislation, regulations, and practices related to immigration and citizenship, work permits, and the international enforcement of custody decisions and child support agreements. At the same time, increasing international concerns about terrorism and trafficking require the state to make greater efforts to protect borders, property, and people. These new measures sometimes restrict family visits and make border crossing more onerous. Additional surveillance and security also require greater public expenditures at a time when governments are pressured to reduce taxes and cut costs. The growing internationalization of travel and communication could alter public-spending priorities as well as family relationships.

Pressure from International Organizations to Reform Family Policies

In the twentieth century, transnational policy coordination and regulation has been intensified by international governmental organizations, especially since the Second World War. The most prominent areas of transnational cooperation are trade, investment, finance, and macro-economic policy, as well as environmental policies and social policies in employment, migration, social security, education, health and social services, population control, and humanitarian aid (Yeates 2001, 95). Townsend (1993) argued that transnational organizations play a key role in how resources are accumulated and distributed globally, which helps to explain global inequality and poverty. The policies of the World Bank, the International Monetary Fund, and the World Trade Organization have also played a major role in the transnational diffusion of neoliberalism, focusing on international competitiveness, free markets, and free trade. While these organizations are important for world trade and development, they seldom have a direct impact on family policies in OECD countries. Nevertheless, they create pressures for restructuring that can influence these policies.

International organizations expand into the realm of family when they make policy or legal judgments on the movement of workers, equal pay among workers, parental benefits, fertility and child welfare issues, and reproductive health. Table 4.5 outlines several areas of family policies in which international organizations have developed an agreement, directive, or convention. This table shows that a number of organizations have developed multilateral agreements or made official statements on family-related issues, including the United Nations, the International Labour Organisation, the World Health Organisation, the Vatican, and the European Union.

The European Union is an example of an international organization that has overtly pressured national governments to reform family policies (Hantrais 2000, 2004; Weiss 2000; Ross 2001). The legislative framework for the European Community was originally designed as market law with little treaty power over family policy, but a number of family

Table 4.5
International rulings or agreements on specific family policy areas

Family policy area	Decisions or agreements by international organization relating to family policy area
Reproductive health, birth control, childbirth	World Health Organisation United Nations (conventions) Vatican* (pronouncements)
Marriage / civil unions, and family benefits	European Union (Social Charter) Vatican* (opposed to civil unions and gay/lesbian marriage)
Maternity / parental benefits	International Labour Organisation (conventions) United Nations (conventions) European Union (Social Charter)
Protection from abuse and neglect (children and women)	United Nations (conventions: 1979) UN 1994 (domestic violence became human rights issue) WHO studies UNICEF studies and publications
Childcare	European Union (disseminates best practices among member nations)
Child poverty	United Nations Convention and UNICEF
Child custody and international adoptions	Hague Convention (since 1980) European Convention
Enforcement of child support for people crossing international borders	Bilateral and multilateral agreements

* These pronouncements affect only Catholic citizens or politicians.
Sources: Various reports and conventions noted throughout this book.

issues underlie the field of social security. Member states pool some of their sovereignty through negotiated treaties, but these often have no constitutional standing. For example, the Social Charter is a 'solemn Declaration' or set of proposals for European social action. Nevertheless, EU institutions do a fair amount of 'soft' politicking, or informing and urging member states to change their family-related policies (Ross 2001).

The European Union has set up numerous measures to promote gender equality in the labour force, and both men and women have been given access to employment rights and benefits. Initially, the EU tried to give priority in social security benefits to traditional nuclear families (heterosexual and legally married), but the European Court moderated discrimination based on family status (Weiss 2000). This court requires parental benefits to be paid to both mothers and fathers, and part-time work to be paid the same hourly wage as full-time work to encourage gender equity. However, unpaid family work (done mainly by women) is always excluded from social security benefits. Weiss (2000) showed that the EU continues to maintain the separation of spheres between paid work and the family even though they are strongly interrelated.

The interconnections between social policy making in the European Union and national policy formation and implementation have been examined, tracing the history of EU documents. Hantrais (2000) noted that similar demographic trends are present in member countries but the pace of change has varied. Governments respond differently to these changes based on their own benefit history. Although the EU cannot focus on all areas of family policy, it has nevertheless introduced policies relating to employment leave for family responsibilities (such as parental benefits) and the rights of migrant workers' families. With some exceptions, there appears to be a trend towards individual rights in social insurance programs and income tax (assessed separately from the family situation) within European Union countries (Hantrais 2000; 129).

Legislation designed to ensure employment equity or to encourage women's career advancement in the EU has neither enabled women to enter the labour force at the same rates as men nor allowed them to be promoted like men. Consequently, occupational segregation based on gender continues (Hantrais 2000, 134). As long as equal pay, equal treatment, and access to social security depend on full-time continuous employment, as they do in many countries, large numbers of women will be disadvantaged, since they continue to do the bulk of unpaid caring work and often arrange their paid work so as not to conflict with these family responsibilities. Legislation granting equality to women can also be used against them, as employers who cannot hire women at lower wages might prefer to hire men.

In 1997, the Agreement on Social Policy (the Social Charter) was reinstated within the Treaty of Amsterdam after the Labour Party won the British election. (In 1992, the agreement had been removed from the main body of the Maastricht Treaty upon British insistence [Hantrais 2000, 219]). The Social Charter gave a new salience to social issues as member states finally agreed after forty years that social rights in the EU should be protected. However, the treaty's ability to override national legislation continues to be contested and constrained. Most of the clauses of the Social Charter require consultation and give member states the right to introduce their own measures. Furthermore, the focus is still on economic integration and workers' rights (Hantrais 2000, 220).

The European Union can impose sanctions for non-compliance but lacks funds to redistribute resources to reduce poverty or to compensate states for making concessions (Hantrais 2000, 233). Member states can also restrict efforts to develop social policy at the EU level through vetoes or court cases against the European Commission. For example, the United Kingdom vetoed the entire Social Charter (Crompton 2004). Consequently, the fact that the Social Charter exists does not mean that all member states are forced to abide by it or accept every directive or decision in it; different welfare traditions and social circumstances continue to exist within member countries. Nevertheless, EU treaties and court decisions have eroded national autonomy over social policy (Hantrais 2000).

One example of the influence of the European Court is the way that decisions relating to sex equality and the movement of workers have served to regulate families. McGlynn (2001) argued that these decisions have been based on a heterosexual couple with the husband as the main breadwinner and the wife as the main care provider even though most families no longer live like this. This ideological construction of family limits the potential of sex equality laws to bring about real changes in the lives of women by reproducing traditional understandings and expectations and limiting entitlements to rights. The dominant ideology of family and motherhood could form the 'normative foundation' for family law across the European Union.

The EU used to focus on 'standard' employment, which disadvantaged many women workers, but it has recently developed equality directives on part-time and temporary work. Male work patterns used to constitute the norm, but now the concept of the parent-worker is becoming embedded in directives relating to the regulation of working time, although the implementation is uneven, with national differences in legal machinery and political will (Walby 2004). Despite limited jurisdiction, the EU has legislated against employment discrimination based on sexual preference, advocated the extension of abortion services, and promoted policies to reduce violence against women. Although strategies 'to mainstream' gender issues are mainly advisory rather than judicially enforceable, many gender issues are now part of legal directives. Support for gender equality does seem to be ebbing in the draft of the new constitution, but these issues, according to Walby, are subject to ongoing debate.

This discussion of the European Union indicates that international alliances and global trade agreements do not necessarily reduce the diversity of state practices because political institutions and industrial relations can critically mediate its impact (Walby 2004). There is evidence of a developing regionalism in the emergence of three major competitive blocs: the United States (and NAFTA), the EU, and Southeast Asia, led by Japan (Hettne, Inotai, and Sunkel, 1999). The development of a world polity may promote the diffusion of some values, but cross-national policy variations remain. Similarities are associated with specific political institutions, opportunities, and projects. Within the European Union, this includes the commitment to social inclusion and successful lobbying efforts by the feminist movement (Walby 2004). Yet Stratigaki (2004) argued that the goals of the feminist movement have been co-opted and altered in the European Union, reflected by a gradual shift from the sharing of family responsibilities between men and women to a market-oriented objective of encouraging flexible forms of employment to enhance work-life balance. This shift makes the earlier feminist goals more consistent with prevailing political and economic priorities.

Canada has vowed that its social policies would not be compromised by its international trade obligations. However, caution is required in negotiations within the World Trade Organization and the Free Trade of the Americas Agreement to prevent social programs from being exposed to greater trade-driven privatization and commercialization (Jackson and Sanger 2003). Many of Canada's social services are delivered by not-for-profit agencies, and negotiators need assurances that the risk of trade challenges will be minimized for social programs delivered in this way rather than directly by government.

Transnational organizations could have considerable impact on social policy and especially employment-related programs but researchers disagree on the extent or importance of these influences. As well, much of the research on the impact of international organizations on family policy has focused on the European Union; the impact of other trade and investment agreements remains largely unexplored.

Freer Trade, Neoliberal Restructuring, and Families

Few researchers have systematically examined the harmonization of social programs in countries with free trade agreements, and when they have they have not focused on family policies. For example, Montanari (1995) compared direct and indirect harmonization of social policies in countries belonging to the European Community and the European Free Trade Association (EFTA) from 1955 to 1985. In this project, a high degree of diversity and variation was found in social policies, but more harmonization was apparent in the EFTA countries, where trade unions and social democratic parties have been relatively strong. However, much has happened in terms of the internationalization of trade and rising rates of international migration since 1985. Recent pressures for harmonization include new international directives and conventions, as well as 'soft politicking.'

Much of the concern from the political left about freer trade and global markets relates to the neoliberal ideologies and practices that usually accompany these multilateral agreements. Neysmith and Chen (2002) argued that globalization and neoliberal restructuring have transformed social policy and social services in many countries over the past twenty years. Comparing Canada and the People's Republic of China, they showed that many of the costs of restructuring have been picked up by women, a fact that is not usually highlighted in the restructuring literature. This theme has been adopted by a number of women scholars.

McDaniel (2002) argued that new, unspoken expectations are being created for women in 'globalizing western democracies.' Decentralization shifts responsibilities further downward, under the guise of democratic accountability. As more states privatize caring activities for children, persons with disabilities, and the frail elderly, women are expected to perform more unpaid caring work within their families. When this work is unpaid, it becomes further devalued. 'Families become the new social safety nets, with women in families the new unpaid social workers' (McDaniel 2002, 143). Individual responsibility is stressed, with punishments for parental neglect or lack of supervision. In addition, employment insecurity and the erosion of social benefits and other protections have led to a 'bullying normativity,' where employed and prosperous taxpayers feel entitled to deride those who have less.

Many researchers have concluded that globalization affects families because it leads to growing inequality, unemployment, and impermanent work. Briar-Lawson et al. (2001) noted that globalization also contributes to declining aspirations, as children realize that education does not automatically translate into employment. Global trade has contributed to rising world poverty, increased national debt, growing corporate profits, and urbanization, as well as the fragmentation of extended family systems. Briar-Lawson et al. argued that the state remains important but must be reinvented to avoid welfare crises, advocating 'partnerships' among policy makers, professionals, and families to ensure family well-being.

The Luxembourg Income Study has been used by many researchers to compare the impact of government transfers on different types of households. Smeeding (2002) used this database to compare the impact of 'globalization' on inequality in OECD countries. He found that the fruits of economic progress have not been evenly spread, but that most 'rich' nations have benefited from the 'trend toward global economic progress.' Rather than blaming trade policy and globalization, he concluded that large differences in inequality could be better explained by social policies, wage distributions, time worked, social and labour market institutions, and demographic differences. Nevertheless, Smeeding found a higher level of inequality in OECD countries in the late 1990s than in the 1980s. He concluded that domestic policies and institutions still have an impact on inequality, even in a 'globalizing world economy.'

Throughout this book, I show that certain international organizations try to persuade national governments to modify their family policies, but their impact has been uneven. Organizations such as the United Nations and the International Labour Organisation have encouraged the development of certain family-related policies and programs in those states considered as 'welfare laggards,' but they have experienced limited success. Some 'rich' countries have refused to sign international conventions on social issues, arguing that it would be too costly to create the necessary institutional infrastructure to ensure that the commitments are kept. Others have signed the agreements but allocated insufficient resources to service delivery or enforcement, and therefore failed to promote family well-being (Hantrais 2000; UNICEF 2005).

Perhaps the greatest impact of transnational organizations has been to promote neoliberal principles as the basic framework for the restructuring of economic and social programs. However, expecting more families to rely on market incomes has had limited success within some households, especially those with one female earner, many children, few employment skills, or limited job experience.

Conclusion

International organizations may not have harmonized family policies, but the creation of common markets, international agreements, and more international travel and communication has certainly altered patterns of work and family life. In recent years, job markets in many countries have become more competitive and polarized, enhancing opportunities and income for employees with internationally competitive skills and experience. Globalizing markets have also led to larger discrepancies between high and low earners, and between those whose income derives from different sources (wages, salaries, state support, or investments). Some employees are able to move themselves and their families to areas with better employment prospects and higher pay, taking advantage of bilateral or multilateral agreements that permit the free flow of labour from one country to another. Others are left with insecure and low-wage jobs if they cannot relocate to improve their prospects due to low assets, poor employment skills, low education, lack of confidence, or family obligations.

Globalizing labour markets often affect men and women differently. When one partner in two-earner families relocates to a new position, the other partner often becomes unemployed, at least temporarily. Husbands are more likely than wives to initiate employment relocations because they usually see themselves, and are seen by others, as the main family earner. Employed wives often perceive their work as secondary to their husband's, and others usually share this perception. Especially lone mothers find it difficult to relocate for employment reasons because the move could disrupt custody and childcare arrangements, children's friendships and schooling, and the family's social support system. Furthermore, many lone mothers feel that they cannot work full time because they lack suitable childcare services, and moving house for part-time employment is not worth the time and money. Yet some women benefit from current economic conditions, and new labour market practices have augmented the gap between women who delay or avoid childbirth, acquire tertiary education, gain job experience, and retain a partner and those who do not (Warner-Smith and Imbruglia 2001).

Governments in most OECD countries have tried to help both employees and employers to compete in global labour markets. Educational programs have been designed to improve general levels of literacy and numeracy, to develop computer skills, and to enhance job readiness and motivation to find paid work, especially for school leavers and former beneficiaries. Some states have subsidized the relocation of workers whose skills are needed elsewhere or have provided childcare subsidies for employed mothers with young children. The state has also offered tax breaks to employers to establish business enterprises in high-unemployment areas, to employ former beneficiaries and school leavers, or to develop childcare services on work premises. Some states have reduced 'compliance costs' for employers and subsidized low-wage workers. They have also assisted employers to modernize their operations, retool, and secure new export markets overseas. At the same time, some of the same governments have reduced entitlement to state income support for those outside the labour force.

As we will see in later chapters, supranational organizations have pressured national governments to develop or enhance their social programs relating to employment, such as paid leave for pregnancy, adoption, childbirth, breastfeeding, family illness, and bereavement. They have also encouraged national governments and employers to expand childcare services for employees and to pay equal wages to part-time workers. Especially the European Union has placed considerable pressure on member states to harmonize their social programs and legislation, and has framed national policy debates by putting certain issues on the EU agenda. Despite this pressure, major cross-national variations remain in family services and policies. Similar economic and political pressures have not always created similar policy solutions because, as we suggested in chapter 3, national politics and institutions always intervene to alter policy outcomes. Family policy restructuring continues to be influenced by existing welfare regimes, ideas about citizenship and family, and the effectiveness of political alliances and lobby groups.

The first four chapters of this book have set the stage by defining key concepts and discussing three main sources of pressure on national governments to restructure family policies. The next five chapters provide more detailed applications of restructuring in selected areas of family policy. In the first area, relating to reproductive health and childbirth, the goals are to understand whether or not there is any evidence of cross-national convergence in policies and practices, and which factors encourage convergence or help maintain national differences.

5 Reproductive Health and Childbirth

This chapter demonstrates that guidelines from international organizations such as the World Health Organisation and United Nations encourage national governments to provide the necessary programs to prevent sexually transmitted diseases, promote contraceptive use, practise safer childbirth, minimize unnecessary technological interventions at childbirth, and extend paid breastfeeding breaks to employed mothers. However, formal agreements among OECD countries tend to focus on some reproductive issues more than others, and especially the rights of parent-workers at the time of childbirth. These agreements pay less attention to more controversial issues such as access to abortion, the rise of medically assisted conception, or the steady increase in induced births and Caesarean deliveries.

Mindful of international guidelines and rising medical costs, states have urged health care institutions to use midwife care for 'normal' pregnancies, to shorten hospital stays, and to limit the use of unnecessary technology in childbirth. However, efforts to reform reproductive and maternity services have not always been successful, antagonizing certain interest groups, health professionals, and patients and their families.

In this chapter, I show that both international directives and government policies influence childbirth practices, but these practices are also shaped by changing labour markets, the desire for medical and corporate profits, and the politics of choice. I argue that childbirth practices are converging cross-nationally but not necessarily in the direction approved by national governments and international health and labour organizations. Some of these practices are also strongly opposed by the 'moral right.' Before I discuss the influences on programs related to

Reproductive Health and Childbirth 85

contraception, abortion, maternity care, and medically assisted conception, some background information on indicators of health and well-being is necessary.

Basic Indicators of Well-being

All OECD countries gather basic information about life expectancies, infant and maternal mortality, contraceptive use, low-birth-weight babies, and causes of premature death. A number of international organizations (such as the United Nations, the World Health Organisation, and the OECD) also collate and publish these statistics, which can be used as basic indicators of family health and well-being.

Since the 1960s, life expectancy at birth, or the average number of years a new baby is likely to live, has increased in almost all OECD nations, from 65.7 to 73.3 years for males and from 70.8 to 79.5 years for females (OECD 2001, 80). Increased life expectancy is related to improvements in sanitation, accommodation, and nutrition; advances in health care (such as the development of inoculations and antibiotics); and improved practices in maternal health. Variations in life expectancies, both within and between countries, are influenced by differences in income, living standards, and lifestyle as well as access to health services.

Females now outlive males in most developed countries. In the OECD, child mortality rates (annual deaths per children aged one to four) are relatively low at 0.5 for girls and 0.6 for boys, compared to rates of 42.0 for girls and 29.4 for boys in a non-OECD country such as India (United Nations 2000a, 56–7). Although life expectancy in OECD countries has converged towards the average, countries such as Korea, Mexico, and Turkey have made greater gains in recent years while eastern European countries have experienced lower gains. These lower gains are attributed to poor diet, unhealthy lifestyles, and excessive alcohol and tobacco consumption (OECD 2001). Lower life expectancy is also related to high levels of pollution, poor enforcement of health and safety measures, soaring unemployment, and cutbacks in social programs caused by economic restructuring or political unrest.

The average age in OECD countries is increasing because birth rates are falling and life expectancy is rising, meaning that people aged sixty and over form a growing percentage of the population in all countries. In Western Europe, for example, about 23 per cent of women and 18 per cent of men were sixty and older in 2000 but this is projected to rise to

Table 5.1
Percentage of population under 15 years and 60 years and older for selected countries, 2000

Country	% under 15	% of females aged 60 and over	% of males aged 60 and over
Australia	21	18	15
Canada	19	19	15
Denmark	18	23	18
France	19	23	18
Germany	16	27	20
Hungary	17	23	16
New Zealand	23	17	14
Russian Federation	18	23	14
Sweden	18	25	20
United Kingdom	19	23	19
United States	21	18	14

Source: Extracted from United Nations 2000, 20–1.

29 per cent of women and 24 per cent of men by 2020 (United Nations 2000a, 4). Instead of viewing rising life expectancies as one of modern society's greatest achievements, policy analysts focus on the negative aspects of 'population aging' and view seniors as a drain on future public resources, often without investigating their incomes or the valuable unpaid services they provide for children and grandchildren. Table 5.1 shows percentages of males and females aged under fifteen years and sixty years and over in selected OECD countries in 2000.

Low income and high poverty rates are often used as indicators of problems with family well-being. Although 'child poverty' is addressed in more detail in chapter 7 when we discuss family income supports, we need to be aware for the discussion in this chapter that growing up in poverty is associated with poorer nutrition and dental practices, more low-birth-weight babies, and higher rates of child neglect, teen pregnancy, and maternal death. In addition, low-birth-weight babies are considered to be at risk of later health and social problems, and therefore are often the focus of special state programs. Poverty is also related to higher rates of smoking, substance abuse, accidents, and premature deaths (Roberts 1997). Low income and problems accessing health and social services are also more prevalent among certain cultural groups and vary by region of the same country. As we will see throughout this chapter, income disparities and variations in access to services become consequential to the discussion of reproductive health outcomes.

Reproductive Health Policies and Services

Contraception Programs and Sexuality

In the last fifty years reproductive behaviour has become widely accepted as a major concern of governments (United Nations 2003). Sexual practices and childbearing were once viewed as private family matters outside the scope of state involvement, except that both the church and state regulated marriage and granted more rights to 'legitimate' children, or those born to married parents. Barrier methods of contraception have been available for centuries, but until the 1960s most churches and states discouraged their use even within marriage.

In the 1960s, women's rights activists demanded more sexual freedom, the eradication of the 'double standard' of sexual practices, and greater access to contraception and abortion, as well as access to tertiary education and employment equity. In Canada, homosexuality between consenting adults, therapeutic abortions in hospitals, and the advertisement and dissemination of birth control became legal for the first time in 1969 (McLaren 1999, 173). More effective hormonal methods of contraception, available for the first time in the 1960s, began to shift public attitudes about reproduction and weakened the link between marriage and childbearing (Dickson et al. 1997). Since the 1970s, sterilization has become a prevalent method of contraception in OECD countries (Balakrishnan, Lapierre-Adamcyk, and Krotki 1993). As Table 5.2 indicates, three-quarters of married women in many OECD countries now use some form of contraception.

A review of United Nations' conference decisions and reports indicates that these have been instrumental in the promotion of greater contraception use. In 1968, family planning found its way into human rights discourse with the UN-sponsored International Conference on Human Rights in Teheran. The groundbreaking Proclamation of Teheran stated: "the protection of the family and of the child remains the concern of the international community. Parents have a basic right to determine freely and responsibly the number and spacing of their children" (United Nations 2003; 14). This recognition of family planning as a human right coincided with the significant progress made in developing new types of contraceptives, including the contraceptive pill and the intrauterine device (UN 2003, 14–15). In 1979 the United Nations urged member states, in the Convention on the Elimination of All Forms of Discrimination against Women, to remove discrimination in the provision of health care services, including access to family

Table 5.2
Fertility and contraception statistics for selected countries, 1995–2002

Country	Total fertility rate (1995–2000)	Teenage births (per women aged 15–19)	% of married women using contraceptives*
Canada	1.6	20.2	75
Australia	1.8	18.4	76
New Zealand	2.0	29.8	75
United Kingdom	1.7	30.8	82
United States	2.0	43.0 (2002)	74
Sweden	1.6	6.5	NA
Netherlands	1.5	6.2	79

* Percentage of women of reproductive age (15–49) reporting contraceptive use by themselves or their partner
Sources: Henshaw, Singh, and Haas 1999; UN 2000a; OECD 2003b; US Deptartment of Health and Human Services 2003

planning. The 1993 Vienna Declaration, adopted by the World Congress on Human Rights, reaffirmed these basic reproductive rights by declaring a woman's right to accessible and adequate health care and the widest range of family planning services (UN 2000b, 59).

This view of reproductive rights as basic human rights was further strengthened in 1994 at the UN International Conference on Population and Development in Cairo and its five-year review of implementation in 1999. Governments were urged to ensure universal access to reproductive health care and access to safe, effective, and affordable methods of family planning. They were also encouraged to provide freedom from sexual violence, to eliminate harmful traditional practices (including female 'genital mutilation'), and to eradicate coercion within the family and society (UN 2000, 59). The 1994 Cairo conference revolutionized the conceptualization of family planning by empowering women in matters of reproduction (United Nations 1995). Reproductive issues became articulated within the discourse of self-determination and individual well-being and rights, rather than the earlier focus on national population control and demographics (United Nations 2003).

This ideological shift can be largely traced to the influence of feminist non-governmental organizations that critiqued the demographic rationale for international population policy, saying that it was coercive and unethical and subjected women's bodies to the attainment of an abstract and quantitative societal goal. Feminists were also critical of the inaccessibility of reproductive health services for some women, as well as the lack of respect and privacy that service providers often showed women at family planning clinics (Finkle and McIntosh 2002). The Cairo conference pushed the notion that family planning and women's health services should be integrated as a single package while giving greater attention to the rights of women (United Nations 2003, 17–18). However, this was not a new idea in some countries. For example, Sweden already had a long history of integrating family planning programs within the broader health care context (Westlander and Stellman 1988).

Women's right to reproductive health was also a central focus in the United Nations' Fourth World Conference on Women held in Beijing in 1995. The platform for action called upon governments to recognize that reproductive health depends partly on available information and services, the prevalence of high-risk sexual behaviour, discriminatory social practices, and negative attitudes towards females. Governments were also asked to address the gaps in the collection and analysis of statistical information on women and health, and to encourage research on these issues (UN 2000b).

Three-quarters of all countries, either member states of the United Nations or non-members, now provide direct support for access to modern contraceptive methods (UN 2003, 7). Direct support entails the provision of family planning services through government-run facilities, such as hospitals, clinics, health centres, or government fieldworkers. Another 17 per cent of countries support family planning programs and contraceptives indirectly, through support of non-governmental activities such as those operated by family planning associations (7). In the last thirty years, nearly all countries have shifted their policies towards increased support for modern contraceptive methods, but despite sizeable growth in government support, the demand for contraceptive and family planning services still greatly exceeds supply. In some countries or jurisdictions, the cost of contraception limits its use among low-income couples and opposition to both sex education and contraceptive use is widespread.

In recent years, neoliberal restructuring, below-replacement fertility rates, and the rise of the Christian right have influenced policies and practices relating to contraception. A number of OECD countries have actually reduced direct government support for family planning initiatives[1] (UN 2003), which may reflect a broader context of privatization, cost containment, and government withdrawal from centralized health and welfare programs. This reduced support could also represent a concern about below-replacement fertility rates and an attempt to counter them. In post-1989 eastern Europe, profound economic and political upheaval has not only hastened the decline in fertility, but the development of market-focused capitalism and privatization has also led to more restrictive laws relating to contraception and abortion. These factors also created opportunities for the re-emergence of some institutions in the public sphere. This is especially the case in Poland, where the Catholic Church has once again become an influential lobby group concerning social policy matters (UN 2003; Albanese 2004).

While the majority of less developed nations continue to view fertility levels as 'too high,' an increasing percentage of the governments of wealthier nations have come to regard national fertility levels as 'too low' (UN 2003, 1). Just over half of wealthier nations now consider their fertility rates to be inadequate, compared with 21 per cent in 1976 (1). Both the changing role of women and the increasing fertility control afforded by modern contraceptive methods have substantively reduced fertility rates. This has contributed to population aging, which many governments (such as Australia) see as a looming crisis, as we noted in chapter 2.

In the United States, fundamentalist Christian interest groups have ensured that state-funded sex education programs focus on celibacy before marriage as the most effective form of birth control. These groups discourage open discussion of contraceptives because they believe it encourages young people to engage in premarital sex. They campaign against contraceptive use outside marriage because they believe that sexual intercourse should be reserved for marriage. The Christian right also believes that the purpose of marriage is procreation and therefore oppose even marital family planning that involves contraceptive devices.

The World Health Organization estimates that about 5 per cent of adolescents contract a sexually transmitted disease each year. This is particularly a problem for young adults, who are less likely than older people to have access to information about these diseases and less inclined to seek early treatment that might prevent more serious infec-

---

1 Austria, Canada, Denmark, France, Japan, Italy, and New Zealand provided direct support for contraception in 1996 but changed to indirect support by 2001 (UN 2003).

tions. In some parts of the world, half of all new HIV infections appear to have occurred in the fifteen-to-twenty-four age group, particularly among women, who may pass it on to their fetus during pregnancy (WHO 1998). Policy makers, educators, and voluntary groups have promoted the use of 'safer sex' and especially the use of condoms to prevent the spread of sexually transmitted disease. There is some evidence that condom use has increased, especially among teenage males in the United States (Murphy and Boggess 1998).

The HIV pandemic has spurred educational campaigns into safer sexual practices in most countries (United Nations 1996, 38). It has also highlighted the need for more effective national and global initiatives to combat sexually transmitted diseases and to prevent their spread. More states are discussing or initiating new policies that require international migrants to be screened for HIV as well as other diseases. More states are also collaborating on research projects that search for a vaccination or medical breakthrough for AIDS patients. In addition, international collaboration is required to decide which drugs are most effective to combat these diseases and which should be subsidized under public health care programs. At the same time, multinational pharmaceutical companies continue to increase their profits through the international marketing of these new drugs.

Increasingly, sexuality has become a marketable commodity in many OECD countries (McDaniel and Tepperman 2000, 132). It is romanticized in the media and sold in the consumer-oriented economy as fantasies and pleasures. Prevalent representations of sex help to explain why premarital sex is becoming widespread in most OECD countries and why some young people fail to use contraception and condoms even when they are available. Sex education programs tend to focus on the rational and clinical aspects of birth control rather than dealing with values and feelings about sexuality and relationships. This contrasts with the romantic and glamorous images of love and sex in the media. Controversies continue in many countries about the nature of sex education and its role in the schools, as well as education about sexually transmitted diseases and access to abortion.

Access to Abortion

The state's role in facilitating legal or 'therapeutic' abortion has been controversial for over forty years. Increasingly, early pregnancy is seen as a health and socio-economic risk to women, but birth rates in OECD

92   Restructuring Family Policies

Table 5.3
Induced abortion rates in selected countries

Country	Rate of induced abortions per 1,000 women aged 15–44	
	1975	1996
Canada	10.5	15.5
Australia	n.a.	22.2
New Zealand	8.6	16.4
United Kingdom	11.2	15.6
United States	21.7	22.9
Sweden	20.2	18.7
The Netherlands	5.2	6.5

Source: Henshaw, Singh, and Haas 1999

countries have generally declined among teenage women. Nevertheless, some young women still become pregnant before they complete their education, especially those from low-income families. Some give birth and raise their children with family or state income, but many have abortions. Especially in those countries where abortion is illegal, young unmarried women are more likely than older married ones to seek abortions from untrained practitioners, to perform abortions on themselves, and to delay seeking medical treatment if complications arise (UN 2000a, 58). Therapeutic abortion rates vary cross-nationally but have increased in the liberal welfare states between the 1970s and 1990s, as Table 5.3 indicates.

Few countries deny women an abortion if the continuation of pregnancy endangers her life, but vast cross-national variations exist in legal availability (UN 2002a). Obtaining an abortion is seldom seen as an ordinary health service. Some jurisdictions require mandatory waiting periods and counselling before abortion, and even third-party authorization, such as spousal consent in Turkey (Rahman, Katzive, and Henshaw 1998). Numerous countries allow abortion on limited grounds, such as when continuation of the pregnancy threatens to jeopardize the physical or mental health of the woman, if there is evidence of fetal impairment, or in the case of rape or incest (UN 2002a). In the Republic of Ireland, abortion is legal only when the pregnancy endangers the woman's life (Mahon 2001).

In countries such as Sweden, Norway, the Netherlands, Denmark, France, Belgium, the United States, and the Russian federation, abortions are available on request, regardless of the reason they are sought (Centre of Reproductive Rights and Policy 2003). However, most na-

Reproductive Health and Childbirth 93

tions that permit abortion on liberal grounds have established conditions that must be met before the abortion becomes legal. These include limits on gestational age (usually before twelve weeks), the type of medical facility where the abortion must be performed (hospital or licensed clinic), and who can perform it (a licensed medical practitioner).

Governments that permit abortion on liberal grounds may not fund the procedure without proof of medical necessity or other extreme circumstances (UN 2002a). Abortion is subsidized by the state to varying degrees in Sweden, Italy, and France, but the United States and Germany will pay for abortions only for low-income women who could not otherwise afford the procedure (UN 2002a). Thirty-two American states have declined to use their Medicaid funds to pay for abortions in the absence of extreme circumstances, such as a life-threatening pregnancy or one resulting from rape or incest (Sullivan 2003). In these states, the limits on gestational age also remain contentious. As more accurate prenatal imaging is developed, age-old controversies flare up about when a fetus becomes a human being or a child with human rights.

Access sometimes varies among regions of the same country (UN 2001b, 73–5). In federal states such as the United States and Australia, state variations are apparent in access, creating a situation of 'abortion tourism' as women travel to those states where the procedures are more readily available (Sullivan 2003). Even where laws converge across states or regions, differences in accessibility may still exist in practice (UN 2002a). In Italy, for example, abortion is legally available on request but the lack of hospital facilities and the high number of gynaecologists who are conscientious objectors create barriers for women seeking abortions, especially in the south.

Both the UN Cairo conference in 1994 and the Beijing conference in 1995 urged reproductive autonomy for women. However, the international community remains reluctant to place any substantive pressure on governments to modify or repeal highly restrictive abortion laws, and international conventions allow nation states considerable cultural, religious, and moral autonomy (Centre of Reproductive Rights and Policy 2003). The United Nations urges member states to grant women access to safe abortion where it is legal, and urges access to quality medical care for women who suffer from post-abortion complications regardless of the legality of the abortion itself (1994, art. 8.25; 1995, art. 106.k). This requirement clearly seeks to address the vast numbers of women who die during unsafe illegal abortions, particularly in poorer nations (UN 1996).

The Beijing conference in 1995 urged governments to 'consider reviewing laws containing punitive measures against women who have undergone illegal abortions' (UN 1995, art. 106.k). Women's right to attain the highest standard of sexual and reproductive health and the right to make reproductive decisions free from discrimination, coercion, and violence was also stressed. Both the 1994 and 1995 conferences confirmed that these rights are grounded in and draw from an extensive body of international human rights instruments and international consensus documents.[2] All of these documents emphasize the human-rights aspect of accessibility to quality health care (UN, 1996: 39–41).

European law displays some ambivalence about abortion. The Maastricht Treaty (Treaty on the European Union) may be interpreted as protecting a nation's right to define its own legal parameters with regard to abortion, as it includes a provision offering protection of national identity and sovereignty (European Union 1992, art. F.1). Furthermore, following the principle of 'subsidiarity,' reproductive health policies remain clearly within the jurisdiction of member states (Girvin 1996, 166). Nevertheless, the European Parliament voted in 2002 to support a report by the Committee on Women's Rights and Equal Opportunities on the state of women's sexual and reproductive health and rights (Centre for Reproductive Rights 2004). Through the report, the European Parliament urged member states to legalize induced abortion under certain conditions, at least in cases of forced pregnancy, rape, or the endangerment of a woman's health or life. The underlying principle is that the woman herself should make the final decision (European Parliament 2002). It remains to be seen how this will influence the member states with more conservative abortion laws, such as Ireland, Switzerland, and more recently Poland.[3] Undoubtedly controversies will continue, considering the tension among women's reproductive rights, men's rights, and issues of cultural and religious identity.

---

[2] These include the Convention on the Elimination of All Forms of Discrimination against Women (1979), the United Nations International Covenant on Economic, Social and Cultural Rights (1966), the European Convention for the Protection of Human Rights and Fundamental Freedoms 1950 and the European Social Charter (1961 and 1996).

[3] Abortion was legalized in Poland in 1956, but after 1990 it was restricted, following consistent lobbying from social groups linked to the Catholic Church. The 1997 law prevents abortion on social grounds.

Aspects of European law outside the realm of reproductive rights have also been applied to further women's right to abortion. For example, the Maastricht Treaty supports the rights of thousands of Irish women who travel to England each year to obtain abortions. This is not because it explicitly protects their reproductive rights, but because it asserts their rights as EU citizens to travel freely between member states (Mahon 2001). The right of access to information is also protected under article 10 of the Convention for the Protection of Human Rights and Fundamental Freedoms (1950). This right was enforced in the early 1990s by the Council of Europe in a challenge to the Supreme Court of Ireland's denial of the right to provide information on abortion (UN 2001b, 68). Despite these small gains for Irish women, abortion is by no means freely accessible, as the costs of travelling to England alongside accommodation and medical costs are substantial (Mahon 2001, 178).

Numerous advocacy groups have lobbied governments to reform or repeal abortion laws, and their legality remains controversial in most countries for several reasons. First, some religious groups believe that the fetus is a 'child' with a right to life and that abortion is a form of murder. Second, some hospitals do not provide abortions, largely for religious reasons, which forces women to travel to other places at greater expense to obtain these services. This situation encourages illegal abortions and also opens the jurisdiction to accusations of inequalities in access to health services. Third, some fathers' rights activists and individual fathers believe that they should have more say in whether or not 'their child' is aborted or has the right to life. In Canada, the courts have generally confirmed that women and their physicians retain the right to decide if the pregnancy should continue, leaving the male partner with few options, especially if he is no longer living with the woman. Fourth, rising costs and health care restructuring have encouraged hospital administrators to help make judgments about state funding for particular services, and abortions become vulnerable to cuts when they are seen as controversial procedures. For all these reasons, abortion policy is a useful illustration of the contradictory political pressures on national governments to restructure family law and policies, as well as the influence of neo-liberal principles on restructuring.

Fertility and the State

Improved contraception and the legalization of abortion have enabled the planning of childbirth and made parenthood more of a choice.

However, most adults become parents, and social research clearly indicates that procreation is still considered intrinsic to heterosexual marriage, gender identity, and 'normal' adult life (Baker 2004b). Researchers have found that parents tend to see childbirth as a natural outcome of adulthood and marriage rather than a conscious choice. They say that having children provides opportunities to pass on their values and knowledge, to expand their social networks, to relive the joys of childhood, to receive unconditional love, and to pass on their name, genes, or family line (Veevers 1980; Callan 1982; Cameron 1990; Morell 1994; May 1995). These ideas become more predominant in cultures that emphasize lineage and rely on extended family for assistance.

The opportunities, costs, and benefits of having children vary by age, gender, economic circumstances, and culture, and some people are less likely to reproduce than others. Women with postgraduate education and high incomes, for example, are less likely to marry and have children than men or women with lower levels of schooling and income (Beaujot 2000). For these educated women, the opportunity costs of having children are higher in terms of lost earnings and seniority. However, Gillespie (1999) argued that women who choose not to procreate are expected to account for their choices in ways that mothers are not.

Most governments encourage their citizens to marry and reproduce because heterosexual marriage and parenthood are assumed to help people mature, to promote stability in families and communities, and to encourage continuous employment in order to finance home ownership and child rearing. However, the economic utility of reproduction began to decline in the nineteenth century with the introduction of child labour laws and compulsory education. These social policies limited parental opportunities to use children's labour to supplement the family income. In the twentieth century, the development of old-age pensions, health insurance, and income support programs further discouraged parents from seeing their children as a means of future financial security. Fertility also declined with urbanization because raising children in cities became more costly than in rural areas. Changing labour force requirements also drew married women into paid work and made larger families more complicated and costly.

Despite valid reasons for couples to have smaller families, concerns about declining fertility are now widespread in a number of countries, especially those that remain ambivalent about maternal employment and/or reject higher immigration as a solution to population increase.

In Australia, for example, considerable public discourse among social conservatives deals with how to encourage women to have more children. When delivering a national budget in 2004, the Australian treasurer recently advocated having more children to resolve the 'problems of the aging population and the low replacement rates' (Dodson 2004). Expanding childcare spaces and enhancing the maternity payment were additional policy solutions from this budget speech.

While some governments have tried to remain neutral about fertility issues, many policy makers remain concerned about the financial implications of an aging population with respect to pensions and medical services. Health care analysts, practitioners, and parents also worry about the growing medicalization of childbirth, with its accompanying public and private costs.

Maternity Care Policies and Practices

Hospitals and/or local governments usually offer prenatal classes and free medical examinations for expectant mothers and their fetuses, and the health costs of childbirth are often paid by the state. In the past few decades, maternity care has improved in many parts of the world, and in developed regions 97 per cent of women receive prenatal care, 98 per cent have their babies in health facilities, and 99 per cent of women are attended by a skilled attendant (UN 2000a, 61). Childbirth experiences vary with health policies, cultural birthing practices, and the social and economic circumstances of the woman and her family. Her age and marital status, her physical and emotional health, the presence or absence of the father, and the family's socio-economic situation are also important factors.

As more women work for pay, parental leave programs become essential for their employment equity, but these programs seldom permit both parents to take leave at the same time. If the couple must decide who takes leave, it tends to be the parent with the lower income (usually the mother), and both husbands and wives typically agree that the mother should stay home, especially if she wants to breastfeed (Beaujot 2000). Many men feel unable to take much time off work at childbirth because the family cannot afford to forfeit any of his income. Furthermore, more men worry about losing credibility with their co-workers or employers if they take time off work for family reasons. In recent years, health practitioners have encouraged husbands to participate in prenatal classes, to be present at childbirth, and to participate more in child rearing (Benoit, Carroll, and Millar 2002). Research suggests that the father's participation throughout the pregnancy creates a stronger lifetime bond between him and the baby (Lamb 1976; Ricks 1985).

Prior to the 1940s, most births took place at home with the assistance of midwives or experienced married women, but medical practitioners successfully argued that the sterile conditions of hospitals and medical interventions were necessary for safer childbirth (Tew 1998). In recent years, more babies have been born in hospitals, although the incidence of home births varies by country. In the United States, less than 1 per cent of births now take place at home, a trend remaining essentially unchanged over several decades (US Department of Health and Human Services 2002, 16). In England and Wales, about 97 per cent of births took place in hospitals in 1997, compared to 62 per cent in 1961 (UK Office for National Statistics 2004). Data on home births in England and Wales show a steady decline from 1961 to the 1980s. In 1961, 32.4 per cent of births took place at home, steadily decreasing to a low of 0.9 per cent in 1985 and remaining constant at that level through to 1988. From this low figure the percentage of home births increased marginally but steadily to 2.3 per cent in 1997 (UK Office for National Statistics 2002).

The British increase in home births in the 1990s can be attributed in part to the influence of the Winterton Report by the House of Commons Health Committee in 1992, which was followed by the UK Department of Health's 1993 report *Changing Childbirth*. Both reports questioned the proposition that childbirth was safer in a hospital setting and argued that women should be given a legitimate choice between hospital and home birth, with balanced and impartial information based on sound research and evidence (Tew 1998). These reports also recommended that midwives be given the right to manage their own caseloads and to take full responsibility for women under their care. The reports argued that home births are as safe if not safer than hospital births for women with 'normal' pregnancies. In addition, home births are less costly and involve lower rates of medical intervention (Tew 1998). However, advocates of home births were disappointed by the slow growth of such births in Britain throughout the 1990s (UK Office for National Statistics 2002). It appears that the medical profession's support for hospital births was more powerful than this parliamentary recommendation or the midwives' lobby.

Restructuring health care services has also influenced women's choices about childbirth and related services. In liberal welfare states such as Canada and New Zealand, health care services are being regionalized and health care responsibility is being shifted from public institutions to informal networks and unpaid caregivers (Armstrong et al. 2002). In some regions, health service delivery and planning has moved from the core to the periphery, with greater emphasis on local control and decision making. Benoit, Carroll, and Millar (2002) argued that non-urban women in British Columbia view the recent regionalization of maternity care services in a largely negative light. Women emphasize the lack of choice in care providers, discontinuous care across the birthing period, inadequate quality of care, and lack of opportunity to have a voice in local health care planning. However, many politicians believe that they can reduce public expenditures by the decentralization and privatization of health services. Increasing use of medical specialists and new technology, especially in private facilities, has raised the cost of childbirth and shifted more expenses from the public purse to the patient and her family.

The 'Medicalization' of Childbirth

In most OECD countries, childbirth now involves a variety of medical interventions, including electronic fetal monitoring, anaesthetics, episiotomies, the induction of labour, and routine procedures such as pelvic shaves and enemas, which are sometimes given without women's consent (Bosch 1998). In Spain, for example, over 90 per cent of first births involve episiotomies, which obstetricians argue are necessary in order to reduce vaginal tears (Bosch 1998). Between 20 and 26 per cent of births in the liberal welfare states are induced and Caesarean deliveries are also becoming more prevalent, as Table 5.4 indicates. In Canada, Caesarean deliveries have increased since 1991, but rates vary considerably by province, averaging about 21 per cent of all births (Health Canada 2003, 34–5).

Steadily increasing global rates of Caesarean births over the last century have become one of the most contested issues in maternity care today (Walker, Turnbull, and Wilkinson 2002). The World Health Organisation suggests that the optimum rate is between 5 and 15 per cent of births (1997, 77), but few countries show rates below this level. In the liberal welfare states, the rate of Caesarean delivery exceeds 20 per cent of all births, while the rates in the Netherlands and Sweden have remained at about 10 per cent since the 1980s (Walker, Trunbull,

Table 5.4
Birth statistics in selected countries, late 1990s–2002

Country	Induction of labour as % of all births	Caesarean sections as % of all births	Infant mortality rate, by sex F	M
Canada	19.7	21	5	7
Australia	25.9	22	5	6
New Zealand	20.9	22	7	7
United Kingdom	21.0	22	6	8
United States	20.6	26	6	8
Sweden	7.9	10	5	6
Netherlands	NA	10	5	6

Sources: Extracted from Tew 1998; Health Canada 2000; Ford et al. 2003; New Zealand Ministry of Health 2003; UN 2000a, 81–2; Stephansson et al. 2003

and Wilkinson 2002, 29). Both these countries provide extensive prenatal care, but the health care funding system in the Netherlands requires normal births to be midwife attended and to take place at home (Tew 1998). These two countries also have among the lowest maternal and infant mortality rates in the world, also shown in Table 5.4.

Caesarean rates in the liberal welfare states vary by the social class, age, and ethnicity of the mother, with older and wealthier women more likely to experience Caesarean deliveries. There are several reasons for this trend. As more women bear their first child at older ages, especially those with higher levels of income and education, Caesarean rates are increasing because doctors consider vaginal births to be riskier among women over 35 years old (Bosch 1998; Health Canada 2000, 23). In addition, older, educated, and wealthier women are more likely to ask for procedures they view as safer or more convenient, whereas lower-income women find these operations unaffordable without state subsidies.

Doctors also try to schedule their medical procedures at convenient times for themselves and the hospital staff. Gemmel (2003) found that American doctors perform Caesarean sections not when women need them but on days that suit their personal schedules. These operations are most prevalent on Fridays and least prevalent on the weekend and holidays. Gemmel also found that for-profit ownership of Ohio hospitals was associated with *fewer* Caesarean sections and suggested that this may be because these hospitals accept fewer high-risk patients. However, Australian research reported that women admitted as private patients have a much higher Caesarean rate than public patients: 29.5

per 100 confinements compared to 19.0 (Ford et al. 2003, 107). The suspicion that obstetricians may prefer induced labour and Caesarean sections because they can control the timing of a birth is also supported by British data showing that induced births are most likely to occur between Tuesday and Saturday. Elective Caesareans are extremely unlikely to take place on Saturday or Sunday, but spontaneous labour shows very little variation between days of the week (UK Government Statistical Service 2003). U.S. data show similar trends (US Department of Health and Human Services 2003).

An illustration of the income and ethnic variations in Caesarean deliveries can be found in the New Zealand statistics, where the percentage had increased to about 22 per cent of births by 2001. Women of Asian and European backgrounds, who enjoy the highest incomes and have their first child at older ages, also have the highest Caesarean rates. Indigenous Maori women have the lowest rates of Caesareans and also have their first child at younger ages. For all women, the Caesarean rate increases with age and was over 33 per cent for women aged forty and older in 2001 (NZ Ministry of Health 2003). Particularly elective Caesarean sections[4] increase with the mother's age. In 2001, over 15 per cent of mothers aged forty or older had elective Caesarean deliveries, compared to 2 per cent of mothers under sixteen years (36).

In 2001, about 73 per cent of New Zealand mothers used midwives at birth, 9.6 per cent used general practitioners, and 17.3 per cent used obstetricians (116). Generally, the percentage of women using general practitioners is falling while the percentage using obstetricians is increasing. However, those using midwives had the lowest rates of both acute and elective Caesarean sections (122). In Australia, 21.9 per cent of births were by Caesareans, but for women aged 40 and over the percentage rose to 37.6. Like in Canada, the Australian rate varied by state, and was the highest in South Australia (Ford et al. 2003, 107).

American statistics also indicate that the Caesarean rate is rising, reaching 26.1 per cent of all births in 2002. One government concern is that after a Caesarean birth, mothers are far less likely to experience vaginal births with subsequent children, and Caesareans cost three times more than vaginal births (Tew 1998; US Department of Health and Human Services 2003, 2). Ethnic variations, related to socio-

---

4 An elective Caesarean section is performed before the onset of labour, whereas an acute Caesarean section is performed urgently for maternal or fetal health reasons once labour has started.

economic status, are also apparent in American statistics. Black mothers in the United States, like Maori women in New Zealand, are less likely to have Caesarean births, but black Americans are far more likely than white or Hispanic mothers to have pre-term and 'very preterm' babies, and low-birth-weight and 'very-low-birth-weight' babies (US Department of Health and Human Services 2003, 89). As we mentioned earlier, these babies are more likely to experience health and disability problems throughout life. British data also show the relationship between lower socio-economic status and poor birth outcomes (Tew 1998).

Considerable research suggests that neonatal mortality rates and childbirth complication rates tend to be lower in jurisdictions where health practitioners perform *fewer* Caesarean sections, where midwives provide continuity of care, and where midwives are permitted to attend both home and hospital births (Jezioranski 1987, 100; Papps and Olssen 1997; Tew 1998). However, more births are being classified as 'high risk' due to the rising age of childbirth, and obstetricians rather than midwives or general practitioners are expected to treat higher-risk maternity cases in hospitals. This raises the neonatal mortality rates of hospital births by obstetricians compared to that of home births by midwives. Yet even with normal births, midwives are less likely than doctors to rely on technological monitoring, drugs, and other interventions. Consequently, the clients of midwives require less postpartum care and recovery time (Fooks and Gardner 1986, 7; Tew 1998). In addition, midwives cost less public money than obstetricians, and for this reason some jurisdictions include them in the public health care system and support midwifery training programs (Baker 1995, 361).

Many health care authorities are concerned about the rising costs associated with elective Caesarean deliveries. Some states have enacted policies or strategies designed to lower the frequency of these births because they are associated with longer hospital stays and additional costs (Walker, Turnbull, and Wilkinson 2002). In Canada, clinical guidelines have been established for Caesarean sections, and efforts have been made to encourage women who have previously experienced a Caesarean section to attempt a vaginal delivery in subsequent births (Health Canada 2000, 21). In Australia, a global obstetric fee was introduced in 1998 in an attempt to reduce Caesarean deliveries in that country, but the rate continues to rise (Walker, Turnbull, and Wilkinson 2002, 37).

Some governments have tried to reduce technological interventions and health care costs by encouraging or requiring the attendance of midwives at childbirth. This has been successfully done in the Netherlands. In New Zealand, the 1990 Nurses Amendment Act restored autonomy to midwives, who were previously limited by legislation that allowed only medical practitioners to take full responsibility for childbirth (NZ Ministry of Health 1990, 1). However, while midwives attend an increasing number of births in the liberal welfare states, obstetric interventions and particularly Caesareans continue to increase (UK Government Statistical Service 2003; NZ Ministry of Health 2003; US Department of Health and Human Services 2003). This suggests that physicians have greater authority than midwives to establish hospital practices. Furthermore, as childbirth involves more technology and physicians become more concerned about legal liability, specialists or obstetricians seem to be acquiring more control over childbirth than general practitioners.

Neoliberal restructuring has enabled the development of private hospitals and birthing centres in certain jurisdictions, where some luxuries may be provided and doctors are permitted to charge patients a direct fee for service. In countries such as the United States and New Zealand, wealthier families purchase private insurance to defray the higher costs of private health care services. Many studies find that women receiving maternity care in private hospitals are more likely to give birth through Caesarean sections (Roberts, Tracy, and Peat 2000; Walker, Turnbull, and Wilkinson 2002).

The higher percentage of Caesarean sections performed on wealthier private patients cannot be explained by an increased percentage of higher-risk pregnancies. Women seek out care in private hospitals when they can afford it because these facilities often provide more comfortable and private accommodation with better meals than many public hospitals. Women request or permit induced labour or Caesarean sections because they are told by their doctors that these are safer than vaginal births for older mothers. In addition, these procedures offer both women and their doctors more control over the birthing process and higher fees for doctors.

In liberal welfare states, private birthing centres may offer more personalized care, but both private and public hospitals now focus on cost efficiencies. In the 1940s and 1950s, women could expect a two-week 'confinement' in hospital, but now they are expected to leave in a few days. This short stay is justified for health reasons but also serves as a cost-cutting measure (Tew 1998). Controversies continue about the licensing of midwives, the growing use of obstetricians instead of midwives or general practitioners, the increasing use of technology in childbirth, and the development of a two-tiered health care system – one for the rich and one for the poor. At the same time, neoliberal restructuring is closing rural hospitals and smaller facilities, offering women less choice in maternity services and providing less continuity of care throughout pregnancy and childbirth. Labour market restructuring has also affected breastfeeding practices.

Breastfeeding Policies and Practices

For decades, both the World Health Organization and the United Nations Children's Fund have emphasized the importance of breastfeeding for childhood and maternal health (WHO 1981, 4). Breastfeeding is associated with numerous health benefits, such as providing optimum nutrition for infants, reducing the incidence and severity of infectious diseases, and lowering infant mortality (WHO and UNICEF 1990). It is also an effective means of spacing children. As well, recent studies suggest that mothers who breastfeed enjoy a reduced risk of breast cancer and possibly of ovarian cancer and osteoporosis (Galtry 2003, 168).

In 1974, the Twenty-seventh World Health Assembly noted a general decline in breastfeeding in many parts of the world (WHO 1994, 4). They related this trend to a wide variety of sociocultural factors, including the promotion of commercially manufactured breast-milk substitutes. The assembly thus urged member countries to review and 'where appropriate' to regulate sales promotion activities of baby foods, through advertisement codes and legislation (WHO 1981, 4). In 1981, the Thirty-fourth World Health Assembly adopted the International Code of Marketing of Breast-milk Substitutes (WHO 1981, 5), which aimed to: 'contribute to the provision of safe and adequate nutrition for infants, by the protection and promotion of breastfeeding, and by ensuring the proper use of breast-milk substitutes, when these are necessary, on the basis of adequate information and through appropriate marketing and distribution' (8). The code asserted that due to the vulnerability of infants and the risks associated with inappropriate feeding practices, the marketing of breast-milk substitutes required special regulatory attention (7). The WHO and UNICEF also introduced the Baby-Friendly Hospital Initiative in 1991 to encourage maternity facilities to become active supporters of breastfeeding practices and to abandon the use of breast-milk substitutes (UNICEF 2004).

One of the factors influencing the duration of breastfeeding is the length of maternity leave and the provision of breastfeeding breaks and facilities for employed mothers (Galtry 2003). The International Labour Organisation (ILO) adopted its original Maternity Protection Convention in 1919, with twelve weeks' leave with cash benefits to ensure continuity of income, protection against dismissal during leave, and two half-hour daily breaks for nursing infants (ILO 2000b). In 1952, the revised Maternity Protection Convention extended leave entitlement to cover illness resulting from pregnancy and expanded upon the types of medical benefits provided (ILO 2000b). It also specified that nursing breaks be paid and counted as working time (International Baby Food Action Network 2000). Under the latest Maternity Protection Convention (no. 183 in 2000), women are entitled to a daily reduction of working hours with full remuneration for breastfeeding, and more categories of women workers are now covered under the convention (ILO 2000b).

Convention 183 requires ratifying states of the ILO to offer a minimum of fourteen weeks of paid maternity leave either at two-thirds of previous income or with social security payments (ILO 2000a). Furthermore, the ILO pressures national governments to improve these entitlements. Recommendation 191 recommends that paid maternity leave be extended to least 18 weeks at 100 per cent of previous earnings. The ILO also recommends that 'where practicable provision should be made for the establishment of facilities for nursing under adequate hygienic conditions at or near the workplace.'

The European Social Charter of 1996 also contains provision for paid maternity leave or social security benefits for a minimum of fourteen weeks, increased from twelve weeks in the original 1961 charter (Council of Europe, 1961, 1996, art. 8). The current charter also stipulates that nursing mothers are entitled to adequate time off for this purpose. Both the ILO convention and the European charter consider it unlawful to dismiss a woman during maternity leave, although there are some conditions attached (Council of Europe 1996, art. 8; ILO 2000a, art. 8). However, not all OECD countries have ratified the ILO convention and some European countries have not signed the Social Charter.

Cross-national differences in the prevalence of breastfeeding are partly influenced by women's employment rates, their access to paid leave, public education programs, ethnicity, and social class. In New Zealand, nearly 80 per cent of mothers breastfeed their new babies, either exclusively or partially, but Maori mothers are least likely to breastfeed exclusively (NZ Ministry of Health 2003, 70). Although low-income women used to be *more* likely to breastfeed their infants than wealthier women, breastfeeding may have become a middle-class phenomenon in some countries as more low-income women find themselves in paid jobs with few benefits and little control over their hours. Another middle-class phenomenon is the use of medically assisted conception.

Medically Assisted Conception

Considerable research has found that parenthood is still used as a rough indicator of maturity, heterosexuality, men's sexual prowess, femininity, mental health, and even moral worth (Callan 1982, 1987; Cameron 1997; Bergart 2000). When people settle with a suitable partner and establish some financial stability, they usually expect to reproduce, and many are distressed if they cannot (Cameron 1990; May 1995; Adair and Rogan 1998; Ulrich and Weatherall 2000; Exley and Letherby 2001).

Low fertility, which seems to be on the rise in OECD countries, is correlated with a number of urban problems and lifestyle choices, including environmental pollution, high stress levels, cigarette smoking, alcohol abuse, sexually transmitted diseases, and prolonged use of birth control pills (Adair and Rogan 1998; Coney and Else 1999). In addition, conception problems become more apparent as the age of marriage rises and older women attempt to conceive for the first time or with a new partner. However, low fertility, like family violence, might also be reported more often. The development of fertility clinics and the media publicity given to new reproductive technologies encourage people to seek medical assistance with conception.

The previous portrayal of assisted conception as new, experimental, or potentially dangerous has shifted, and it is now viewed more as mainstream medical practice. Several researchers have examined popular representations of medically assisted reproduction, showing that they appeal to scientific progress, medical expertise, humanist cures for disease, and the politics of choice. All these representations help to normalize the procedures (Franklin 1995; Albury 1999). Both Bharadwaj (2000) and Van Dyck (1995) argue that the discourses used within medicine and journalism are complementary, with the media shown to be a key site through which assisted reproduction has been legitimated.

Detailed information about medically assisted conception is now available from the Internet, including the location of clinics, the procedures they offer, the probabilities of success, the potential risks, and the costs. Those with money and employment leave can afford to travel to clinics far from home, even to another country, to purchase the services they believe will help them. This could raise expectations about the effectiveness of procedures but also reinforce the belief that people have the 'right' to bear children. The increasing demand for fertility services also necessitates more state regulation of related research and services, the licensing of clinics, the eligibility rules for treatment, and access to state subsidies.

Fertility treatments can be expensive, disruptive, and time consuming, involving several medical appointments per week and drugs that alter normal functioning. As techniques have been perfected, success rates have increased. Unfortunately, clinics have sometimes fostered misunderstandings by making public their pregnancy rates rather than live birth rates, despite the fact that about one in four of such pregnancies ends in miscarriage (Baird 1997). British and Australian research indicates that *in vitro* fertilization (IVF) ends in success for less than a third of those who embark on it (Doyal 1995, 149), only 15 per cent per treatment cycle (HFEA 1997; Ford et al. 2003). In Australia, the viable pregnancy rates were 14.9 per cent after one cycle of IVF, 15.9 per cent for insemination with sperm, and 18.1 per cent for egg transfer. If these products are frozen or thawed, the pregnancy rates fall (Ford et al. 2003, 100). Australian research also shows that adverse infant outcomes, such as pre-term delivery, low birth weight, stillbirth, and neonatal death, are higher among assisted-conception births compared to all births (Ford et al. 2003).

The direct cost of fertility treatment to patients varies by the procedure, the use of drugs, and state subsidies. *In vitro* fertilization is one of the most expensive and, unless subsidized, can cost patients many thousands of dollars.[5] The small minority who end up with a healthy baby from reproductive technologies may find these costs acceptable, but 'we know little about the majority who go away with empty arms' (Doyal 1995, 149). Governments typically distinguish between medically necessary interventions and those requested for social reasons. Patients with no medically diagnosed reason for infertility or who are

---

5 In New Zealand, this procedure cost about NZ$8,500 per treatment in 2002, but has since increased to over $12,000.

not at risk of passing on a genetic disease may be unable to receive publicly funded services. For example, only one cycle was paid by state-funded health care in New Zealand in 1997 when the average duration of treatments was 1.6 cycles (Gillett and Peek 1997). Now two treatments are paid by the state if fertility problems are caused by a medically diagnosed or genetic problem.

Patients sometimes say that the very treatment designed to solve their fertility problem is unaffordable, is usually kept secret from most relatives and co-workers, and interferes with their paid work and relationships (Baker 2004b). Being unable to conceive while their siblings and friends are having children makes them feel 'abnormal,' but unsuccessful fertility treatments can compound their feelings of social exclusion. Low-fertility couples whose treatment is unsuccessful can accept their circumstances and move on with their lives, yet living in a childless marriage is considered socially undesirable, particularly among certain cultural groups.

Couples can keep trying with medically assisted conception, but this can be emotionally draining and financially costly. They can apply to adopt, but there is a shortage of able-bodied infants and long waiting lists in most OECD countries (Baker 2001b, 20). In addition, the adopted child is not genetically connected, which is important to many people. Couples can become foster parents, but this is a temporary arrangement. They can look to overseas adoption, but this option is expensive and governed by complex international agreements. Couples can find a surrogate mother, but the legality of this pursuit is dubious and the process can be time consuming and expensive. For would-be parents, there is no easy solution to infertility problems.

Some jurisdictions have permitted a broader category of family types to receive publicly funded fertility treatment. This has occurred after political pressure from cohabiting and lesbian couples demanding equal access to assisted conception, plus pressure from fertility clinics, and with growing public concern about the consequences of declining fertility rates for the nation. Yet access to fertility procedures remains much higher among wealthier couples that are heterosexual and legally married. Some states view these treatments in the same light as cosmetic surgery and argue that people have no 'right' to reproduce, especially if their attempts are costly for the state and/or have a low probability of effectiveness. Even privately funded treatments sometimes have public costs, especially when things go wrong, such as ectopic pregnancies and miscarriages (Baird 1997). Furthermore, some patients continue to request treatments even when the probability of success is very low (Baker 2004b). In other words, many social policy issues arise from new procedures in medically assisted conception, which is increasingly normalized and legitimized by the medical profession, journalists, and some patients.

As more people seek medical assistance with conception, political pressure grows to develop new laws governing eligibility for state-funded services, the duration of treatment, the rights of donors and surrogate parents, and offspring's access to information about sperm and egg donors. Many of these issues have already been legalized and contested in the courts, but the speed of change in genetic research and reproductive techniques has exceeded that of the law. However, wealthier patients can travel to other jurisdictions with less stringent regulations in order to seek treatment.

In OECD countries, two opposing demographic trends are occurring at the same time: more young people in the general population are choosing child-free lifestyles and more couples and individuals are becoming parents through medically assisted conception. Reproduction is now possible for a larger percentage of the population and for more diverse families. Now that fewer people legally marry, procreation remains one of the few distinguishing badges of maturity and stability, and medically assisted conception may help to solidify this status. While many educated middle-class couples are unable to reproduce or attain their desired family size, the state worries that some parents have more children than they want or can care for, either financially or emotionally. Policy makers continue to strive to encourage the 'right' people to reproduce, which usually means able-bodied, heterosexual married couples with adequate incomes.

Conclusion

In this chapter, I argued that health and well-being statistics for individuals and families are converging. For example, life expectancies are rising in most OECD countries, with women living longer than men. Infant and maternal mortality rates have declined since the 1930s, teen pregnancy rates and adoption rates have fallen since the 1970s, and most married women now use contraceptives. In some countries abortion rates have remained steady in recent decades, but they have increased in the liberal welfare states since the 1970s. Medical intervention in childbirth is also rising in most countries, and this includes induced labour, elective Caesarean sections, and medically assisted conception. However, vast cross-national differences remain in these trends, reflecting different health policies and practices.

The apparent convergence in health statistics, reproductive services, and childbirth practices has been influenced by similar social, economic, and political factors. Improvements in living standards and health care have reduced some types of premature death, especially maternal deaths from pregnancy-related complications and childbirth. Higher education for women is related to more effective contraceptive use and a later age at first birth. In addition, international organizations, such as the United Nations and the World Health Organisation, have pressured national governments to carry out research related to health and well-being, to gather basic health statistics, and to sign international agreements on a number of issues now viewed as human rights. All signatory states have been urged to ensure access to health and reproductive services, to provide a variety of services relating to family health, and to ensure their effectiveness.

In addition to international pressures, similar funding concerns have influenced reproductive policies and practices within each country. Most governments have become more mindful of rising health care costs with new and expensive equipment and higher labour and operating costs. Policy makers have also reacted with growing concern to the health care cost implications of population aging, but have responded as well to the public demand for lower taxes. Consequently, health ministers have encouraged health care institutions to shorten hospital stays, to use midwife care for 'normal' pregnancies, and to limit the use of unnecessary technology in childbirth. However, state efforts to reduce the costs of reproductive and maternity services have sometimes antagonized professionals, who worry about patient care, their professional autonomy, and legal liability costs. Efforts to reduce health care expenditures have not always been successful in countries where the medical profession forms a powerful interest group.

In this chapter, we have seen that numerous factors influence policies and practices relating to conception and childbirth. Firstly, neoliberal restructuring has achieved some cost savings but also encouraged the rise of private hospitals and clinics in certain jurisdictions (such as New Zealand). Under these conditions, doctors have been able to offer a wider range of services to patients who are able and willing to pay. With respect to maternity services, some doctors have been able to convince women over thirty-five years old that Caesarean deliveries are safer than vaginal births and that the effectiveness rates of assisted conception are high enough to justify the cost. Wealthier patients may even ask their doctors for induced labour or elective Caesareans in order to alleviate the unpredictable timing, the pain, and some of the side-effects of childbirth. Others have successfully pressed their physicians to continue fertility treatment even when the probability of pregnancy is low.

These interventions have increased the cost of private health care for patients, but the 'politics of choice' have also influenced public expectations about health policies and practices. If some couples can afford to have a much-desired child, shouldn't these services be available to everyone? Costs also rise for the public health care system if the unexpected occurs and women are sent in emergency situations to public hospitals. Furthermore, doctors and clinics clearly make profits from reproductive interventions in private clinics, emphasizing their scientific effectiveness and the politics of choice in attracting and keeping patients. Similarly, marketing of infant feeding formulas has played on maternal guilt by focusing on the products' nutritional content and easy preparation for busy mothers. These companies have also made huge profits.

Secondly, childbirth policies and practices are influenced by professional competition between doctors and midwives but also between obstetricians and general practitioners. Midwives promote women's right to home births and continuous care from pregnancy until several months after childbirth. They argue that childbirth is a natural act that should not be medicalized or controlled by physicians, but that women benefit from the presence of a qualified and supportive midwife at the time of childbirth. General practitioners encourage continuous care by family doctors but favour hospital births.

On the other hand, many obstetricians believe that delivering babies should be confined to specialists who understand the risks and can effectively use the new technologies. They view births to mothers over the age of thirty-five as risky and strive to provide quality care using the latest technological interventions. All three parties endeavour to protect themselves from malpractice lawsuits, to preserve their working conditions, and to retain professional autonomy and control. Fertility specialists and obstetricians tend to use more interventions and create more lucrative practices. At least in the liberal welfare states, these medical specialists have become a powerful lobby in the childbirth process despite the state's desire for cost-cutting measures.

Thirdly, policy makers and hospital officials are confronted with different views on the morality of contraception, abortion, elective Caesarean births, and fertility interventions. While feminist groups have fought for women's right to control their own bodies and often promoted care by midwives, social conservatives seek to ensure that sex remains within marriage, that procreation takes place within committed heterosexual relationships, that married couples continue to reproduce the next generation, and that both patients and doctors enjoy maximum choice in health care services and procedures. Some politicians continue to see reproduction as a patriotic duty despite the current socio-economic conditions that make it more complicated and costly. These politicians strive to ensure that declining fertility does not interfere with the country's ability to finance social programs in the future.

Finally, this chapter has shown that economic, professional, and political factors tend to counter some of the pressures on health care institutions and practitioners to provide safe, necessary, and cost-effective reproductive and childbirth practices. Although some international organizations have been arguing for years for specific reforms, national governments have not always been able or willing to implement parts of their agendas. International studies and statistics indicate that reproductive and childbirth practices are converging, but not always in the direction desired by governments or international organizations such as the World Health Organisation. Instead, conception and childbirth have become even more governed by medical practices, new technologies, private funding, and patients' ability to pay.

6 Work, Gender, and Parenthood

This chapter focuses on parenthood and work, including the strategies parents, policy makers, and employers have developed to more effectively integrate caring and employment. We first note how gender interacts with parenthood in paid and unpaid work and then explore policy options for paid parental leave from employment. (Childcare issues are discussed separately in the next chapter.) Despite international pressure on governments to help parents integrate paid work and family responsibilities, substantial cross-national differences remain in employment statistics and work/family policies. Generally, the liberal welfare states have been the most resistant to regulating employment conditions and acknowledging that parents (especially mothers) have legitimate concerns about balancing paid work and family life. This chapter shows that women's increased participation in employment conceals the fact that they still trade off employment and family involvement. Women's entry into employment may have changed their own lives but has had little impact on the structure or organization of employment (Daly and Rake 2003, 172).

Parenthood and Paid Work

The employment rates of men and women in most OECD countries have been converging since the 1960s as men's rates declined slightly while women's increased. Men's declining rates can be attributed to prolonged schooling, more non-standard work, and earlier retirement. Women's employment and self-employment increased because more families needed a second income as living costs increased, including children's prolonged education. In addition, fewer pregnancies enabled

Table 6.1
Economically active mothers and fathers with a child aged 0–10 years, 1985–93

Country	Mothers 1985 (%)	Mothers 1993 (%)	Fathers 1985 (%)	Fathers 1993 (%)
Austria	NA	64	NA	97
Belgium	66	71	97	96
Denmark	85	84	97	99
Finland	NA	77	—	95
France	62	70	98	98
Germany – West	41	50	98	97
Germany – East	NA	88	NA	97
Greece	42	51	97	98
Spain	38	49	97	97
Ireland	26	43	96	94
Italy	42	49	99	97
Luxembourg	36	45	99	96
Portugal	28	51	97	95
Sweden*	NA	59	NA	93
United Kingdom	48	59	97	95

*With children under seven
Source: Leira 2002, 52

women to continue their education and use it to find better-paying jobs. Rising female employment also represents a response to the growing desire for higher living standards and to ideologies that associate women's employment earnings with self-fulfilment, independence, and 'liberation.' The labour force also expanded to create more service jobs considered appropriate for women, and the development of part-time work assisted mothers to earn money while retaining domestic responsibilities.

The main increase in women's employment has been among married women and mothers. Table 6.1 shows the changes in European OECD countries between 1985 and 1993 in the percentages of 'economically active' parents, a term that includes both self-employment and employment. We can see that during these eight years of economic restructuring and rising costs, rates increased noticeably for mothers and declined slightly for fathers, but variations among countries are also apparent. Despite women's increased economic activity, the labour force remains 'gendered.' Table 6.2 indicates that the hourly earnings of women employees in OECD countries average 84 per cent of men's, whether we

Table 6.2
Hourly earnings of women vs. men, 1998–2001 (gender wage ratio)

Country	Full-time wage and salary employees	All wage and salary employees
Australia	91	89
Belgium	91	93
Canada	82	81
Denmark	89	89
Finland	82	82
France	87	89
Germany	80	81
Italy	85	91
Netherlands	80	79
New Zealand	86	84
Portugal	92	95
Spain	88	86
Sweden	86	83
Switzerland	76	78
United Kingdom	80	75
United States	79	78
OECD Average	84	84

Source: Extracted from OECD 2002, 97, Table 2.15.

compare full-time employees or all employees. However, substantial cross-national differences are apparent. The difference between male and female mean full-time earnings varied from just 8 to 9 per cent in Portugal, Belgium, and Australia to 24 per cent in Switzerland. The gender wage gap reported as a percentage of median earnings is close to 40 per cent in Japan and Korea (OECD 2001, 69).

Even with equal-pay-for-equal-work provisions and anti-discrimination legislation, the wage gap continues for both full-time and part-time workers. This wage gap reflects a segregated labour market in which men and women often perform different kinds of jobs. Men's jobs range from high-level business and professional positions to low-level manual labour jobs, while women tend to be clustered in service, administrative, and semi-professional positions. In addition, men tend to work longer hours and receive more promotions, while women work shorter hours and sometimes experience lower bargaining power and discrimination when they attempt to progress through the ranks. In Australia, the centralized bargaining system used to be an effective instrument in maintaining high wages and narrowing the gender gap, but it has been under threat since the advent of enterprise bargaining (Mitchell 1995).[1] However, the Industrial Relations Reform Act, which came into effect in 1994, retained minimum wages for Australians at a higher level than Canadians experience (O'Connor, Orloff, and Shaver 1999, 104).

Beaujot (2000) noted that Canadian men and women with neither spouse nor children experience similar rates of full-time employment, but that mothers make more concessions than fathers for the integration of earning and caring. Furthermore, unpaid housework is one of the important bases on which we 'do gender.' Mothers with young children, but not fathers, often reduce their working hours or opt out of paid work for caring and household responsibilities. However, this pattern varies cross-nationally, reflecting different social attitudes, institutional arrangements, job opportunities, degrees of financial need, and social policies. Employment rates for mothers with children under six years of age varied from a low of about 35 per cent in Japan to over 75 per cent in Sweden (OECD 2001, 45). In some OECD countries, most maternal employment continues to be part time, whereas working part time is unusual in others. In 2001, for example, 89.4 per cent of employed mothers with at least one child younger than six years worked part time in the Netherlands compared to 9.1 per cent in Hungary (OECD 2003a, 37).

Gendered life patterns and expectations are reflected in employment rates, job categories, and earnings, but opportunities and attitudes are changing. In Canada, Fast and Da Pont (1997) found that women continue to experience work interruptions for family reasons but that these are becoming shorter and more concentrated at childbirth. The size of the gender gap in earnings is declining over time with the rise in educational attainment and job tenure for women relative to men. Brooks, Jarman, and Blackburn (2003) also noted that occupational segregation based on gender declined in Canada from 1981 to 1996, as women strengthened their full-time participation in paid work and improved their earnings relative to men. At the same time, there was a slight increase in part-time work for men and some tradi-

---

[1] In centralized bargaining, all employees in the same job category belong to the same union regardless of their place of employment. After successful negotiations, they all receive the same wage settlement. In enterprise bargaining, the employees of each workplace bargain separately with their employer. This means that wages might be different for similar categories of workers living and working in different parts of the country.

tional male occupations experienced both a decline and an influx of female workers.

Household specialization associated with parenting has also declined but is still apparent. Lundberg and Rose (1998) noted that the first birth reduced American mothers' paid working hours by 45 per cent but did not affect fathers' hours. In fact, fathers' wage rate *increased* by 9 per cent after the birth of a child while mothers' wage rate fell by 5 per cent (Lundberg and Rose 1998). In OECD countries in 2000, an average of 2.9 per cent of employed fathers aged between twenty-five and fifty-four worked part time, compared to 28.7 per cent of employed mothers with one child and 36.6 per cent of mothers with two or more children (OECD 2002, 77). Clearly, having children alters women's employment patterns more than men's.

Labour markets have become more competitive, making it difficult for employees to take time out for childbearing and child rearing. As more women move into 'non-traditional jobs', the organization of work in these occupations makes having children more complex (Ranson 1998). Rather than changing the 'long-hours culture' or altering meetings times or work goals, women workers have been expected to match the work patterns of their male counterparts. In addition, Hochschild (1989) showed that many mothers working full time experience a 'double day' or a 'second shift' when they arrive home to unpaid housework and caring responsibilities. Since Hochschild's study, many researchers in other countries have confirmed that mothers rather than fathers shoulder the responsibility for caring work even when they work full time, partly through the belief that it is women's work but also because it is difficult and expensive to find anyone else to do it.

Concerns about Maternal Employment

In many OECD countries, childbearing, child rearing, and domestic work have been seen as priorities for married women. Consequently, these women's entry into paid work has always been influenced by factors other than paying the bills or pursuing personal ambitions. Such factors include whether or not they have a partner, their partner's wages relative to living costs, whether or not they have children, the number and ages of their children, marriage breakdown rates, the household's financial need, women's educational attainment, and ideologies about the importance of paid work for women's autonomy and fulfillment (Everingham 1994; Bittman and Pixley 1997). Maternal employment is further influenced by the nature of state support. States that promote the male breadwinner/female caregiver model of family often encourage maternal child rearing at home. Those that support the mother/worker model offer better enforcement of pay equity, more generous maternity benefits, and affordable childcare, all of which encourage girls to see lifelong employment as feasible and normal for mothers.

Public debate and policy initiatives about maternal employment date back at least a century, despite the fact that Taylor-Gooby (2004) identified it as a 'new risk' for social policy. In the nineteenth century, social conservatives were concerned that strenuous working conditions would interfere with women's reproductive health and reduce the birth rate, and early trade unionists argued that women's lower wages would edge unionized men into unemployment. In the 1960s, social conservatives worried that working mothers would neglect their children and that lack of (maternal) supervision would increase children's opportunities for delinquency. Feminists have noted that none of these concerns would become realities if governments, trade unions, and employers supported maternal employment and gender equity. Over the years, women activists fought for paid maternity benefits, pay equity, subsidized childcare services, and after-school programs.

Now, most trade unions and governments have ensured that male and female workers are entitled to the same employment rights, but gendered differences remain in employment outcomes. Some social reformers argue that both mothers and fathers experience problems balancing work and family life in the twenty-four-hour economy and argue for a 'level playing field' between employees with responsibilities for children and those without, regardless of their gender. However, research shows that mothers experience more employment problems than fathers do.

Although most women are now employed, many mothers with young children work part time or accept casual positions because earning money is considered secondary to their main role as care providers and homemakers. These mothers have few incentives to work full time or seek promotion because they retain responsibility for most of the housework and childcare at home (Bittman and Pixley 1997). This means that they have less freedom to accept job promotions, especially those that involve moving to another city or country. Women's lower earnings or sporadic work throughout their lifetimes often lead to reduced or no retirement incomes, especially in those countries where the major old age pension is financed through social insurance and based on previous employment. Lower earnings increase the chances of poverty in old age, which requires the state to provide income support for older unattached women. For this reason, governments and organizations such as the OECD are trying to encourage both women and men to see a lifetime of paid employment as normal and desirable.

Not all women can accept this advice unless family leave and alternative caring arrangements are already in place. The fact that large cross-national differences are apparent in the employment statistics of women and mothers reflects different labour market conditions, caring arrangements, social programs, and public attitudes about working mothers and the responsibilities of fathers.

Making Adaptations for Earning and Caring

Over the decades, employed parents have used at least three different strategies to reduce their combined workloads of caring and earning. The first is for mothers to opt out of paid work while raising children and to enter or re-enter when their youngest child enters school. The second is for mothers to work part time or accept temporary or undemanding jobs when their children need close supervision and care, and to accept full time work only when all their children are in school or become self-sufficient. And thirdly, parents can hire assistance with childcare or housework, freeing them to work full time or pursue other activities.

Many women still leave their paid jobs for several years when they give birth rather than taking a short maternity leave. At a national level, this pattern has been called a 'two-phase work cycle,' as women's employment rates tend to be high during their early twenties (before most have children), low in their thirties (when children are young), and higher again in their forties and fifties (when children are in school or have left home). This pattern has diminished in North America but is still widespread for women in Britain, Australia, and the Netherlands (O'Connor, Orloff, and Shaver 1999; Millar and Rowlingson 2001).

If women opt out of paid work when they reproduce, their successful re-entry depends on the length of absence, their age when they leave and return, their family size, their qualifications, previous employment experience, and their current skills and job contacts. Women who have children before they establish themselves in full-time work may eventually enter the labour force with outdated education and skills, competing for jobs with youthful graduates. These mothers could still upgrade their qualifications, but many would have to begin at the bottom of the employment hierarchy. By the time they accrue work experience, financial assets, or pension credits, they could be fifty years old, and if they live with an older male partner, he could be contemplating early retirement. Women who raise children at home for ten or more years also tend to establish a traditional division of labour at home, which then becomes difficult to alter once they return to paid work (Shelton and John 1996; Beaujot 2000, 175).

If women develop their work experience before they become pregnant, they are more likely to qualify for maternity/parental benefits and to have established a shared division of household labour with their partner. Once a career is established, however, giving up employment income, occupational status, and regular contact with co-workers is not easy for women or the household budget. Furthermore, delayed conception sometimes leads to fertility problems. So both scenarios – rearing children before entering paid work or developing employment experience first and then taking time out for child rearing – offer challenges for mothers and their families.

A second strategy to avoid the 'double day' is for mothers to accept part-time, temporary, or undemanding jobs when their children are young. In current labour markets, greater 'flexibility' is often perceived to be against the interests of employees, but many mothers (and students) see temporary jobs and part-time hours as compatible with their own interests (Wolcott and Glezer 1995). However, these jobs often pay lower wages than full-time work and include fewer opportunities for training and promotion. Also, they sometimes require employees to be 'on call' or to work unpredictable hours, leading to problems with caring arrangements, family time, or other activities. More mothers than fathers also opt for self-employment as a way of managing care (Arai 2000), but these jobs include low-paid piecework done at home and other marginal business ventures.

New technologies and opportunities to 'telework' (or to use computerized linkages from the office to home) could help manage the integration of work and family, but could also mean that work intrudes in all activities and increases stress levels. Mirchandani (1999) found that Canadians who telework at home tend to establish strict physical and mental boundaries to separate work and domestic activities. Ironically, she found that men teleworkers isolate themselves from domestic activities even more than men who work outside the home, but that women maintain more permeable boundaries between paid and unpaid work.

The Social Charter of the European Union states that part-time workers should be paid comparable hourly rates to full-time workers, but not all EU member states have signed this agreement. In North America, part-time workers typically receive lower pay than full-time workers, accept less prestigious positions, and continue to work with little chance of promotion or employment-related benefits (such as retirement pensions). Duffy (1997) and Vosko (2000) also found that many Canadian part-time workers find it difficult to move into full-time work if they wish to increase their hours and income.

Finally, higher-income families can purchase relief from the double day by hiring childcare and home-cleaning services. Although the cost of childcare varies cross-nationally, this option becomes feasible for many parents only if services are subsidized by the state. Another possibility is inexpensive market-based care, but these caregivers often lack professional qualifications and state regulation. Bradshaw et al. (1996) and Bradshaw and Finch (2002) showed that the cost of childcare was particularly high in New Zealand and the United Kingdom, two countries with relatively low rates of full-time employment for mothers with preschool children.

If parents must pay the full cost of high-quality childcare, the price is unaffordable for average-income earners. Consequently, low-income parents tend to rely on informal care by sitters, neighbours, friends, or relatives, and sometimes pay them through reciprocity rather than cash (Edin and Lein 1997; Baker 2004a). Families can also purchase takeaway or ready-made meals to save preparation time, but the nutritional value can be lower than that of home-cooked food and the cost is almost always higher. Home-cleaning, household repairs, grass-cutting, or snow removal services can also be purchased in most countries, sometimes through franchised businesses or self-employed individuals. These services, however, are typically too costly even for moderate earners and therefore remain options only for higher-income families.

Marriage and fatherhood usually encourage men to take their earning obligations more seriously, but mothers often reduce employment hours and spend more time on caring work. When mothers with several children accept a paying job, they tend to work weekends or part time or to alternate shifts with their husbands, in order to integrate paid work and family life (Marshall 1994; Drolet and Morissette 1997). Yet family conflict is highest if couples work shifts over which they have no control because coordinating childcare, leisure, and other family activities becomes more difficult (Marshall 1998). Employment leave is sometimes the only way to deal with family emergencies, but mothers are far more likely than fathers to disrupt their work schedules to balance this conflict (Akyeampong 1998).

The OECD average for part-time work was 3.6 per cent of male employees compared to 23.2 per cent of women employees in 2000, but large differences exist among countries as well as between all women and mothers with young children (OECD 2002, 78). Part-time work is prevalent among mothers in countries such as the Netherlands, Switzerland, Germany, and Australia where the male breadwinner family has been privileged in social policy. In these countries, women are far more likely than men to work part time, and mothers with young children at home are more likely than other women to work part time. For example, 38.3 per cent of women without children in the Netherlands worked part time in 2000 compared to 82.7 per cent with two or more children. For men, the trend is in the opposite direction: 6.2 per cent of men without children and 4.6 per cent with two or more children worked part-time (78).

In Nordic countries and North America, labour force participation rates for both mothers and fathers tend to remain high throughout the childbearing years, with mothers taking one or two short maternity leaves and fathers taking much less time off. In North America, employment rates are now higher for women of prime childbearing ages than for older women (Beaujot 2000, 151), representing a generational shift in work patterns. Higher employment rates for young mothers suggest that these 'work rich' families probably suffer from 'time poverty.'

Wolcott and Glezer (1995, 181) argued that Australian mothers who work part time can best integrate work and family, and that 'the majority are satisfied with this solution.' Although many mothers with young children opt for this 'choice,' fathers seldom make these adjustments. If the pattern of more paid work for fathers and less for mothers is maintained, many women will continue to experience insecure work, low pay, and financial problems in old age, reinforcing their dependence on male partners and the state (Baker and Tippin 1999).

Policy Approaches to Working Parents

OECD countries have adopted at least two broad policy approaches to help families integrate earning and caring. The first views the 'normal' family arrangement as one in which the husband/father earns household income and the wife/mother retains primary responsibility for the home and children, although she may also earn money. Within this family model, the state might provide tax benefits for the family breadwinner and 'his dependants,' while the female caregiver might be given a small caring allowance if the household income is low. However, the state makes only a gesture towards the needs of employed mothers, such as subsidizing childcare for employed mothers with low household incomes. In this first category, we could place countries such as Australia, New Zealand, the United Kingdom, the Netherlands, and Japan.

The second approach assumes that both husbands and wives are employees capable of self-support and that both are responsible for supporting any children they produce. This model of family offers varying degrees of public support for childcare, parental benefits, and employment leave for family responsibilities, but does not usually assume that adult partners are 'dependants' or that gender roles are substantially different. This approach can be further divided into two subcategories: jurisdictions that expect mothers to become workers but provide few public supports, and those that offer more generous statutory benefits and services for employed mothers. The United States fits into the first subcategory while Sweden, Finland, Denmark, and France fit into the second (Baker 1996; Christopher 2002).

Countries that view women primarily as housewives and mothers, and/or accept a residual role for the state in social provision, tend to offer few public supports to help combine child rearing with full-time employment. In these countries, at least four structural barriers have made it difficult for employed mothers: ungenerous or no statutory maternity or parental benefits, the shortage of public childcare facilities, the high cost of these services, and persistent cultural attitudes that children are somehow damaged by non-maternal care.

In New Zealand, for example, all four barriers existed until recently. Most social programs assumed that families had a male breadwinner and female caregiver even though maternal employment rates had increased (Baker 2001b). The childcare subsidy for low-income families did not cover full-time working hours until 2003, despite the focus on paid work and self-sufficiency in welfare-to-work programs established in 1997 by the conservative National government. This subsidy still remains targeted to low-income families rather than all families requiring childcare services. New Zealand offered only unpaid maternity leave to female employees until July 2002, when twelve weeks of paid parental benefits were introduced for those with continuous employment with the same employer for one year (Baker 2005). This legislation originated as a private member's bill from a female member of the (left-leaning) Alliance Party (Baker 2001a), but was implemented by the Labour-led government (with a female prime minister).

The cultural expectation that domestic and caring responsibilities are female concerns continues to shape girls' 'choices' about education and employment. Conservative discourse in many countries still emphasizes the importance of having children and women's choice to mother at home, which could discourage some girls from seeing themselves as future employees. At the same time, current welfare requirements sometimes encourage young mothers on social benefits to accept any paid position in order to earn money rather than to prepare for a lifetime of earning. However, gendered work patterns may diminish in the future as labour markets offer less security to both men and women.

Within the liberal welfare states, noticeable differences are apparent in support for maternal employment. Canadian social programs have supported maternal employment more effectively than similar programs in Australia, New Zealand, or the United Kingdom. The Canadian provincial governments continue to subsidize childcare spaces for low-income families[2] with financial assistance from the federal government, which also pays a substantial income tax deduction to defray the cost of childcare necessary to maintain paid work. Federal maternity benefits have been paid through the Unemployment Insurance Program since 1971 for fifteen weeks to eligible female employees. In 1990 ten weeks of parental benefits were added, and these were recently expanded to thirty-five weeks. This makes a total of fifty weeks' paid leave available to eligible mothers[3] (or thirty-five to fathers) in Canada compared to fourteen weeks' parental benefits in New Zealand[4] and no statutory parental benefits in the United States or Australia.

Canadian benefits for employed mothers were won after years of lobbying by organized groups such as the Child Care Advocacy Asso-

---

2 However, there are never enough subsidized spaces to meet the demand.
3 In recent years, the percentage of paid workers eligible for Employment Insurance has declined considerably.
4 The Labour government increased paid leave to fourteen weeks in 2005.

ciation, the National Action Committee on the Status of Women, and Legal Education Action Fund for Women. Politicians were forced to listen to these groups because maternal employment rates had increased earlier and faster in Canada than in Australia and New Zealand, and high-quality childcare was considered to be crucial to women's employment equity as well as early child development (Baker and Tippin 1999). In Australia and New Zealand, the women's movement tended to focus on gender differences and on pensions for mothers caring for children at home.

Social programs in European countries such as France and Sweden support employed mothers with effective employment training, high wages for women relative to men, enhanced leave for family responsibilities, and more generous state-funded childcare (Kamerman and Kahn 2001). The European Economic Commission (EEC) made recommendations relating to equal pay in the 1960s and expanded this in the 1970s to access to training and employment, employment conditions, and social security. By the 1980s, women were becoming a strong constituency in Europe, but the 1990s marked the beginnings of 'mainstreaming' gender into European Union policy, with discussions and the adoption of measures to help parents reconcile work and family life (Hantrais 2000, 114). Considerable debate has occurred about the impact of these measures, as the extent and pace of change in behaviour and attitudes about women's status vary with labour markets, wider policy environments, and national family structure and policies. By 1998, employment guidelines contained measures to help workers better integrate paid work and family life, including leave for family responsibilities, part time work, parental leave, more flexible hours, childcare services, and policies to facilitate the return to work.

OECD countries vary considerably in their support for different categories of employed mothers, some offering better support for lone mothers than partnered mothers (Gornick 2000). Finland, Sweden, and France offer the most generous employment supports for all mothers, and these countries also demonstrate the lowest poverty rates for mother-led families and the lowest poverty ratios between married and single mothers (Christopher 2002). Although the International Labour Organisation has long argued that statutory maternity benefits are basic requirements for women's employment equity, some states continue to provide minimal protection for the incomes and job security of pregnant employees.

Differing Models of Maternity/Parental Benefits[5]

Although feminists disagree about many issues, they do agree that some form of cash benefit at birth is essential for women's employment equity and their continuing role as mothers. What remains contentious is whether social policies focusing on equality of opportunity with men will lead to equity and justice for women. Men do not become pregnant, do not bear children, and do not breastfeed. Consequently, some feminists argue that if women are to gain equality of *outcome*, special benefits must be created to consider these biological differences.

'Liberal feminists' have focused on equality of opportunity: equality before the law, equal access to higher education, and equal pay and promotional opportunities in the labour force. More radical and socialist feminists have argued that women's biology and life experiences are different from men's, and that policies should emphasize equality of outcome rather than equality of opportunity. Legal, political, and economic institutions have been designed by men to suit their interests and needs, radical feminists say, which suggests that equal access will not lead to equity or equitable outcomes. Women need to acquire policy-making positions and help redesign laws, programs, and practices to focus more on childbearing, consensus, cooperation, human needs, and environmental protection and less on hierarchy, competition, and profit making. These two theoretical stances have been simplified for this discussion but remain important in the debate over maternity and parental benefits.

Feminists also agree that men have designed much of the welfare state, even in Scandinavian countries (Hernes 1987). This is noticeable in maternity and parental leave programs, as some still assume that employees are full-time workers with a continuous attachment to the labour force. This has meant that many mothers are ineligible for statutory maternity benefits because they are recent entrants to the labour force, are self-employed, work part time or in temporary positions, or do unpaid work at home (United Nations 2000a, 133).

Many European countries are more likely than liberal welfare states to provide generous employment-related benefits and special support for children and families, as Table 6.3 indicates. Sweden, Denmark, and France have long recognized that when mothers are abandoned to

---

5 An earlier version of the ideas presented in this section was previously published in Baker (1997b).

Table 6.3
Maternity/parental leave benefits in selected OECD countries

Country	Date of first legislation	Length of maternity/parental leave	Percentage of wages paid in covered period	Provider of coverage
Australia	1973 unpaid leave	1 year	No federal statutory requirement for paid leave but some unions pay	–
Canada	1971 maternity benefits 1990 parental benefits	15 weeks maternity + 35 weeks parental	55% to a ceiling	Social insurance (employment insurance)
Denmark	1915 maternity benefits	18 weeks maternity + 10 weeks parental	100% to a ceiling	Social security
France	1909 maternity leave 1913 maternity benefits	16–26 weeks	100%	Social security
Germany	1883 parental leave 1927 maternity benefits	14 weeks	100%	Social security to ceiling and employer pays difference
Japan	1926 maternity benefits	14 weeks	60%	Social security or health insurance
New Zealand	2002 parental benefits	12–14 weeks parental	Flat rate	Social security
Norway	1909 maternity benefits	18 weeks maternity + 26 weeks parental	48 weeks at 100% or 52 weeks at 80%	Social security
Sweden	1937 maternity benefits 1974 parental benefits	480 days parental	390 days at 80% and 90 days at flat rate	Social security
United Kingdom	1975 maternity benefits	14–18 weeks	90% for 6 weeks, flat rate thereafter	Social Security
United States	1993 parental leave	12 weeks	No federal statutory requirement for paid leave but some state/unions pay	–

Source: Ayusawa 1966, 195; Bock and Thane 1991, 5; United Nations 2000a, 142–3; Sainsbury 2001, 122; various websites

market forces without state protection and services, these mothers often cannot compete with employees who do not become pregnant, have no family responsibilities, and are free to seek better opportunities elsewhere. In addition, countries such as Sweden have focused on full employment policies and provided more generous legislation for wage protection, social benefits, and family leave (Baker 1995; Christopher 2002). These additional benefits and laws have helped to protect mothers from income loss, whether or not they are in the labour force.

Political pressure from rising female employment rates during the 1960s and 1970s and declining fertility in subsequent decades led to improvements in parental leave policies in most countries. Yet there is no correlation between women's employment rates or total fertility rates and the jurisdiction's choice of maternity or parental leave model. The OECD total fertility rate has declined since the 1970s to about 1.6 in 2002 (OECD 2005, 28). Sweden has a high rate of female employment and a relatively high rate of fertility, as does the United States. Yet Sweden developed social insurance programs to protect employees from income loss at childbirth while the United States did not.

In the next section, I outline three policy models to deal with the integration of pregnancy, childbirth, and employment, originally discussed in an earlier article (Baker 1997b). The first is paid maternity leave.

Targeting Benefits to Mothers

About a hundred years ago, Bismarck first established cash maternity benefits for employed women in Germany. By World War I, several European countries, including France, Italy, and Britain, already had passed some form of national maternity insurance for working women. The first and most influential international standard that recognized the needs of working mothers emerged from the 1919 International Labour Organisation Maternity Protection Convention. This ILO agreement laid down such basic principles as women's right to maternity leave, nursing breaks, wage compensation, and job protection (Heitlinger 1993, 190).

In 1952, the ILO convention was revised to include a twelve-week minimum leave period, including six weeks after the birth. Additional leave was to be provided in cases of pregnancy-related illness, and medical benefits were to be provided by qualified midwives or medical practitioners. Employers could not give notice of dismissal during maternity leave, and work breaks had to be given for breastfeeding. The convention was amended again in 2000 to include fourteen weeks' leave (ILO 2000b). The European Union Social Charter also provides for a minimum of fourteen weeks' paid leave or social security benefits (Council of Europe 1996, art. 8).

Maternity benefits arose partially from concern over the health of children whose mothers were employed, but the development of cash benefits within social insurance reflected the view that maternity contributes to societal needs as well as those of individual parents. In addition, social insurance for maternity reflects the view that income loss at childbirth is a social risk that should be shared by the state, employers, employees, and their families (Kamerman and Kahn 1989). Maternal leave policies are gender specific and assume that childbirth is a physical ordeal for women requiring preparation and recuperation, and that protective legislation is needed to prevent risks to unborn fetuses and to the health of pregnant women. In addition, maternity benefits are often viewed as a form of employment equity, or an attempt to grant women equal opportunity in the workforce rather than penalizing them when they become pregnant. Finally, maternity leave and benefits can be an inducement to reproduce by ensuring that employed women do not respond to the difficulties of combining work and child rearing by choosing to remain childless.

Targeting Benefits to Parents

Paid parental benefits, as opposed to maternity benefits, incorporate some concerns about the biology of childbirth but do not see childbirth as something that happens only to women. Rather, they emphasize the gender-neutral processes of nurturing and bonding. The philosophy behind parental leave is that fathers should be encouraged to be present during childbirth, to bond with their newborn infants, and to participate in their daily care. Parental benefits are justified with the argument that childbirth leave and benefits directed only to mothers could discourage employers from hiring women of childbearing age, discourage gender equality, and discriminate against men who want to care for their newborn infants. The right to parental benefits has been fought on the principle of gender equality for men and equal rights for biological and adoptive fathers (Baker and Tippin 1999). Political pressure, especially from legal reformers and fathers' rights groups, has required many jurisdictions to ensure that program eligibility is gender neutral.

With growing unemployment rates, some jurisdictions have extended unpaid parental and child-rearing leave in order to reduce unemployment, share jobs, and create temporary positions for unemployed workers. However, lone mothers and low-income parents can seldom afford to take advantage of unpaid leave or leave on half-wages. Even when wages are fully replaced, fathers are far less likely than mothers to take parental leave, especially for extended periods (Haas 1990; Beaujot 2000). This suggests that long-term leave (whether paid or not) could perpetuate a gendered division of labour.

The Laissez-Faire Model

Under the laissez-faire model, pregnancy and childbirth are considered private or family matters, of little concern to either employers or the state. Proponents of this view argue that asking employers to share the expense of childbirth leave and benefits would be too costly and would encourage discrimination against female employees. Employed women might also get pregnant or work the required number of hours simply to take advantage of access to maternity benefits, causing extra expenses and disruptions for employers. If the state were to provide such benefits, taxes would rise significantly. Such arguments have prevailed in the United States where, despite high levels of lone-parent households, high fertility rates, and moderately high female employment rates, the federal government has created no national program of maternity or parental benefits. Instead, unpaid leave is provided by the federal 1993 Family and Medical Leave Act, and individual states, employers, professional associations, and trade unions are left to decide whether or not to offer paid leave (Baker 1995, 179). Similar arguments prevented paid parental benefits from being established in New Zealand until recently (Baker 2001a).

Some of the assumptions behind the laissez-faire position have been tested in research. For example, Phipps (2000) examined Canadian micro data from 1988 to 1990 to see if changes in the Canadian maternity/parental benefit system influenced behaviour. Maternity benefits were first introduced in 1971, and parental benefits were added in 1984 and extended in 1990. Until 1997, eligibility rules for Canadian maternity/parental benefits under Unemployment Insurance required twenty weeks of paid employment with at least fifteen hours per week or minimum weekly wages. The switch to 'Employment Insurance' in 1997 means that applicants now require seven hundred hours of employment with no minimum earnings – the equivalent of twenty weeks at thirty-five hours per week. From an analysis of the data before and after parental benefits were extended, Phipps concluded that fertility behaviour was not significantly influenced by the availability of benefits, and there is no evidence that women adjusted their labour supply behaviour in order to gain access to such benefits. Furthermore, teenage mothers, women with little education, and those experiencing difficulty in the labour market continue to be less likely to become eligible for these benefits. Phipps used these conclusions to argue that governments should ease access to maternity and parental benefits.

Maternity and parental benefits can fulfil several different policy goals. They can be perceived as an attempt to improve maternal and child health, a form of employment equity for women, an inducement to reproduction, and a citizenship right for every employee. They can also be seen as an expense and aggravation to employers or as a deterrent to hiring women. Which model is chosen by a jurisdiction depends mainly on the political ideology of the government in power and the strength of various advocacy groups. Political pressure may be national, or it can originate from supranational organizations such as the International Labour Organisation and the European Union, who both try to encourage member states to develop a minimum standard of employment benefits (Hantrais 2000). However, the policies chosen by governments fit in with their priorities and the model of family they support. In the next section, I argue that certain policy choices suit some political interests more than others.

Whose Interests Are Protected by Various Leave Policies?

The introduction of maternity and parental leave legislation has served several vested interests. Maternity leave policies are based on a concern for maternal and child health and welfare. Allowing pregnant women to take job-protected leave recognizes health risks to fetuses and mothers from overwork or exposure to work-related hazards. Permitting recovery time acknowledges that childbirth is physically and psychologically exhausting. Consequently, health and safety advocates, religious groups, and conservative women's groups have argued for gender-specific maternity leave.

Maternity leave legislation can also be used to secure and sustain the labour force participation of women. If, after working for a designated period of time, women are guaranteed paid leave while their positions are held open, they are more likely to enter the labour force and to ensure that they have met eligibility qualifications before becoming pregnant. Leaving paid work for childbearing and child rearing and returning years later was only feasible for women when the labour force was expanding (enabling women to re-enter more easily), technological change was slower, men were paid a family wage, and divorce rates were lower.

Now, women experience more difficulty re-entering the workforce after five to ten years because of shrinking labour markets, increased global competition, and rapid technological change. Furthermore, a smaller percentage of households can survive on one income and fewer mothers can depend on another wage in the household, especially where separation and divorce rates are high. Although women have always paid a heavy price in lifetime earnings for moving in and out of the labour force, maternity leave provisions have improved their economic status considerably. Consequently, all feminist groups, 'progressive' reform groups, and trade unions have fought for paid maternity leave, although there has been more debate about the wisdom of long-term leave for promoting gender equality in the home and workforce.

Parental leave as opposed to maternity leave legislation has been motivated by movements to increase the rights of fathers to care for their children with a minimum of lost income. The creation of gender-neutral benefits in Canada resulted from a constitutional challenge focusing on the differential entitlements between adoptive parents and biological fathers, rather than any substantial change in men's caring roles (Baker 1995, 162). Traditionally men have been encouraged to give priority to earning a living rather than caring for their children, but parental leave legislation acknowledges that some men want to play a larger role in their children's care and development. However, research from Canada and Sweden has indicated that only a minority of fathers take their full entitlement of parental leave. Men who take full parental leave tend to spend more time caring for their children after that leave ends, but they may be a self-selected group who are more interested in nurturing (Haas 1990; Beaujot 2000).

Despite the different interests and origins of parental and maternity leave, caring work continues to be gendered, partly through the effects of early socialization but also because legislation in all countries has been implemented within a gendered labour market. In all OECD countries, women tend to take responsibility for 'kin-keeping,' childcare, and housework; they more often work part time; and they continue to be marginalized in some aspects of the labour force, even in Scandinavia (Hernes 1987; Leira 2002). Feminists and progressive reformers agree that paid maternity or parental leave is essential in order to promote gender equity. The availability of generous social benefits can encourage young women to establish full-time employment before pregnancy and delay their first birth. In comparative analyses, paid maternity/parental leave and adequate childcare are important factors in determining the lifetime earnings of women (Dalto 1989; OECD 2001). Paid leave also contributes to poverty reduction, especially in lone-mother households, as there is no need to resign from employment in order to have a family.

Of course, women's employment rates are influenced by other factors than the availability of maternity or parental benefits. These include high divorce rates, low wages or unemployment of male partners, feminist ideologies emphasizing work and self-sufficiency for wives, a woman's educational qualifications, and lack of state support for raising children at home. Policies that pay mothers to stay home and care for their children for extended periods of time (more than several years) serve to reinforce patriarchal relations. After several years at home, a woman's role as care provider and homemaker tends to become solidified and her job skills, employment experience, and earning capacity are subsequently eroded.

Wide variation is apparent in the motivating philosophy behind maternity and parental leave and benefit programs, as well as the duration of benefits and compensation level. Yet the underlying structure of the legislation remains essentially patriarchal because it assumes that male work characteristics are the norm. Entitlement is sometimes based on a lengthy work record in standard employment even though many women work in temporary or part time positions with fewer than the required hours to qualify (Chaykowski and Powell 1999; Bashevkin 2002b).

Reforming Parental Leave Policies

Recent reforms have attempted to remove some of the obstacles and patriarchal biases from parental leave legislation. France, Germany, and Sweden now offer government benefits to pregnant women regardless of their labour force attachment. Several Canadian provinces have reduced or eliminated the requirement of a lengthy employment record because it disqualified so many women from leave and benefits. Canada also reformed its employment insurance (EI) program to base eligibility on the number of hours previously worked rather than the number of weeks. This could help non-standard workers to become eligible for EI, although benefit levels were reduced in the process (Baker and Tippin 1999, 97). The Canadian government also extended the length of parental benefits from ten weeks to thirty-five weeks in January 2001 (Lawlor 2003). In contrast, New Zealand's parental benefit, first introduced in 2001, requires one year's continuous employment with the same employer and pays a flat rate for only twelve weeks, which was the International Labour Organisation's 1952 minimum (UN 2000a, 133). In 2005, this was extended to fourteen weeks after pressure from the ILO.

The gendered nature of paid work and different use of parental leave by men and women preserve the unequal sharing of economic and practical parenting. When parenting is divided, fathers usually assume economic parenting, acquiring full-time paid work. At the same time, mothers perpetuate their dependency through practical parenting (performing routine household tasks and caring for the children), because they want to, because it is still seen as 'women's work,' but also because women are less able to find high-paying and permanent full-time jobs. If only one parent at a time is permitted to take parental leave, which is usually the case, the family is better able to survive on the father's higher wages. In addition, both men and women view mothers as the logical choice for leave recipients. As mothers must already take some time off work for childbirth and recovery, the decision to take *all* of the leave could easily follow.

Two trends have been apparent in employment leave for pregnancy and parenting. First, gender-neutral terminology is increasingly used within leave policies in an attempt to create equal employment opportunities for males and females, and paid parental leave has replaced gender-specific maternity leave in some jurisdictions and workplaces. In the United States, for example, maternity benefits have been perceived as discriminatory to fathers unless they are incorporated into sickness and disability insurance. This insistence on treating men and women equally in terms of employment benefits is ironic considering that women give birth and lactate while men do not. However, the U.S. Constitution requires equal treatment of men and women despite biological differences and the inequalities perpetuated by the present economic system. Radical feminists argue that this insistence on equal treatment of people who experience life differently is counterproductive for women and perpetuates the male bias in social policy.

A second trend is the extension of unpaid parental leave for one to five years, which addresses several policy concerns. Offering extended leave is an attempt by the state to resolve childcare problems without providing public funding for these services. Extended leave also allows mothers who choose to care for their own children and who can afford temporarily to forfeit their earnings to do so without giving up their jobs. Extended parental leave reduces absenteeism by temporarily replacing parents of infants or young children with employees who have fewer domestic responsibilities. And finally, extended leave helps reduce unemployment by offering short-term contracts as maternity replacements. This can provide invaluable job experience to otherwise unemployed or marginally employed people. Yet extended unpaid leave is only an option for middle-class and two-parent families, and could work against women's equality by solidifying traditional gender roles.

Although some form of maternity or parental benefit is essential for women's employment equity, these programs will not resolve the gender-based inequalities either at work or at home. Social programs must also focus on raising girls' interest in occupational achievement, reducing occupational segregation based on gender, improving pay equity, providing affordable and accessible childcare, and increasing the participation of both boys and men in childcare and housework. In addition, changes need to be made to the structure of work to remove the assumption that it is separate from personal life. The design of leave programs must therefore consider that employment opportunities have never been the same for most men and women. Women's labour market activities have always been influenced by their marital and parental status to a much greater extent than have men's. Traditionally, obligations to children and husbands have caused women to accept part-time or temporary employment, limit overtime work, take unpaid leave, relocate with their husband's occupation, and accept lower wages.

The gendered division of labour within and outside the home suggests that neither gender-neutral nor gender-specific benefits for employed parents can resolve this problem. Tying these programs to the traditional male model of work will not be effective without other equity measures. These include statutory maternity benefits for women not fully attached to the workforce, other programs guaranteeing income security, measures to promote employment equity, equal pay for jobs of comparable worth, and universal health care. Only when states intervene to help counteract market forces can both mothers and fathers achieve employment equity.

The Gendered Division of Domestic Work

Research from many OECD countries concludes that men have increased their share of domestic work in recent decades (Sullivan 2000). However, much of this increase can be explained by the fact that more men live alone, given later marriage and higher rates of separation and divorce. Research shows that in heterosexual couples, female partners continue to do most of the housework and caring work even when they also work for pay (Bock and Thane 1991; Dempsey 1997; Baker and Tippin 1999; McMahon 1999; Leira 2002; Gazso-Windle and McMullin 2003). Husbands will 'lend a hand' if their wives are pressed for time, but housework and childcare remain the responsibility of wives (and female relatives) throughout much of the world.

Early studies of housework (Lopata 1971; Oakley 1974) redefined it as 'work' rather than a natural extension of women's role or an activity motivated by love. They also noted its characteristics as unpaid, low status, potentially isolating, and not always chosen by those who perform it. For example, Luxton (1980) examined family life in an isolated Canadian mining town, showing that housework was 'more than a labour of love' because it also involved power relations and gendered and class-based expectations. Hartmann (1981) argued that American men have not only resisted doing housework but create more housework for their wives than they actually do themselves. Hochschild (1989) used the term 'second shift' to describe the housework and childcare performed by most American women when they come home from a day in the labour force.

Social researchers have studied the amount of unpaid domestic work done by husbands and wives through qualitative interviews and time-budget studies. Although national variations are apparent, the general trends are the same: wives do more housework and caring work than husbands and also accept more responsibility for the organization and completion of these tasks. The Australian Bureau of Statistics has carried out extensive time-budget surveys, and their analyses conclude that Australian women perform about 70 per cent of unpaid domestic work, which has been largely unaffected by women's increasing labour force participation rates. No matter how many hours of paid work a wife does, her husband's contribution remains relatively constant (Bittman 1991, 1995; Baxter 1994; Baxter and Bittman 1995).

Despite the increasing use of new equipment such as dishwashers, microwaves, automatic washers, and clothes dryers, Australians in the early 1990s spent about the same amount of time in the kitchen and laundry as they did in 1974. From 1974 to 1991, women on average lost one hour of leisure time per day because more were working for pay, but women also retained responsibility for domestic duties. Men worked more in the kitchen and laundry, but two-thirds of their unpaid work was done outdoors (Bittman 1991). Using the 1997 Australian Time Use Survey, Bittman and Rice (1999) continued to show that men have not taken up the slack even though women have increased their paid work. Instead, 'domestic outsourcing' or the purchase of market substitutes for domestic labour helps women resolve the time pressure created by an increasing commitment to paid work. This conclusion has also been found in other countries.

Research also suggests that children do not contribute substantially to household work, even when they are older. Mothers spend more time and energy persuading their children to do household tasks than it would have taken if they did the work themselves. Nevertheless, parents feel that children should do housework in order to learn to take responsibility. If a child neglects to perform a designated task, the mother usually does it herself rather than trying to get another child or her husband to do it (Goodnow 1989; Goodnow and Susan 1989).

Why do wives continue to accept most of the responsibility for housework even when they work for pay and prefer a more shared division of labour? Dempsey (1999) concluded, based on interviews with Melbourne women, that although a few women clearly want to retain control over the domestic realm, most wives are unable to persuade their husbands to take more responsibility for indoor household tasks. He found that husbands tend to use a variety of tactics to avoid these duties, such as waiting to be asked each time by their wife, saying they do not know how to do it, arguing that the task does not really need doing, and delaying completion. Dempsey concluded that relative power differences in heterosexual relationships continue to influence patterns of housework.

The division of labour in dual-earner households in Canada and the United States was studied by Davies and Carrier (1999) to understand which factors influence the apportioning of household tasks between husbands and wives. Based on 1982 data,[6] they concluded that the hours of work and the income earned by marital partners are less

---

6 There was no acceptable explanation why the data were so old in this 1999 publication.

important than 'marital power relations' in determining the allocation of household tasks. They argued that power relations are influenced by gender expectations, opportunities, and experiences in the larger society, and that gender intersects with race, ethnicity, and social class to influence these relations.

Gazso-Windle and McMullin (2003) used 1995 Canadian social survey data to explore the relationships among time availability, relative income, gender ideology, and the time spent on housework. They concluded that there is some evidence that wives and especially husbands 'trade off' time they spend in housework by doing more paid work. However, women and men with higher incomes and education spend less time on housework but more time on childcare. Ironically, wives spend more time on housework when their wages are higher or closer to their husbands', suggesting that being a successful family earner means something different for husbands than wives. Some women may feel that they have to compensate for their success in the (male) breadwinning role by performing extra domestic tasks. Alternatively, the husbands of high-earning women may resent their 'intrusion' into family breadwinning and consequently may resist sharing domestic work. The authors concluded that egalitarian notions about gender behaviour are more likely to influence men's participation in childcare than in housework.

Crompton (2004) studied work/life stress among full-time workers who were partnered, had at least one child, and lived in the United Kingdom or continental Europe. She found that this stress was the highest among women, parents, and professional men who worked overtime. Work/life stress levels were lower among employees who worked shorter hours and lived in countries with institutional supports for employed parents (such as Finland and Norway). Stress was also lower among employees who said that they shared housework and childcare with their partner.

A gendered division of labour within the home and the workplace has many implications for both men and women. More mothers than fathers develop close lifetime ties with their children from years of physical and emotional caring work. In addition, some wives may be able to pursue their own hobbies, charitable work, and friendships during the day if they work part time or are outside the labour force. At the same time, accepting most of the responsibility for housework and childcare reduces women's chances of obtaining employment qualifications, working full time or overtime, or being promoted to higher-paying or more responsible positions. Being female also seems to reduce women's chances of enjoying special favours within the family or an exemption from housework if they become successful breadwinners.

The fact that wives and mothers tend to work fewer hours for pay and earn lower incomes than their husbands means that their access to a large portion of family resources is dependent on the goodwill of their partners. Daly and Rake (2003) demonstrated through their own analysis of Luxembourg Income Study data that wives contributed between 25 to 41 per cent of family income in the seven OECD countries they studied, varying considerably by country. Women's contribution to family income was the highest in Sweden and the lowest in Italy (128), reflecting women's higher employment rates in Sweden. However, the authors also noted that women's contribution was often higher in families reliant on state income support than in those depending solely on earned income.

For non-employed or marginally employed wives, the lack of personal income could translate into less decision-making power in their marital relationship, could reduce confidence in their ability to protect their interests or support themselves outside marriage, and could lead to less income in the event of widowhood or divorce. Furthermore, when women accept most of the responsibility for domestic work they reinforce traditional role models for their children (Duffy and Pupo 1992). Yet many women who would prefer their husband to accept a larger share of household and caring work feel that they have little control over their household division of labour (Dempsey 1999).

Some countries have attempted to encourage men to increase their share of domestic responsibilities through social policy initiatives. One means is to ensure that fathers as well as mothers are entitled to employment leave at the time of childbirth or adoption, in the hope that they will take it and also form a closer and lasting bond with their child. Secondly, some governments have tried to encourage fathers to take some parental leave by legislating days that *must* be taken by the father or be forfeited by the couple ('daddy days'). Thirdly, most governments have encouraged joint custody and tried to enforce paternal child support after separation and divorce. All these policies, however, focus on the care and support of children. Social policies to encourage men to accept more responsibility for housework have been much more difficult to develop and enforce.

Conclusion

In this chapter we have seen that more men than women work for wages in the full-time labour force and men typically work longer hours and earn higher wages. While women's participation rates have increased substantially in recent years, the gender gap remains in pay, job status, and working hours, although it is eroding as more younger women gain credentials and develop lifetime careers. Men's work patterns have recently deteriorated in some OECD countries with the erosion of union protection, the flight of capital, competition from women workers, or political unrest in their country. In addition, men in the liberal welfare states are now working longer hours and consequently spending less time with their families.

Globalized labour markets are polarizing families: some are 'work poor' or have unemployed or marginally employed adults, while others are 'work rich' but have insufficient time for caring activities or leisure (Bittman 1998; Torjman and Battle 1999; Kay 2000). Increased employment migration and global trade have benefited young men and women who are child-free, educated, and geographically mobile, but low-income mothers and certain cultural minorities remain disproportionately represented among low-wage workers and low-income families. As labour forces in OECD countries now contain more mothers with young children than in previous decades, governments and employers have had to create new policies to deal with potential conflicts between work and family.

Some OECD countries have been more successful than others in developing social programs that help parents combine paid work with childbirth and childcare. Sweden and Denmark, for example, have provided broader legal protection for employees who become new parents and more generous funding for childcare services, while Belgium and France have offered strong support for all families with children through child allowances and tax concessions, as we will discuss in chapter 8. More governments are now talking about children as a 'future resource' and making promises about reducing 'child poverty,' but not all states are developing effective social programs to counteract global market forces that tend to diminish family income. Placing more emphasis on national productivity measures, global competitiveness, interest rates, the erosion of the work ethic, and reduced public spending tends to diminish the effectiveness of any family policy initiatives.

Providing statutory supports and services for parents who are trying to balance work and family life is essential for women's employment equity, but these initiatives require political commitment, public regulation, the coordination of social programs, and the investment of public money. Integration between family policy and labour market policy is needed, but this requires effective lobbying and coalition building, which is especially difficult in an era of neoliberalism with demands for smaller government and lower taxes. New programs such as expanded parental leave or childcare services require either new public money or the reallocation of spending, and competition is always fierce for public resources.

The cross-national trend towards governments expecting more adults to enter paid work may be complicated and risky for mothers, especially those on low incomes living in the current economic environment of liberal welfare states. In some cases, moving from social benefits to paid work may result in a net financial loss for their families (Evans 1996; Baker and Tippin 1999; Millar and Rowlingson 2001). The extent of the complications (both perceived and real) is not always recognized by policy makers, because a full understanding requires some acknowledgment of the lack of training to allow workers to move to better positions, of the insecurity of many jobs, and of the psychic damage caused by dead-end and low-paid work. Recognition of these complications also requires an acknowledgment of the wider social environment experienced by low-income mothers. This includes the fact that low-income people tend to be less healthy than higher-income people but that even full-time workers are not always eligible for paid sick leave. Those who work in temporary jobs, who begin a new job, or whose children are ill must often take unpaid leave for family sickness. Despite the low wages received by many lone mothers, non-resident fathers often pay no child support, as we discuss in chapter 9. In addition, availability, quality, and affordability of childcare remain problems for many families

In some jurisdictions, social conservatives have expressed concern that encouraging women to take paid work will further reduce fertility rates and induce mothers to neglect their 'family duties.' At the beginning of chapter 1 of this book, we saw that this concern was expressed in a recent Vatican report. Social conservatives also insist that there must be equal support for the one-earner family where the other parent cares for children at home. The state must be seen as fair and equitable when providing social benefits and tax relief, ensuring that children receive high-quality care regardless of their parents' employment status. Nevertheless, the persistence of gender differences in the labour force raises questions about the adequacy of the welfare state in securing women's welfare (Daly and Rake 2003).

7 The Care and Welfare of Children

As more mothers work for pay or are encouraged to see themselves as future employees, the daytime care of children becomes a pressing social policy issue. However, the improvement of public childcare services is not the only policy concern in this realm. Public discourse suggests that family problems such as child abuse and delinquency are increasing as more parents are unavailable to supervise their children during working hours. Ideally, states and voluntary organizations develop programs to prevent parents and their children from falling into dire circumstances, but resources for preventive services are often stretched to the limit. This is especially true where neoliberal ideas and practices have reduced income taxes, contracted out social service delivery, and targeted state support to those considered to be 'at risk.'

In this chapter, we focus on five policy issues relating to the well-being of children and their parents: the daytime care of children with employed parents, programs for lone mothers caring for children at home, adoption programs, foster care, and child abuse programs. Although many other family service issues could be discussed, these provide some insights into national and international trends in service delivery and some of the pressures on national governments to standardize and improve these services. Although some states provide social services and income support to all families with children, the liberal welfare states tend to focus public resources on families 'in need' or considered to be 'at risk.' These may mean that children are neglected, families have insufficient income for food or shelter, the home is violent, a lone parent is experiencing problems coping with children, or parents or children are involved with drugs or alcohol or are in trouble with the law. However, state support for the daytime care of children with employed mothers has become a more universal need, as most mothers now also participate in the labour force in OECD countries.

Childcare Policies for Employed Mothers

Funding and Regulating Childcare

As maternal employment increases, debates about the state's role in childcare services have become prominent. Some conservative politicians have always asserted that childcare is a private matter that should be of no concern to governments or employers (Timpson 2001). Nevertheless, conservative lobby groups in the past successfully argued for income tax relief for one-earner families as well as income support for low-income mothers caring for young children at home. In addition, early intervention programs (such as Head Start) were seen as one solution to childhood development problems, helping to ensure the social inclusion of children from impoverished or deprived families. At the same time, feminist groups have pressured governments to view the accessibility, affordability, and quality of public childcare services as employment equity issues for women, as well as providing early education for children. As a higher percentage of families require non-parental childcare, more people accept the idea that the state needs to be more involved in funding these services.

There are essentially two types of state-funded childcare programs: one emphasizes parental care while the other supports the development of non-parental care and services (Jenson and Sineau 2001a). Parental programs include the payment of income support that enables low-income parents (mainly mothers) to care for their children at home, such as the Domestic Purposes Benefit in New Zealand or the Parenting Allowance in Australia. Programs such as family allowances and maternity grants could also be seen as a form of state support for child rearing, although they focus on financial support for parenting rather than the actual care of children.

Non-parental childcare programs may involve day nurseries, group care within a family, and public support for in-home care by sitters and nannies, including temporary work permits for carers from overseas. The most prevalent form of state support is a subsidy paid directly to care establishments in the form of capital grants for building or renovating facilities, operating expenses, wage subsidies for care providers, or subsidies for low-income children. State support usually privileges not-for-profit services sponsored by local government, charitable organizations, or employers rather than assisting commercial care or franchise operations. Some states offer vouchers directly to parents, who must then find their own care services, while others provide income tax rebates or deductions for services already purchased.

In addition to funding or providing childcare as a public service, states also regulate childcare facilities, care providers, and the programs or services they offer. This may involve inspecting the physical site to ensure that the space is adequate for the number of children, the yard is fenced, there are a sufficient number of toilets, the food preparation areas are sanitary, and there are enough toys and educational materials. Governments also regulate the qualifications and pay rates of care providers, parental fees for care, the staff/child ratios, and the quality of the educational program.

Kindergarten and childcare services enjoy a long history, although the lobby for state support has been a contentious struggle in some countries. Preschool or nursery school has been seen as a necessary and enriching part of early education since the nineteenth century, especially in Europe, but many preschools have been sponsored by private educational foundations rather than the state (Baker 1995, 189). Countries with a socialist tradition (such as East Germany) or a tradition of social democracy (such as Sweden) have long expected women to earn a living and contribute to the nation's economic productivity. To enable mothers to remain in the labour force, these states have provided public childcare services, which came to be seen as a citizenship right (190).

In the liberal welfare states, governments continued to view preschool childcare as a private family issue until the 1960s, or much later in some countries, expecting mothers to care for their own children at home. Opposition to married women's employment was briefly challenged during World War II in countries such as Canada and Australia, when women's labour was needed in war industries and to replace male workers who joined the armed forces (R. Pierson 1977; Kedgley 1996, 132). Some governments offered tax incentives and subsidies to encourage married women to accept these jobs. For example, the Canadian government revised the Income Tax Act to allow husbands to claim their wives as dependants regardless of how much money the latter earned. Federal cost sharing was also extended to the provinces to enable them to provide daycare centres for mothers working in war industries, and this was later offered to all employed women. However, only Quebec and Ontario took up this offer, and the day nurseries were closed after the war (R. Pierson 1977).

The political importance of childcare increased in Canada in the 1970s, with rising rates of maternal employment and greater public concern about work/family conflicts, children's supervision, and early childhood education (Baker 1995, 201). From 1966 to 1996, the Canada Assistance Plan provided federal government funds to the provinces for social services and income support, and some of this was used for the childcare services of low-income families. However, the demand for subsidized spaces always outstripped the supply. The federal government has also offered relatively generous income tax deductions since 1971 to employed individuals who submitted receipts for non-family childcare.

In the early 1980s, two Canadian commissions studied childcare issues and, after considerable lobbying by childcare advocacy groups, in 1987 the Conservative government under Prime Minister Brian Mulroney introduced a National Strategy on Child Care. However, only the tax reforms were implemented from this strategy, and the proposed national childcare program was delayed. As childcare falls under provincial jurisdiction, the federal government was unable to persuade the provinces to create a program with national standards. This meant that federal childcare subsidies to the provinces continued to be channelled through the Canada Assistance Plan, which was a program for funding welfare. Since this program ended in 1996, the federal government has been giving block grants to the provinces to use for a variety of health, social, and educational services. Friendly (2001) argued that after many years of lobbying, Canadian childcare programs have not developed beyond a rudimentary level, and even deteriorated in the 1990s. She attributed some of the problems to disputes over federal-provincial jurisdiction. In the 2004 Canadian election, however, childcare shortages became a major election issue for the Liberal Party, which won a minority government.

Public debates have continued in many countries about how childcare services should be funded, who should provide them, and whether public money should privilege non-family daycare for employed parents. Many social conservatives argue that 'families' (read: mothers) should be given a choice of caring for their own children at home or hiring someone to look after them while they enter the workforce. However, if governments wanted to offer mothers a real choice, the payments for caring at home would need to approximate women's potential earnings in the labour force. This would require much higher taxes than individuals pay in all of the liberal welfare states, especially in the United States or New Zealand. Since the 1990s, most liberal states have *reduced* their highest marginal tax rates, leaving less public money for improved childcare or other social programs. In addition, governments would be unable to regulate the quality of parental care at home or to compensate for parental neglect of children. The less expensive option would be to subsidize regulated childcare facilities.

Cross-national Variations in Childcare Programs

Despite years of research and practical knowledge about what constitutes quality care, considerable variation exists in state childcare policies and programs. Countries such as France have provided half-day preschool for children aged three to the compulsory age of school attendance as part of the education system, and about 99 per cent of children of these ages attend (Leira 2002, 62). In the Nordic countries, parties on the political left have advocated for public childcare services and benefits in order to promote gender equity, while parties in the political centre and on the right have promoted equal subsidies to all families with young children, regardless of their choice of childcare. Sweden, Denmark, France, Belgium, Iceland, and the former East Germany have provided more extensive services for preschool children at a lower cost to parents than have other OECD countries, although some focus their public facilities on children aged three and over (Gauthier 2001; Jenson and Sineau 2001a; Leira 2002).

The liberal welfare states usually subsidize the cost of childcare only for employed parents in low-income or one-parent families, generally in not-for-profit centres or licensed homes regulated by the state. Two-parent families without low incomes usually pay the full cost if they require non-family care. Some governments (such as Canada) also provide tax benefits for the childcare expenses of employed parents, regardless of family income. Yet these tax benefits require official receipts from caregivers, which are sometimes difficult to obtain because some carers work informally in the underground economy.

In 1996, the Quebec government (under the Parti Québécois)[1] an-

---

1 Policies of the former Parti Québécois government were seen as more social democratic than those in other Canadian provinces. The Parti Québécois also advocated sovereignty for Quebec.

nounced a new family policy package for the Canadian province of Quebec, which included a childcare program that initially required parents to pay only five dollars per day for care whether or not parents were in paid work. This program was phased in from 1997 until 2001, when the provincial government increased the number of spaces, the wages of educators, and its childcare budget. Quebec became the only province in Canada to develop such a universal system of childcare for preschool children (Childcare Resource and Research Unit [CRRU] 2003). However, in April 2003 the Parti Québécois lost the election to the Liberals, who announced that they intended to slow the expansion of the childcare program, increase parental fees, and encourage for-profit childcare (CRRU 2003). After considerable public protest, the new government released a consultation paper in August 2003 with several proposals to alter the childcare system. The Quebec childcare debate has continued unresolved since then, the only change being to the fees, which were raised to seven dollars per day.

The European Union began with very few social policy commitments, and none in the area of family or childcare policy. By the early 1980s, the European Commission began to institutionalize its equal opportunity work. Drawing from networks such as the Childcare Network, the EU installed experts and advocates who sought to expand the concept of equal opportunities to include access to paid parental leave and childcare (Ross 2001). By the 1990s, the European Council was making recommendations on childcare programs and policy regarding parental leave. As unemployment increased, the provision of childcare became justified as a form of job creation in the 'social economy' as well as an issue related to gender equity and women's citizenship. Ross (2001) argued that in recent years EU institutions have become facilitators for disseminating best practices in employment matters rather than legislators, as some member states have resisted intrusion into social policy.

Vast differences were apparent in the cost of preschool childcare to parents in the twenty-two countries studied by Bradshaw and Finch (2002). They found that few countries subsidize informal care even when it is the most prevalent form of childcare. At the time of their research, a number of countries offered no state subsidies for the most prevalent form of care, including Israel, Italy, Spain, and the United Kingdom, although some income-related subsidies were available in Israel and Italy. Yet preschool childcare was high on the political agenda of OECD countries, and Bradshaw and Finch noted that nearly all reported plans to expand services and reduce the costs to parents (88). Three countries (Denmark, the Netherlands, and England) expressed their intentions to extend or introduce a 'childcare guarantee.' This was a legal guarantee or merely a promise that all children within a certain age (or the children of lone parents entering employment) would have access to a childcare place by a certain date, although this guarantee could refer to part-time or full-time care. In addition, several countries have promised to increase childcare places or to reduce childcare costs to parents. For example, Norway announced that it would reduce parental payments from 37 per cent of total costs to 20 per cent by 2005 (89).

Out-of-school childcare has become an area of recent reform in many countries. Norway now requires all municipalities to provide daycare for school-age children, while New Zealand pays a small portion of childcare costs for employed lone mothers. Finland and Sweden provide free meals for all preschool children in childcare facilities, and several other countries offer free or subsidized meals only for children from low-income families (91). Bradshaw and Finch noted that access to childcare and its affordability remain important policy concerns in the countries they studied. In most places, however, the cost of care falls mainly on parents, albeit to a lesser extent for low-income families.

The Growing Demand for High-Quality Childcare

Even when governments subsidize childcare, the number of applicants usually outstrips available spaces. Daycare facilities that are highly recommended and not-for-profit often have long waiting lists, especially in the liberal welfare states. This is why childcare activists usually object to vouchers or payments to parents as a solution to the childcare problems of employed parents. If the state subsidized not-for-profit providers rather than parents who need the services, more facilities would become available. The shortage of spaces means that most employed parents with preschool children must rely on unregulated sitters in the liberal welfare states, but parents seldom have the time or opportunity to monitor the quality of these arrangements. In some jurisdictions (such as the Canadian province of Alberta), neither the employees of childcare centres nor child minders (sitters) are required to have special training. These jobs generally pay the minimum wage or less, and consequently have difficulty attracting and retaining trained and committed care providers.

A number of advocacy groups have formed around childcare concerns, such as the National Family Day Care Council (Australia) and the Canadian Day Care Advocacy Association. In recent years, some labour unions have become advocates for improved childcare services for their members. These groups have asked governments to tighten regulations; improve the training, fringe benefits, and pay for childcare workers; and allocate more public money to childcare for employed parents. Advocacy groups have also tried to upgrade the qualifications and the salaries of childcare workers, which in some jurisdictions are much lower than the salaries of kindergarten teachers. Kindergarten teachers have typically been unionized and paid through funds from education ministries, while childcare workers are less often unionized and are usually paid through funds from social services or voluntary organizations (Baker 1995; Brennan 1998).

In countries with high immigration or a high percentage of indigenous people, many parents expect to find culturally sensitive childcare services. In New Zealand, Maori language preschools (*Te Kohanga Reo*) are well established, but elders continue to argue that special immersion schools should be expanded and that their language should be taught as part of the national school curriculum (Baker 2001a). Immigrant parents (especially the mothers) also need childcare to enable them to take language training to improve their employment opportunities and to help them integrate into their new country or become more independent from family. Employees who have little control over their working hours or who are required to work evening or weekend shifts also need childcare services, but most centres schedule care well in advance and operate during regular office hours. If parents work on different shifts, they may be able to share child rearing, which can save money but may also restrict family activities and time together as a couple.

Grandmothers are sometimes able and willing to provide childcare while the child's parents are at work, and care by grandmothers can save parents money, provide culturally sensitive care, and solidify the bond between generations. It could also lead to intergenerational disagreements about child-rearing techniques and traditional values. Increasingly, grandmothers themselves are working for pay and many are unavailable (or unwilling) to provide childcare services for their grandchildren.

Suitable childcare is especially difficult to find for children with disabilities or 'special needs.' Mothers used to be the main caregivers of children with disabilities, before special hospitals and institutions were established in the 1950s and 1960s, and this source of unpaid labour is being re-examined as a way to reduce health and chronic care costs, with policies of de-institutionalization established since the 1980s. However, many mothers are now fully employed, which means that more public services are needed to care for children with disabilities and the frail elderly. Furthermore, more parents expect local daycare centres or state-run schools to accept special needs children so that they can receive the same education as other children. Increasingly, these schools receive insufficient state resources to provide this kind of individual attention and must rely on private fund-raising or special short-term grants from the state.

Some mothers continue to care for their own children at home for a variety of reasons. Some view raising their own children as their main joy or career, and can afford to leave the labour force because they have another breadwinner in the household. Yet others care for their own children at home because most daycare centres will not accept infants or children under the age of two unless they are toilet-trained. Even if space is available, parents want to ensure that the quality of care is high and that the centre employs an adequate number of staff to keep the infants clean, fed, and stimulated. In addition, parents are often concerned about the spread of infectious diseases with infants in centre care.

Finding a qualified babysitter to come to the child's home or who will welcome an extra child in her home is also difficult. Licensed family homes are available in most jurisdictions, but childminders or sitters usually operate outside state regulations. Sitter care is seldom regulated by any level of government yet remains the most prevalent type of childcare for employed parents (Baker 1995, 235; Millar and Rowlingson 2001). Increasingly, employers and governments are promoting longer parental leaves because infant daycare is expensive and controversial. Consequently, many mothers stay home for the first two years because affordable and high-quality infant care is difficult to find.

Researchers have explored the connection between childcare services, active labour market policies, and women's employment, using cross-national data. For example, White (2001) showed that access to childcare increases the labour supply, increases women's labour market participation, and therefore raises national productivity. She argued that state support for childcare should be seen as an active labour market policy in Canada as it is in many European countries, rather than merely a mechanism to promote child development or to reduce family poverty.

Krashinsky and Cleveland (2003) examined eight common myths about and objections to publicly funded childcare in Canada. They showed that childcare is under-funded compared to government spending on education at other levels, and that access to subsidized care is unevenly distributed to parents across the country because priorities and funding levels vary by province. Except for Quebec's seven-dollars-per-day childcare program, most Canadian provinces provide subsidies only for low-income families. Other families do not qualify for subsidies and must make their own arrangements, but some may qualify for a federal income tax deduction.

Finding accessible and affordable childcare services remains a problem for employed parents in many countries. A recent survey by Recruit Ireland found that 63 per cent of the 350 employed parents surveyed said that they would leave their current job if they could find an employer who provided childcare facilities (Keane 2004). Many also said they would take a pay cut for such a situation. The Irish government is promoting employer-sponsored childcare as a solution to the 'childcare crisis,' as maternal employment has rapidly increased in recent years. In this study, 94 per cent supported tax cuts for employers providing childcare facilities. Almost 30 per cent said that they currently pay more for childcare than for their mortgage or rent, and a further 30 per cent said they pay about the same amount. Three-quarters of the sample claimed that they worried about taking full parental leave for fear that it could hinder their chances at work.

In 2004, the Blair (Labour) government in the United Kingdom expressed the need to draw up plans for emergency childcare for working mothers if their usual arrangements fail at the last minute (Hinsliff 2004). This would prevent women from calling in sick if their childminder was ill or their child could not attend the nursery; only wealthier families can afford private 'back-up nanny services.' State-subsidized emergency services were proposed by backbench women members of Parliament, consulted by Labour staff in preparation for the next election. Julie Mellor, head of the Equal Opportunities Commission, had previously called for a childcare system 'as reliable as NHS' (National Health Service), which would fill the gaps in the patchwork of arrangements that harried working mothers have to make (Hinsliff 2004).

Clearly, the major impediment to improved childcare services is the cost. Consequently, many governments have focused on subsidizing care for low-income families or lone mothers rather than all families needing services, or expanding parental leave and benefits to encourage parents to care for their own infants. However, political pressure is mounting in many jurisdictions to offer public preschool for younger children, safer childcare, more out-of school services for older children, and holiday care. Lobby groups also argue that governments must recognize that parents cannot be expected to earn a living without reliable care for their children. As maternal employment rises in OECD countries, social activists demand more state support for childcare as both an equity issue for employed mothers and an investment in children.

State Support for Childcare at Home

Although most countries have raised state support for public childcare services, politicians cannot afford to ignore the needs and sacrifices of parents who care for their children at home. In some jurisdictions, these parents (usually mothers) remain an important political constituency who expect public recognition for their work and public assistance to help defray their costs. One policy to recognize mothers' desire to care for their infants at home is the expansion of paid parental leave. Sweden assumes that parents will work for pay, but their paid parental leave program allows parents to care for their infants at home for almost a year and a half, although few fathers take more than a few weeks. We have also noted that Canada's parental benefits now extend for almost a year. Australia has been more supportive of maternal childcare than the other liberal welfare states, offering a parenting allowance to care for children at home, which we discuss in more detail in chapter 8. However, Australia has provided much less public support for non-family childcare than countries such as Canada, Sweden, or France.

Many countries provide additional support for lone mothers caring for children at home, as these families are more likely to experience poverty and other family problems. The percentage of lone-parent families among all households has increased in most OECD countries, especially since 1985 (OECD 2001, 35). Mothers head 90 per cent of these families, which are vastly over-represented in the poor population of nearly every country (34). The impact of long-term poverty on children is an important policy concern in most OECD countries but especially in liberal welfare states, where poverty rates are the highest (UNICEF

2000). However, political discourse voices less concern for the children's parents.

Living with one parent does not mean that children experience problems, but being involved in protracted parental conflict, losing touch with a father, and living in poverty can be quite detrimental to children's development (Amato 2004). Having paid work reduces the risk of poverty in mother-led families, but maternal employment rates and women's wages relative to men's vary considerably by country, as we saw in chapter 6. National variations in the employment rates of lone mothers can largely be explained by the following variables: labour market conditions, the effectiveness of cash and in-kind benefits, the provision of maternity benefits and subsidized childcare services, and public attitudes towards maternal employment (Hantrais and Letablier 1996; Christopher et al. 2001; Millar 2001).

Lone mothers are less likely than partnered mothers to be employed, especially full time in the liberal welfare states (Millar and Rowlingson 2001). Even when lone mothers do find paid work their poverty rates are higher than those of couple families, largely because they do not have a male earner in the household. Although welfare-to-work policies are based on the assumption that paid work will permit beneficiaries to exit from poverty, many researchers have questioned this assumption for lone mothers (Edin and Lein 1997; Hunsley 1997; Baker and Tippin 2002; Walter 2002; Ziguras 2003).

The extra expenses required to retain a paid job mean that low-wage mothers seldom improve their incomes by much when they exit from social benefits. They may gain higher self-esteem, develop new social networks and time management skills, and become favourable role models for their children (Bryson and Warner-Smith 1998). However, many are pressed for time as well as money and often worry about the supervision of their children. Australian research indicates that many mothers exiting from social benefits into paid work return to benefits before the end of a year (Chalmers 1999). Our New Zealand research suggests that the requirement to maintain employment without the support of adequate public childcare elevates stress levels, undermines health, and inhibits the ability to retain paid work (Baker 2002a, 2002b).

Well-conceived social programs can certainly influence the integration of maternal employment and childcare. Morissens (1999) compared the influence of several policies including childcare on the employment situation of lone mothers in Sweden and Belgium. Although Esping-Andersen (1990) placed these countries in different welfare regimes, Morissens found similar outcomes. In both countries, lone mothers enjoy high employment and low poverty rates. Social policies facilitate the combination of paid employment and caring, and the network of childcare provisions has expanded in recent years. However, Sweden offers publicly subsidized daycare mainly in municipal centres, while the Belgian state plays a smaller role in childcare services. Yet both countries offer a variety of social benefits for families with children: child allowances, maternity grants, maternal and parental leave benefits, and child support if the father is absent. Furthermore, lone mothers are not treated differently than mothers who are married or cohabiting. Their status as mothers is the basis of their entitlement, but some benefits are also related to earnings. Morissens concluded that the best way to guarantee good economic outcomes for lone mothers is a combination of generous social benefits for all families, combined with policies that support parental employment.

All OECD countries show higher child poverty rates for one-parent households than for two-parent households, especially when the one parent is the mother (UNICEF 2000). Would the financial problems of lone-mother families be resolved by higher levels of state support for their employment? Or do favourable taxes and transfers for all parents with young children make more of a difference? Most research concludes that both employment supports and favourable taxes and transfers are essential for all mothers to live above the poverty level in autonomous households. Both are especially important for lone mothers (Christopher 2002). However, low income, parental employment concerns, and the daytime care of children are not the only issues facing some families.

'Legitimacy' and Adoption

In recent years, more children have been born to parents who are unmarried or not even living together. Under both common law and civil law, governments used to label children born outside marriage as 'illegitimate,' which meant that they acquired no automatic right to their father's surname, his financial support, or any inheritance from him. Furthermore, the unmarried father had no legal right to decide how his children would be raised. Before the 1970s, many unexpected pregnancies led to (illegal) abortions or hastily arranged 'shotgun' marriages. Public acknowledgment of premarital pregnancy was discouraged, especially for middle-class women, and it was difficult for unmarried mothers to raise a child without a male breadwinner.

If unmarried pregnant women were unable or unwilling to have an (illegal) abortion or to marry, they often left their community, gave birth surreptitiously, and permitted the infant to be adopted by a (middle-class) two-parent family. Private or church-run maternity homes often assisted unmarried mothers through childbirth and quietly arranged for the adoption of their children. Otherwise, these women would have been subjected to social disapproval or ostracism, and would have brought shame upon themselves and their families (Swift 1995; Little 1998). 'Closed adoption' practices early in the twentieth century sometimes meant that birth certificates were altered and no further contact was allowed between adopted children and their birth mothers.

Before the 1970s, supporting a child through paid work was difficult for mothers, as they were expected to resign from their jobs upon pregnancy. 'Fallen women' (those who gave birth out of wedlock) were excluded from certain occupations, such as school teaching, because they provided a poor example to others. Women's access to high-paying jobs was also more restricted, women's average wages were lower, and public childcare was generally unavailable. Without financial assistance from the child's father or the mother's family, raising a child outside marriage was too challenging for most women.

Throughout the 1960s, social reformers and feminist activists lobbied for better access to birth control, legal abortion, divorce, and entitlement to government benefits for lone mothers. By the early 1970s, when many national economies were prospering, the number of lone mothers struggling to support their children increased with higher rates of separation and divorce. Some governments listened to the lobby groups arguing for state income support for lone mothers. In 1973, for example, both Australia and New Zealand gave lone mothers the statutory right to state income support, enabling them to raise their children at home without giving them up for adoption (Baker and Tippin 1999). Throughout the 1970s and 1980s, births to unmarried mothers began to increase in many countries with the liberalization of sexual attitudes, the weakening of public disapproval of unmarried mothers, and the expansion of state income support.

By the 1970s, social workers and psychologists were arguing that closed adoption was an unsuitable solution to birth outside marriage because it created negative psychological consequences for both children and mothers. Newborn infants were permanently separated from their birth mothers, kin groups, communities, and sometimes from their culture. Birth mothers disappeared during pregnancy and were expected to pretend that they had never given birth. With closed adoptions, mothers lost contact with their children because identifying information was withheld from all parties. Throughout the 1970s, social reformers began to argue that children should not be punished or stigmatized by their parents' sexual activities or marital decisions, although legislative changes were slow in some countries.

By the 1990s, most jurisdictions in the liberal welfare states had removed legal distinctions for children based on their parents' marital status, and most unmarried mothers now raise their own children. Laws expect fathers to support their children even if they have never lived with or married the child's mother (Baker and Phipps 1997, 118). In addition, new ways have been developed to establish paternity, and some states spend vast quantities of public resources trying to ensure that fathers acknowledge their children's existence and contribute to their support. Welfare benefits are sometimes withheld from mothers who refuse to identify the child's father (a minority of unpartnered mothers feel that they are at risk of violent retribution from the child's father if they identify him).

While adoptions in the 1950s usually involved 'illegitimate' children of unmarried mothers, most domestic adoptions now are by relatives or step-parents in blended families (Baker 1995, 255). In non-family situations, many jurisdictions promote 'open adoption' in which children and birth mothers can retain some contact if they choose. Also, if birth mothers feel they must relinquish their infants for adoption, they are offered counselling and ample opportunity to reconsider. Declining teen birth rates and new adoption practices have reduced the number of infants available for adoption within OECD countries. This has encouraged potential adoptive parents to consider accepting older children, but some of these children have experienced difficult early years with abusive or neglectful families or with a series of foster parents. Consequently, many potential parents now search internationally for infants to adopt.

Multilateral or bilateral agreements govern the processes of international adoptions, and these agreements generally stipulate that suitable parents should be sought first within the child's extended family and/ or culture. Children cannot be sold into adoption, and their health must be assessed before as well as afterwards. Birth parents, if available, must give their informed consent and have time to change their minds before international adoptions can be finalized. Adoptive parents must visit the child's country and be carefully screened by adoption agencies within that country as well as at home. In some cases, there are strict residence requirements for adoptive parents in the child's country and the payment of hefty 'administrative fees' before adoptions can be finalized. Some jurisdictions also offer post-adoption services (Speirs and Baker 1994).

Increasingly, international adoption procedures are becoming more legally complex and expensive for prospective parents. Host countries are under international pressure to improve their child welfare services and foster home systems, and local lobby groups often object to foreigners removing young children because they are considered to be the nation's future resource. Adoptive parents also find that raising a child from another culture and country could bring a number of health-related and disciplinary challenges. Some of these children previously lived in the streets or in orphanages lacking resources and staff to provide a stimulating and healthy environment for the children. Consequently, more couples that might have adopted in the past are now approaching fertility clinics in their own communities to help them conceive, often with donor sperm or eggs. However, medically assisted conception, like international adoption, tends to be a middle-class option, as the costs to potential parents tend to be high.

From Foster Care to Kin Care

Before the 1920s, many local authorities removed children from families who presented a danger to them or could no longer care for them, and placed them in children's institutions run by charitable organizations (Swift 1995; Connolly 2003). Some of these residential institutions were given local government or state subsidies to care for the children, but they also served as adoption centres, searching for permanent adoptive parents from unrelated families. Gradually, child welfare workers and social researchers came to believe that residential care in institutions was not beneficial to the children, although some of the religious-based institutions continued to raise children well into the 1960s and 1970s. Many provided adequate care, but others have been accused of giving children insufficient care and attention, using unnecessary force when disciplining them, and abusing them sexually. In recent years, some church-based institutions have been forced to make public apologies or to pay restitution for the past deeds of their staff.

When the state became more involved in family services and professional social work training after the 1960s, definitions were clarified, including 'the child in need of protection.' New principles also guided state intervention into families, such as the 'principle of least intrusion' and 'family preservation' (Krane 2003). Detailed procedures to deal with family casework were prepared, and higher educational standards were required of social service workers. Some states provided their own child protection programs, while others mandated private agencies to offer these services on behalf of the state.

After the 1970s, children were less often placed in orphanages or large institutions and more often left within their own families, with the support, guidance, and supervision of visiting professionals. Other children were placed in the care of unrelated foster families. The state often subsidized some of the expenses of foster care, but this form of care was always seen as a temporary solution, and children were generally encouraged to maintain contact with their birth parents and siblings. The state or its mandated agencies were also involved in screening and regulating foster parents, ensuring that the family environment was 'suitable' for the child's well-being and development.

Suitable foster families usually included two heterosexual parents living in a stable relationship with a steady income. Often, the father was the breadwinner and the mother was a full-time caregiver, and both were young and healthy (Speirs and Baker 1994). As more women entered the labour force in OECD countries, foster parents became more difficult to find. In addition, concerns were raised about the implications of placing children with strangers, especially if they were outside the child's cultural group. Consequently, in the past two decades many states have encouraged kin members or extended families to care for these children (Connolly 2003).

The trend to kinship care has been noted in many countries, accounting for over 11 per cent of care placements in the United Kingdom (UK Department of Health 2003), 24 per cent in Australia (Hunt 2003), over 31 per cent in the United States (Clark 1995), and 32 per cent in New Zealand (Statistics NZ 2002). This practice is often justified by 'the best interests of the child,' and more specifically by the concept of 'family preservation,' or providing a sense of family support and cultural continuity in the children's lives. However, kin carers tend to receive fewer services and social supports than non-related caregivers (Connolly 2003). Therefore, the practice of relying on kin members to care for these children could be seen as a form of neoliberal restructuring designed to save public funds previously spent on institutional care or unrelated foster care.

One concern with kin care is that standards of care are less rigorously applied than in foster or residential care. Care providers are approved who would not have been acceptable as foster parents because of their low income, older age, single-parent status, poor health, parenting problems, or substandard accommodation (Hunt 2003). In addition, children cared for by kin are more likely to continue living in poverty, whereas foster care usually meant moving into a middle-class home with a stable family income. Considerable research indicates that remaining in impoverished households can be detrimental to children's health, well-being, and life chances, as we will discuss in chapter 8.

In countries such as Australia, New Zealand, and Canada, indigenous and minority group children have been over-represented among those coming to the attention of the child welfare system. The former practices of keeping indigenous children in state-regulated residential schools or having them adopted by 'white' families have fallen into disrepute. This is largely because many children suffered from cultural confusion after living with white foster parents and/or reported some form of abuse in both foster families and residential schools. State agencies now tend to see kin care as less contentious because it keeps children within their local community and cultural group. Consequently, considerable effort has gone into trying to appy foster care processes and standards to kinship care. Although research comparing child well-being in kin care with that in foster care is underdeveloped, sometimes contradictory, and not fully reliable (Connolly 2003), governments continue to encourage these practices in an attempt both to reduce state expenditures and to preserve family life.

Children's Rights and Programs to Counter Abuse

Child abuse within families includes physical, sexual, or emotional injuries inflicted by parents, other relatives, or guardians. Although some parents and guardians have always mistreated or neglected their children, child welfare laws no longer permit them to treat children as their property. In many jurisdictions, children's rights have expanded, and neither parents nor teachers have the right to physically punish children under their care (UNICEF 2003). However, we do not really know whether the initiatives by national governments and international organizations to curb child maltreatment have been effective.

Many jurisdictions now maintain registries, but child protection workers and victimization studies indicate that these registries record only a fraction of cases. The number of reported cases has risen dramatically every year, but it is not known whether this indicates an increase in the actual number of abuse cases or is a result of new reporting requirements.

In the 1980s and 1990s, considerable public attention focused on the sexual abuse of children after government-mandated reports (such as the Canadian Badgley Report in 1984) concluded that the percentage of adults who had been the victims of 'unwanted sexual acts' as children was much higher than previously acknowledged. Studies also noted that sexual abuse tends to occur during the daytime, in the home of the victim or a friend, and by a (male) relative or family friend. While girls are more vulnerable than boys, many young boys are also sexually abused. Recently, school and church leaders have become concerned about sexual abuse by teachers, youth workers, and priests and are looking for ways to identify potential abusers before an incident occurs and to deal effectively with perpetrators. However, allegations are sometimes made decades after the incident, with few reliable witnesses, which makes them difficult to verify.

In the past, public concern about child abuse focused on face-to-face interactions between adults and children. Now parents and children need to be even more vigilant because the Internet can be used to make illicit contacts with young people, with sexual and harmful intent, and children can be sexually mistreated through photography. The Internet enables the viewing, dissemination, and sale of child pornography on a much wider scale, and drugs and alcohol are more easily available to entice young people into illegal or sexual acts. At the same time, the state has become more involved in hunting down child pornography, child abuse, and prostitution rings, and now uses computer and DNA technologies to identify perpetrators. More children are also given lessons in self-protection at school, and public tolerance of child abuse has plummeted with widespread media attention.

All OECD countries have acknowledged the need to protect vulnerable family members. In addition, organizations such as United Nations have been instrumental in pressuring national governments to clarify the rights and duties of parents and children and to protect children from abuse and neglect. For decades, they have pushed governments to provide public education on these issues and to offer interventions for families in need of assistance. Although some welfare states have been proactive and focus on the prevention of family poverty, disharmony, and children's behavioural problems, others have been content to deal with family-related problems after these are drawn to the attention of authorities. The liberal welfare states generally fit into the second category, where services are targeted to 'at-risk' families who have already come to the attention of the police, teachers, social workers, visiting homemakers, medical staff, or local government officials (Baker 1995).

Some of the measures designed to prevent and control child abuse include the appointment of children's ombudspersons, the establishment of children's telephone helplines, the integration of home-visiting services, and closer monitoring of children considered to be at risk. The Council of Europe has launched a campaign to combat all forms of violence, and the United Nations Committee on the Rights of the Child regularly reports on child protection measures within industrialized countries. The UNICEF report (2003) on child maltreatment argued that the problem of child abuse and neglect needs to be made more public. It also suggested that effective strategies include home visits to *all* families with young children by a variety of qualified health, education, and social service staff, rather than targeting children assumed to be 'at risk.' Finally, the report argued that child abuse strategies must address the economic circumstances of parents, as those living in impoverished and stressed conditions are statistically more likely to abuse their children (21).

Considerable debate continues about whether the new interventions to deal with child maltreatment have actually reduced it. The 2003 UNICEF report showed that rates of child death from maltreatment have fallen in fourteen out of twenty-three countries, but the rate has remained stable in four countries and has actually increased in five others (9). For non-fatal child abuse a trend is more difficult to establish, because new reporting requirements and intervention programs have increased the visibility of abuse. Some programs might prevent serious maltreatment, but others may bring to light maltreatment that was previously covered up or not apparent to officials.

The UNICEF report concluded that the general decline in child deaths through maltreatment and 'of undetermined intent' might suggest that general levels of child abuse have declined in most countries, despite increased reporting. The alternative explanation is that advances in emergency and medical services have reduced the child death rate, but serious abuse and neglect continue (UNICEF 2003, 10). Child death rates through maltreatment also correlate well with adult homicide

Table 7.1
Child maltreatment deaths for selected countries, 2000

Country	Average no. of deaths over 5-year period per 100,000 children under 15 years
Spain	0.1
Italy	0.2
Norway	0.3
Sweden	0.6
Australia	0.8
Denmark	0.8
United Kingdom	0.9
Canada	1.0
New Zealand	1.3
United States	2.4
Portugal	3.7

Source: UNICEF 2003, 4.

rates and reflect the level of violence prevalent in a society (11). Comparing child deaths through maltreatment and through injuries, the Report found a weaker correlation but suggested that these are two different measures of care and protection that societies afford to their children. Countries such as the United States and Portugal have high rates on both measures, as Table 7.1 illustrates (11).

The causes of child maltreatment are difficult to determine, but the UNICEF report noted that most adults who were abused as children do *not* turn out to be child abusers. However, various factors in people's circumstances accumulate to augment the risk. Parents who abuse alcohol and drugs and live in impoverished and violent homes are more likely to maltreat their children. Maltreatment also contributes to depression, anxiety, and hostility in children, as well as certain types of behaviour such as physical inactivity, smoking, alcoholism, drug abuse, risky sexual practices, and suicide (UNICEF 2003, 19). There is clear evidence of growing concern across industrialized countries about the cost of such behaviours to individuals, families, employers, and taxpayers.

Developing a culture of non-violence seems to be a significant factor in preventing and reducing child maltreatment. Consequently, some states have banned the physical punishment of children, including by parents, and have initiated educational campaigns about alternative forms of punishment. Sweden did this in 1979 (UNICEF 2003, 24), and a 1999 study found that physical punishment and public support for physical punishment have both declined substantially in that country since the 1970s. The reporting of child abuse has increased (as in other countries), but youth drug and alcohol abuse rates and youth crime rates are down. However, these figures have been disputed and challenged by other researchers, indicating the difficulty of measuring the impact of such legislation (UNICEF 2003, 24).

An international shift towards awareness of the effects of domestic violence upon children has been both reflected and fostered by a range of international conferences (Jaffe, Sudermann, and Geffner 2000, 2; Graham-Bermann and Edleson 2001; Krug et al. 2002, 103). With this shift, many countries have amended child custody policies to take into account the parent's history of domestic violence. However, as we discuss in chapter 9, cases governed by the Hague Convention that involve a parent's flight with children across international borders primarily focus on returning children to their place of residence and give little credence to a history of domestic violence (Jaffe, Lemon, and Poisson 2003; Kaye 1999). Mothers who experience domestic violence often report fear for their children's safety, which is generally minimized in a complex and frequently hostile court system (Radford and Hester 2001; Jaffe, Lemon, and Poisson 2003, 17).

Although most governments have voiced concern about domestic violence against women and children, the absence of public money remains the major impediment to establishing effective programs and services. In the liberal welfare states, private donations as well as public funds support transition houses for battered women, but these safe houses are often staffed by volunteers and operate on the verge of closing due to lack of funds. Follow-up therapy and counselling may be necessary for the entire family, yet these services also cost money to establish and maintain. Despite acknowledging the serious nature of this kind of violence, states have not always delivered sufficient program funding to deal with the rising number of reported cases (Sev'er 2002). These women and children need protection, but they also need help to find housing that is affordable, in good condition, close to schools, and in a neighbourhood that is safe for children.

Conclusion

This chapter has discussed several issues related to the care and welfare of children, searching for convergence in the trends and social programs to deal with those issues. Some convergence is apparent in basic principles of childcare provision in Belgium, France, Italy, Sweden, and the European Union (Jenson and Sineau 2001a). This includes a trend towards less costly services, decentralization of services from central governments to local authorities, greater diversification in types of programs and access to them, more flexibility in the use of childcare, and maximizing of parental choice of services. As states rethink their relationship to citizens and the mix between private and public responsibilities, childcare has become the key testing ground for new thinking about equity (17).

High-quality preschools can be crucial to early child development, but employed mothers suffer if childcare is seen mainly as an educational issue. Employed mothers clearly need childcare services during their working hours in order to compete effectively in the current labour market. State support for childcare could be in the form of subsidies paid directly to care providers or tax rebates to parents, but it must cover the cost of *full-time* care and the subsidies need to cover a larger percentage of the actual costs.[2] While the demand for childcare services has been rising with maternal employment, policy responses are not automatic. The level of provision and policy design varies cross-nationally with welfare institutions, political interests, and ideas about appropriate parenting and state intervention in family life.

States as well as lobby groups have their own interests in providing childcare, including the promotion of gender equity rather than early childhood education or the well-being of future generations (Jenson and Sineau 2001, 15). Many states have given priority to childcare over elder care, but disagreements continue about which social policies promote high-quality care and how these programs can be funded. Over the past decade, appreciation of the importance of public childcare services has been building. Yet this acceptance has been set back in some jurisdictions by public concerns over the high cost of childcare (especially infant care), quality assurance, and the potential of child abuse when 'strangers' care for children.

In recent years, most OECD countries have also redefined parental responsibilities and children's rights, formalized procedures to deal with family relationship problems, and placed more emphasis on the training and regulation of social service work. States have also rejected both the institutional care of children and legal adoption by strangers in favour of extended family care (UNICEF 2003). More domestic violence

---

[2] In New Zealand, childcare subsidies for low-income parents have covered only a small fraction of the cost (Baker 2004a).

is being reported, but this does not necessarily indicate that it is becoming more prevalent. States have developed more effective mechanisms to investigate and deal with accusations of abuse and neglect among children, and women's organizations have urged the state and women themselves to take violence against women more seriously. Increasingly, governments are entering into partnerships with voluntary organizations and cultural communities to provide child protection and family violence services. Clearly, intolerance of domestic violence is growing, but there is less agreement about funding priorities and policy solutions.

Ideas about how to reduce family conflict and improve children's outcomes are widely shared among researchers and policy analysts around the world. International conferences among social workers, health professionals, psychologists, human rights activists, and social policy analysts provide opportunities to discuss ideas about health, well-being, and care. Cross-national research projects such as the study by Bradshaw and Finch (2002) involve state or multi-country funding as well as collaboration among researchers from different jurisdictions. All these factors contribute to the discussion of 'best practices' and the sharing of policy options, placing pressure on governments to harmonize social programs relating to family well being.

Despite new programs for family well-being, mothers are still seen as the main care providers for children and blamed when children misbehave or are abused or neglected (Krane 2003). There is also little recognition, at least in the liberal welfare states, that contradictory expectations are placed on mothers when they are pushed into the labour force with inadequate childcare services but also expected to remain the primary caregivers of their children. Raising children while living in poverty requires stamina, parenting skills, and resourcefulness, yet lone mothers are often seen as 'dependants' and 'poor role models' for their children, especially in the United States. Children from low-income, lone-mother, and visible-minority families continue to be over-represented in child welfare systems, but few state-sponsored programs in the liberal welfare states seriously focus on eliminating poverty or involving more fathers in child rearing. Nor do many concentrate on reducing stress, anger, and racial/cultural discrimination (Baker 1995).

The neoliberal demand to reduce income taxes has left less public money for family-support services and income support payments. Block funding arrangements may place social service agencies in competition with hospitals or universities for public money. These kinds of restructuring strategies have encouraged many states to form partnerships with non-governmental organizations to share the delivery of social services. Although these partnerships are sometimes effective, they often operate with fewer state resources and rely more on voluntary organizations and unpaid family members to supply complicated services that formerly were provided by trained professionals. Furthermore, the effectiveness of these new decentralized arrangements is seldom evaluated.

Governments have been urged by international organizations to sign multilateral or bilateral agreements relating to numerous family issues, such as international adoptions and child protection measures. These agreements encourage the convergence of national policies and practices, although they always leave room for governments to develop their own initiatives. Identical programs are not the goal, but even if they were, enforcement would be difficult. In the next chapter, we examine the provision of social housing and income support, noting the changing discourse in these policy areas.

8 Social Housing and Income Support

This chapter discusses housing and income support programs in OECD countries. The two issues are combined in one chapter because 'welfare' payments (or income support for low-income families) often include a housing allowance or supplement. The chapter begins with four arguments used to justify state income support for families with children, which are based on different assumptions and political priorities. The main contention of the chapter is that similar welfare regimes generally promote comparable income support programs, although numerous variations arise from historical differences in the development of the welfare state, the relative strength of local interest groups, and the influence of other political agendas within the nation. Two liberal welfare states (Australia and Canada) are used to illustrate this argument. The chapter then draws some conclusions about the most effective forms of income support.

The provision of income support and social housing dates back to the early twentieth century in many OECD countries. Over the years, much has changed in public discourse about the purpose and value of this support, and numerous modifications have been made to the original social programs. Before World War II, income support was usually targeted to the poorest households and seen as the last resort for families who could not cope on their own, at least in the liberal welfare states. From the 1940s to the early 1990s, most of the liberal welfare states supplemented the incomes of parents with children through universal child allowances or tax breaks, in order to preserve equity between those with dependants and those without. Throughout the 1960s and 1970s, new tax benefits and poverty-reduction programs were created, but after the 1980s many governments began to return to the practice of targeting child benefits to moderate- or low-income families.

Child benefits are now delivered through the taxation system in many countries, based on household taxable income, and paying the maximum to employed parents rather than those with the lowest incomes, who might not be paying taxes. Income support systems are also more frequently designed and administered by economists, who are typically more socially conservative than welfare workers. Income support for low-income families has become less generous in many jurisdictions as the state expects more citizens to prepare for paid work and become self-supporting. Although housing benefits are sometimes included in welfare payments, many low-income families are living in private accommodation with high rents. In this chapter, I show that more governments are now reinforcing 'personal responsibility' for economic well-being instead of trying to prevent poverty or reduce income inequality. Once again, the state is relying on the efforts of extended family members and voluntary organizations (such as food banks) to supplement social services.

Recent Arguments about Family Income Support

Four major arguments about income support, none of which is new, are widely used in policy discussions. The first argument is that reducing 'child poverty' is necessary because the adverse outcomes from growing up in low-income households are costly to the state as well as families and their communities. The second argument is that 'social exclusion' is a bigger problem than low income. Social programs need to keep people socially and economically active in order to avoid the development of an 'underclass' that is marginalized from mainstream society. Thirdly, neoliberals have argued that the cost of state income support has become unsustainable and more people need to become self-supporting through paid work if countries are to prosper in a global economy. Finally, a number of governments are now talking about investing in children. Although other public discourses are also used to justify improvements or reductions in state income support in OECD countries, I will focus on these four major ones.

The Need to Reduce 'Child Poverty'

For several decades, the United Nations has urged national governments to protect the rights and well-being of children. The UN had declared 1979 as the 'International Year of the Child' and in 1989 created a Convention on the Rights of the Child as a binding international agreement. This Convention was given a ceremonial launch in the United Nations and prepared for member country signatures with speeches about the progress in children's status and rights throughout the past decade, as well as the continuing barriers. This event pressured many government leaders to make public statements about eradicating child poverty in their own countries.

In 1989, for example, Canada's Prime Minister Brian Mulroney promised before the United Nations and again in Parliament to seek to eliminate child poverty by the year 2000. This prompted the organization of a lobby group to ensure that this promise was honoured (Baker 1995, 68–9). Periodically, these kinds of promises are repeated, especially when national or international reports indicate that child poverty continues to flourish. A decade later, New Labour in Britain promised to reduce child poverty by half in ten years and eradicate it in twenty years (UNICEF 2000, 5). In 2003, the French government and quasi-government agencies focused on child poverty in a national conference (Jenson 2004). These examples indicate that the discourse of child poverty has been prevalent for nearly two decades in OECD countries.

The United Nations Children's Fund (UNICEF) supports research on children's well-being and publishes periodic reports. The Innocenti report on child poverty in rich nations (UNICEF 2000, 2005) noted that many OECD countries that have the resources to reduce poverty have permitted children to live in households that are deleterious to their development and well-being. In fact, the most recent report states that the majority of OECD countries 'appear to be losing ground against child poverty' (2005, 14). Poverty rates among children living in two-parent families have been higher in North America, the United Kingdom, and Australia than in many other 'rich nations' such as Sweden, Norway, Belgium, or Finland. For one-parent families, these rates are even higher: over 55 per cent of children in American one-parent families and about 52 per cent in Canadian one-parent families live in poverty, compared to 6.7 per cent in Sweden and 7.1 per cent in Finland (2000, 4, 10). These cross-national variations, shown in Table 8.1, suggest that child poverty rates, which are the highest in liberal welfare regimes, can be influenced by socio-economic policies.

In this kind of cross-national comparison, relative poverty rates are used, defined as household incomes of less than 50 per cent of the national median after taxes and government transfers and adjusted for family size. That being said, considerable debate continues about how poverty should be measured. Social conservatives usually argue for an

Table 8.1
Child poverty* in lone-parent families and other families

Country	Poverty rate in lone-parent families	Poverty rate in other families
Sweden	6.7	1.5
Finland	7.1	3.9
Hungary	10.4	10.3
Norway	13.1	2.2
Belgium	13.5	3.6
Denmark	13.8	3.6
Poland	19.9	15.1
Italy	22.2	20.4
Netherlands	23.6	6.5
Greece	24.9	11.8
France	26.1	6.4
Mexico	27.6	26.1
Turkey	29.2	19.6
Czech Republic	30.9	3.6
Luxembourg	30.4	2.9
Spain	31.6	11.8
Australia	35.6	8.8
United Kingdom	45.6	13.3
Ireland	46.4	14.2
Germany	51.2	10.4
Canada	51.6	10.4
United States	55.4	15.8

*Percentage of children living in families where the household income is less than 50% of the national median income
Source: Extracted from UNICEF 2000, 10

absolute measure – enough income to buy nutritious food, adequate housing, basic clothing, and public transport. Despite considerable debate about what constitutes 'poverty' within certain regions, most OECD countries contribute data to the Luxembourg Income Study (LIS), which is an international database using a relative measure of poverty. This database includes details about household incomes, tax benefits, and income support programs, and therefore enables and facilitates cross-national comparisons.

The Innocenti Report noted the strong relationship between child poverty and living with only one parent, as well as having parents who are unemployed, outside the labour force, or earning 'low wages' (defined as full-time wages that are less than two-thirds of the national median). Other research has highlighted the fact that poverty rates are higher if the lone parent is female, especially if she is relying on state income support (Smeeding et al. 1998; Millar and Rowlingson 2001; Baker 2002; Esping-Andersen 2002). Social activists and researchers have focused on poverty among children in recent years, but the Innocenti Report makes it abundantly clear that children are living in poverty due to their parents' circumstances.

Clearly, more can be gained politically from highlighting the consequences of poverty for children rather than adults. Children cannot be blamed for their lack of employment skills or initiative (Baker and Tippin 1999). Also, research evidence shows that children from low-income families are at a higher risk of a variety of negative behavioural outcomes, including learning problems, early school leaving, premarital pregnancy, and delinquency (Lipman, Offord, and Dooley 1996; Hobcraft and Kiernan 2001). If children leave school early, they are more likely to experience unemployment and low income throughout their lives, as well as other problems. These negative outcomes cost additional money to the state in the form of truancy programs, family services, juvenile detention centres, adult jails, social housing, and state income support. Therefore, child poverty action groups, who have organized internationally, have made the compelling argument that the long-term costs of doing nothing about child poverty will be higher than the short-term costs of reducing it.

Child poverty rates are related to parental unemployment and low wages, but also to social programs that fail to protect parents against income loss due to sickness, disability, or unemployment. Even when they are employed, lone mothers are particularly vulnerable to poverty in liberal welfare states and often need wage supplements and social services. In countries such as Canada and the United States, the level of social assistance or 'welfare' is set well below the poverty line (Daly and Rake 2003). Furthermore, social insurance programs do not protect people against the risk of separation, divorce, or becoming a single earner, although for decades they have protected women against the risk of widowhood.[1] Throughout OECD countries, lone mothers with

---

[1] Social insurance programs such as the Canada Pension Plan include survivor benefits paid to the spouse of a deceased contributor, but separated or divorced women must rely on their own wages or state income support. Divorced people can also apply to divide their former spouse's CPP pension credits, giving divorced men lower retirement pensions but providing a small pension for their divorced wives in old age.

low education risk relatively high rates of poverty because they cannot find high-paid jobs or combine full-time work with their family responsibilities. However, the most important reason for the poverty of lone mothers is that living costs have increased in most countries and two full-time earners are now needed to pay the household bills.

The focus on 'child poverty' has also appealed to research funding agencies, and numerous studies have used the multi-country Luxembourg Income Study database to make comparisons. For example, Immervol, Sutherland, and de Vos (2001) examined the role of family benefits in influencing child poverty rates, including child benefits, maternity benefits, and carers' benefits. They noted that in some countries, child poverty rates would rise significantly if family benefits were removed but argued that it is difficult to separate the effect of child benefits from the entire social benefit system. The availability of paid work and relative wages must also be factored into any discussion of family poverty. Jeandidier and Albiser (2001) concluded that the more generous and universal benefits for families with children in France and Luxembourg are particularly helpful to large families and lone-parent households. In contrast, they noted that social transfers in the United Kingdom and the United States are less generous, and that these countries maintain a 'political position of neutrality towards family life.'

Beaujot and Liu (2002) concluded that effective child poverty reduction requires more than state income support. Several simultaneous approaches are needed, including a reduction of teen pregnancies and more opportunities for lone mothers to find and keep employment. They focused on the importance of special provisions for lone parents, including advance maintenance schemes for child support, but also noted the significance of more generous income support for all families and individuals. Nordic countries keep child poverty at a relatively low level through a combination of family benefits and high maternal employment rates (Esping-Andersen 2002). Generally, families in which both parents work for pay are least likely to be poor, and wives' employment is becoming more important with the growing insecurity of male unskilled workers. Employment for lone mothers would not eradicate child poverty, but it would be less expensive for the state to deal with the residual poverty if mothers were employed. Preventive strategies, such as enriched daycare and incentives for school attendance, are also needed to counteract the poor life chances of children living in low-income families and to create a more productive workforce in the future (Esping-Andersen 2002).

Our New Zealand research illustrated the negative impact of family poverty in lone-mother households where mothers were receiving social benefits but were also expected to seek employment (Baker 2002b). Through personal interviews, we found that these mothers tried to shield their children from the worst consequences of poverty, but many lived in unsafe neighbourhoods under stressful family circumstances. Mothers admitted that they are not always successful in protecting their children or keeping them healthy, as the stresses and deprivations of living on low or unreliable incomes led to unhealthy diets and the deterioration of physical and mental health. Without universal health services (including free counselling) or affordable childcare services, life became a struggle. Family poverty was perpetuated by a mother's sporadic work record, but many of these mothers could not make the difficult transition from income support to full-time work despite relatively high levels of personal motivation.

Researchers have focused on lone-mother families as the poorest households, but Cantillon and Van den Bosch (2002) showed that in some European countries (such as the United Kingdom, Italy, and Spain) poverty rates are often as high among families with three or more children. This is important because there are usually more large families than one-parent families in these countries, and by definition they contain more children. The authors showed that Belgium and France have effectively reduced poverty for large families through universal family allowances paid to the mother for each child, rather than a flat rate per family.

These studies and others show that realistic solutions to family poverty must also address the barriers to sustaining employment and improving the social circumstances of low-income parents. Yet in the current economic climate of freer trade and global markets, many employers are minimizing payroll costs by hiring part-time or casual workers. Part-time jobs might enable mothers to fulfil their domestic responsibilities, but they seldom pay enough to support children. However, state income support programs can stabilize and supplement earnings and can help raise children out of poverty, especially when these programmes are combined with other social services.

Preventing 'Social Exclusion' Is More Important Than Reducing Poverty

A second prevalent argument is that growing social problems such as poor school performance, truancy, vandalism, delinquency, teen pregnancy, and the marginalization of certain groups will not be resolved merely by increasing income support to families because no direct correlation exists between household income and adverse child outcomes. Children's emotional and behavioural problems arise from a number of sources and develop over a long period. In addition to low household income, negative child outcomes are also influenced by parental conflict, problems such as depression and substance abuse, and poor parenting skills. Children's behaviour and attitudes are also influenced by their relationships with their siblings, peers, family friends, relatives, teachers, and other care providers as well as by substandard housing, unsafe neighbourhoods, and a negative school environment.

Advocates of the social exclusion argument suggest that researchers need to better understand why some children and youth respect their parents and elders, are law abiding, want to stay in school, eventually find meaningful work, and continue to participate in their communities while others are excluded or choose to exclude themselves. Public discourse and social programs in liberal welfare states have focused on families considered to be 'at risk' of negative outcomes. For example, indigenous people and certain visible minorities have been the focus of special programs because they are less likely than other groups to finish school, find high-paying jobs, and lead healthy and disability-free lives.

Equity programs, culturally sensitive social services, and special scholarships have attempted to reduce social exclusion within 'at-risk' groups. Yet these programs have had marginal success, partly because low income and poor living conditions remain widespread among these groups. Furthermore, programs seldom consider the impact of social and cultural discrimination, and program funding is sometimes tenuous and easily jeopardized by politics. In 2004, for example, the new leader of the National Party in New Zealand (the then Official Opposition) publicly discredited social programs 'based on race rather than need.' When he received considerable public support for these statements, the Labour government placed special programs for Maori and Pacific Island peoples 'under review,' as they were concerned about losing votes in the 2005 election.

Social exclusion discourse has been widely used in the OECD, especially when referring to unemployed youth. Gallie's (1998) European research concluded that social exclusion among the unemployed is less likely to become a social problem when they receive adequate income support and social services. He found that unemployed people are not particularly socially isolated, but they tend to form relationships with other unemployed people who cannot help them financially or assist them back into paid work. By comparing unemployed people and policies in European Union countries, Gallie concluded that strong income security programs can help people retain their confidence and self-respect, reduce their anger and feelings of desperation, participate more in community activities, and search for work during periods of unemployment. This research suggests that cutting social benefits for unemployed people could actually *encourage* social exclusion and the development of an underclass.

The concept of social exclusion, like 'social development' and 'social capital,' is seldom clearly defined in policy discourse. Bradshaw (2003) argued that 'social exclusion' is not merely another word for poverty, although a strong correlation remains between living on a low income and being unable or unwilling to participate in the wider community. However, governments have sometimes focused on social exclusion to avoid acknowledging high poverty rates, low social benefit levels, or the lack of success of existing social programs. The concept of social exclusion permits conservatives to focus on individual or family solutions, such as parenting education and budget counselling, rather than investigating why certain cultural groups are disadvantaged and what can be done to raise their opportunities and relative prosperity.

The discourse of social exclusion can justify placing more resources into fighting truancy, child abuse, and early school leaving at the community level. Diversion programs for young offenders can be developed, and equity programs created for certain categories of people in post-secondary institutions and the labour market. Government partnerships with employers, voluntary organizations, and cultural groups can encourage greater employability and community participation. These programs are essential, but they seldom alter the realities of economic and social inequality. Furthermore, they are not always evaluated to see if they actually reduce social exclusion and/or save public money. This suggests that part of the intended neoliberal goal is to redirect public attention away from the need to raise state income support, and instead to emphasize greater community and family responsibility for welfare and well-being.

Admittedly, social exclusion can be a problem. If people do not feel that they belong or are rejected by others, they will not make an effort to adopt community standards of behaviour. If they cannot find a job or obtain credit, they are excluded from other social activities and opportunities. However, social exclusion is often exacerbated by low income and inability to maintain community living standards. Studies from many countries reveal that children living in families with few material and cultural resources typically experience multiple disadvantages throughout life compared to children from more prosperous households. These include lower achievement in school, higher rates of behavioural problems and delinquency, early school leaving, higher unemployment rates, poor physical and mental health, and premature death rates (Ross, Scott, and Kelly 1996; Roberts 1997; Hobcraft and Kiernan 2001). Furthermore, countries with large gaps between the rich and the poor – such as the United States – tend to have higher rates of child maltreatment, delinquency, and adult crime (UNICEF 2003).

In the 1960s and 1970s, social scientists and policy analysts used to talk more about the ways that social class and socio-economic status (or SES) influenced children's life chances. SES was a combined measure of household income, parents' educational attainment, and their occupational status. 'Social exclusion' may be another way of saying that the socio-economic circumstances of one's family of origin still matter in terms of motivation and future achievement. Perhaps young people from low-SES families cannot be expected to wholeheartedly embrace the globalized economy if they are unlikely to benefit from it. In addition, young people receiving little parental love, supervision, or respect might experience extra difficulties in respecting others and require extra counselling or guidance. However, conservative politicians and taxpayers sometimes promote the concept of social exclusion to justify reducing state income support and encouraging more personal responsibility for welfare.

Benefit Recipients Should Become More Employable

As a part of neoliberal restructuring, many OECD countries have re-emphasized the importance of paid work in assuring well-being, by promoting enhanced skills training and developing 'welfare-to-work' programs. In doing so, they have created programs to encourage school leavers and beneficiaries to move more rapidly into paid work. These programs have actually reduced the numbers of benefit recipients, especially employment-ready individuals with good educational qualifications living in areas with low unemployment rates (Torjman 1996). However, research has found that many program participants are unable to find permanent jobs or exit from poverty even when they rely on paid work. Prime examples are early school leavers from low-income families and lone mothers who had a child before finishing school (Edin and Lein 1997).

As we noted in chapter 6, many lone mothers cannot earn enough to support their families, especially in the current economies of North America and the United Kingdom. The jobs they find are often temporary, low paid, and part time and seldom include flexible work hours, paid sick leave, or extended health benefits (Dooley 1995; Harris 1996; Vosko 2000). Their qualifications are typically lower than those of lone fathers and partnered mothers, and many lone mothers experience childcare and family problems that interfere with keeping a job or progressing through the ranks. Also, lone mothers suffer more often than partnered mothers from both physical and mental health problems. These symptoms are aggravated by low income, substandard accommodation, violent homes and communities, high stress levels, poor diet, and lack of preventive health care (Dorsett and Marsh 1998; Whitehead, Burström, and Diderichsen 2000; Cook, Raine, and Williamson 2001; Curtis 2001; Marsh 2001; Sarfati and Scott 2001; Baker 2002a).

'Welfare mothers' who move into paid work are less likely to leave their jobs and return to social benefits if they had prior work experience, more than twelve years of schooling, and fewer than three children (Harris 1996; Cancian et al. 1999). Riccio and Freedman (1999) found that health and personal problems made continuous employment impossible for about one-third of the participants of a California welfare-to-work program. Whitehead, Burström, and Diderichsen (2000) compared lone mothers in Britain and Sweden in the 1970s and the 1990s, finding more poverty and poorer health in Britain, and more problems in the 1990s than the 1970s. Nevertheless, lone mothers in both countries reported poorer health than married mothers. The authors presented three hypotheses about the relationship between lone motherhood and poor health. Lone mothers (including the employed) suffer from 'time poverty,' which elevates stress levels and leads to illness. The kind of work they do is more stressful and dangerous, and they suffer from lower social support than married mothers. These factors may help to explain the poorer health of Swedish lone mothers compared to married mothers, despite low levels of poverty, high standards of housing, and relatively generous social services.

In our New Zealand study (Baker 2004a), we found that parenting on a meagre income without a partner is challenging for most parents, but especially without affordable childcare. Many of these lone mothers receiving income support felt that being a 'good mother' required them to constantly supervise their children and that paid work brought poor financial returns, leaving them with a myriad of household problems and childcare dilemmas, especially during school holidays or children's illness. All three factors of time poverty, stressful work, and lack of social support seem to impede effective coping mechanisms and to encourage poor health. The challenges and perceptions of these lone mothers were not unique to New Zealand, but mirrored the concerns of lone mothers in studies from other liberal welfare states.

Income support programs are being restructured to shorten the period of benefit receipt and tighten work expectations. For lone mothers, this often means that when the youngest child reaches a specific age, the mother will be expected to find part-time or full-time work unless there are extenuating circumstances. For some, the transition to paid work is perceived as too risky unless they can retain some income support and social services (such as subsidized childcare and health costs). If former beneficiaries lose their jobs and then experience delays re-enrolling for income support, they may be worse off than if they had remained on social benefits. However, for political reasons, governments need to ensure that the services offered to welfare recipients are not more generous than the ones for low-wage workers.

Investing in Children

For years, some European countries such as Denmark, Sweden, and France have invested public resources into relatively generous income support and social services for parents and children. This has led to improvements in family outcomes, including lower poverty rates for both one-parent and two-parent families, and lower rates of abuse, neglect, and child health problems. In recent years, other welfare states have shifted away from expecting parents to take full responsibility for their children to a focus on 'public investment in children,' where children's well-being is shared between families and the larger community (Jenson 2004). This paradigm involves different policy choices, including the provision of child benefits to parents, subsidies for public childcare services, legal advocates for children, children's helplines and child protection services. Jenson (2004) argues that Canada has accepted this new paradigm, but the above programs have been offered in that country for many decades.

Investing in children clearly requires public expenditure. Although no direct correlation is apparent between state social spending and higher family incomes or lack of problems, the Innocenti Report (UNICEF 2000, 14, 15) shows that countries with the lowest child poverty rates allocate the highest proportions of their gross national product to social expenditures. The social democratic countries of Sweden, Denmark, and Finland top this list, while Mexico, Turkey, and Japan fall below the liberal welfare states of Canada, the United States, the United Kingdom, and Australia. Notable cross-national variations are also apparent in the effect of tax and social programs in reducing child poverty, which has led to considerable research on the effectiveness of various measures (much of it using Luxembourg Income Study data).

In Canada, recent policy discourse about investing in children has been influenced by international reports showing continuing high levels of child poverty, growing problems with work/life balance, and changing labour markets. Jenson (2004) argued that the Canadian government has learned from the results of the National Longitudinal Survey of Children and Youth and comparative research. In addition, the efforts of lobby groups such as the Child Poverty Action Group have influenced Canadian public policy. However, she noted that those provinces with neoliberal governments (especially Ontario and Alberta) have been less likely to accept the investing-in-children discourse and less inclined to reform policy for early childhood education and care. I would add that some governments in other countries are using the discourse of investing in children at the same time that they deregulate the labour force, expect more parents to work for pay, and reduce eligibility for income support. All of these measures can reduce household income and limit the time parents have available to supervise their children (UNICEF 2005). This suggests that a gap often exists between what governments say they are doing and the actual social programs.

Social Housing and Family Well-being

For over a century, welfare advocates have argued that reliance on the private housing market means that many low-income families are forced to live in unhealthy, overcrowded, and unsafe accommodation. Living in damp, mouldy, and overcrowded housing can encourage the development of respiratory ailments, depression, and antisocial behaviour and the spread of infectious diseases. Substandard housing can have negative and permanent consequences on children's health, behaviour, and development (Jackson and Roberts 2001). For these reasons, welfare states have helped to expand housing stocks and to improve the quality and affordability of housing in a number of ways.

The type of state housing assistance varies by welfare regime and country but has also changed over the decades. Historically, local authorities and other levels of governments have been involved in urban renewal projects, slum clearance projects, capital grants for new homes, construction and maintenance of state-owned housing, and provision of subsidized loans for private and public housing construction, including cooperative projects. Because current income support programs often include housing subsidies, accommodation allowances, and/or income-related rents, I am including a discussion of social housing along with income support programs.

The value of state contributions to housing and accommodation is difficult to compare cross-nationally. Housing subsidies are sometimes calculated into income support programs, but housing costs vary by country, region, city, and neighbourhood as well as by the size and structure of the dwelling and its state of repair. Researchers making cross-national comparisons need to consider the value of state rent controls (if they exist) and any subsidies for repair and alterations. Bradshaw and Finch (2002) reported that the majority of the twenty-two countries in their study had a housing benefit scheme that reduces gross rent paid by low-income households, and that rent reductions are usually greater when children are in the household. They explored the effect of housing benefits on family expenditures relating to housing and property taxes, noting that OECD studies often assume families spend about 20 per cent of their gross earnings on accommodation. Using this figure, they found that housing benefit systems would substantially reduce housing costs for low-income families with two children living in Australia, Austria, Denmark, Finland, France, Germany, Norway, and Sweden (65). They would make a smaller contribution in Greece, the Netherlands, and the United States, and would not help families in the United Kingdom because the earnings threshold was set so low. The authors noted that Canadian cash and tax benefits for housing are among the lowest of the twenty-two countries, which helps to explain the high child poverty rates in that country.

Governments have long struggled with the problem of assisting low-income families with accommodation without stigmatizing them in their communities. In 1938, New Zealand's first Labour Government attempted to humanize the market place through state planning and social security, and to free social provision from the stigma of charity

(Cheyne, O'Brien, and Belgrave 2000, 36). Part of this agenda included a dramatic house-building program that provided middle-class amenities to the poor rather than minimal shelter. Social housing was located in pleasant areas with desirable outlooks, and each house was solidly constructed and included a large garden. This building project raised the status of working-class housing and altered subsequent building designs for the private sector. The New Zealand government also subsidized mortgage payments and ensured that male breadwinners received a wage large enough to support a wife and two or three children (36).

Canada was one of the last industrialized nations to fund public housing, but by the 1990s three levels of government supported such programs (Baker and Phipps 1997, 170). During the 1930s Depression, the federal government offered loan guarantees for new housing starts and provided enabling legislation for the provinces to become involved in low-rental housing projects (Guest 1997, 101). In 1946, the federal government created the Canada Mortgage and Housing Corporation to administer housing policy and fund research on housing (Baker and Phipps 1997, 171). From 1971 to 1978, the federal (Liberal/Trudeau) government provided direct grants to non-profit companies and co-operatives with 100 per cent financing. The federal government also initiated a program to help homeowners and landlords make repairs to comply with minimum health and safety standards, but this aid was restricted by the Conservative government to low-income households by 1986 (171). Several provincial governments also introduced rent controls in the late 1970s. Now, housing costs are usually factored into provincial social assistance payments, but most Canadian beneficiaries must obtain private housing.

Although many low-income families are renters, some states have promoted home ownership to ensure social and financial stability. Rising housing costs have also encouraged state-sponsored interest-free loans, low-interest loans, or rent-to-buy programs. Neoliberal practices in the 1980s and 1990s encouraged some conservative governments to sell off state housing and to rely more on the private sector to provide low-income housing. British prime minister Margaret Thatcher, for example, endorsed the sale of council houses to long-term tenants (Pierson 1994), and New Zealand's National government in the 1990s sold state housing and introduced market rents for people on income support (Cheyne, O'Brien, and Belgrave 2000). These experiments may have benefited those with secure jobs or assets, but they left many families with little money for food or clothing. In New Zealand, the Labour-led government once again expanded state housing, as the price of private housing surpasses the incomes of most families, especially in central Auckland.

Lefebvre (2003) found that home ownership rates in Canada tend to increase as people age but decline after they are sixty-five years old. About 67 per cent of households owned their own home, and half of these are mortgage free. On average, tenants spend a greater proportion of their income on housing costs than owners, and renting a home in most parts of Canada is associated with low income. Low income is also associated with overcrowded conditions and housing that needs repairs. Of all family types, lone mothers have the lowest rate of home ownership, at 37 per cent compared to 80 per cent for couples.

Although many low-income families require housing support, only 4 per cent of Canadian households live in state-subsidized housing. Low-income home owners who were mortgage free spent 28 per cent of their after-tax income on housing costs. Low-income tenants in government-subsidized housing spent 31 per cent of their income on housing costs while those in private housing spent 48 per cent, which would leave little money for other necessities (Lefebve 2003). Clearly, many Canadians are struggling to pay for housing, illustrating the importance of accommodation subsidies for the economic well-being of families.

Affordable housing is a growing problem for those living in urban conditions, especially families with more than three children, new immigrants, and mother-led families. Temporary solutions include sharing accommodation with relatives or friends or staying in transition housing provided by voluntary organizations. Lack of affordable housing can keep women and children living in abusive households and can create overcrowded conditions that heighten family tensions and promote contagious and chronic diseases. Moving too many times through inability to pay the rent has detrimental consequences for children's school performance and their peer relationships, and for parental employment and relationships.

Housing problems have always been caused by wars, natural disasters, a high number of refugees and immigrants entering a country, and family emergencies. Now more families with moderate incomes living in stable democracies cannot find adequate and affordable housing as accommodation costs soar in major cities. Although cross-national researchers have focused on 'child poverty' to indicate low levels of family well-being, overcrowded and unaffordable housing remains an under-researched family policy issue.

State Income Support

Most countries provide some form of state income support for families with children, and some have done so for over a century. Early programs were designed for widows, deserted mothers with young children, and disabled war veterans with dependents because these people were considered to be more deserving (Bock and Thane 1991; Gauthier 1996). A number of countries also offered income tax relief to taxpayers supporting children or a financially dependent spouse. These family policies were intended to create some measure of horizontal equity between taxpayers with dependants and those without, as well as to supplement family income at a time of growing labour unrest and demand for higher wages (Ursel 1992). Table 8.2 shows the development of income support programs in various countries.

State support for all families with children, regardless of household income, became widespread by the 1940s. Universal allowances for each child in the family were paid monthly or bimonthly directly to the mother or main care provider (Baker 1995). The idea behind universal child allowances was that bearing and raising children was not just something parents did for their own satisfaction; but that reproduction within marriage was an expectation of citizenship, providing the nation with future workers, consumers, and taxpayers. Paying the allowance to the mother was an attempt to ensure that it was spent on children and household needs, but this practice also socially recognized caring work by mothers. After fertility declined in the 1930s and countless lives were lost in World War II, governments wanted to encourage childbearing by offering financial assistance to help parents defray the costs of rearing children. Income support programs were also developed for impoverished individuals and families, and family services and social housing were expanded during the prosperous decades of the 1960s and 1970s.

By the 1980s, more competitive markets led business groups to argue for lower social spending, less stringent labour laws, and lower income taxes. These neoliberal ideas and practices were expected to increase business productivity and national competitiveness in global markets. Business people wanted a better-trained, more motivated and flexible labour force. They also lobbied for lower 'payroll taxes,' which included social security deductions and the 'compliance costs' associated with implementing state-mandated programs for employees (such as pay equity). Employers' groups assumed that lower income taxes would give consumers more money to spend on goods and services, which would raise national spending and productivity.

Several states embraced these neoliberal principles and restructured their family income support programs accordingly. For example, Canada, Australia, and New Zealand – all 'liberal' welfare states – removed the universality from family allowances and targeted them to middle- or lower-income families. The Conservatives in the United Kingdom tried to reduce universal child allowances but were strongly opposed by welfare groups on the political left (Baker and Tippin 1999). Supporters of targeted child benefits justified them by arguing that paying income support to all families with children was wasting public money by 'paying welfare to the rich.' New Zealand and several Canadian provinces also cut the absolute levels of welfare benefits in the 1990s, including those given to lone mothers caring for young children (Baker and Tippin 1999).

Two case studies[2] illustrate the ways that national and regional politics shape income support programs within welfare regimes considered as similar. Australia and Canada share a common heritage, and both are federal states with parliamentary democracies. Nevertheless, national and regional politics have varied, creating dissimilar social programs. These two examples illustrate that local politics, political structures, and the strength of lobby groups influence the development of income support programs for families with children.

Restructuring Family Income Support in Canada

Both federal and provincial Canadian governments hold jurisdiction over different income support programs, although they share the cost of some, while income support is under federal jurisdiction in Australia. Essentially, the Canadian provinces control 'welfare' or income support for low-income families, while unemployment benefits, maternity/parental benefits, and old age pensions are controlled by the federal government. In 1984, the Conservatives won the federal election and began to focus on neoliberal policies and practices. Beginning in 1985, the federal government modified the cost-sharing programme that paid for welfare (the Canada Assistance Plan, or CAP), in order to permit the provinces to include work incentives in their welfare programs (Lord 1994).

---

2 This section contains an updated version of part of an earlier article (Baker 1998).

Table 8.2
The development of income support programs in selected countries

Country	Family income support	Child allowances	Widows' pension	Benefit for lone mothers	Maternity/parental benefits
Canada	• 1941 (Federal) Unemployment Insurance (contributory) • Income support varies by province as part of their social assistance or 'welfare' program • Payments are means tested on family household and additional payments are made for each child • 1996 'Workfare' permitted with demise of Canada Assistance Plan • 1990s – Several provinces cut benefit levels	• 1945–93 Universal • 1993 Converted to income-tested tax credit (Child Tax Benefit [CTB]) • Beginning 1993, CTB contains a Working Income Supplement (WIS) • 1997, WIS increased and paid per child • 1998 CTB and WIS combined to create the Canada Child Tax Benefit (1st child receives more money than subsequent children)	• Varies by province but 1920 in Ontario and British Columbia • 1966 Canada Pension Plan includes survivors' benefit	• No federal benefit • Provinces provide social assistance to all low-income individuals and families (some pay lone mothers at higher rate)	• 1971 Federal maternity benefits (social insurance with unemployment benefits) • 1985 Entitlements for adopted parents • 1990 Parental benefits added • Eligibility changed to include more part-time workers in 1997 and length of leave increased
Australia	• 1944–91 (Federal) Unemployment Assistance (means tested) • 1991: Unemployment Assistance converted to Job Search Allowance and NEWSTART • 1993: Basic Family Payment replaced Family Allowance • 1994: Partner Allowance and Home Child Care Allowance • 1995: Above payments combined to form Parenting Allowance	• 1941 For families with 2 or more children • 1947 Made universal • 1987 Targeted to middle- and lower-income families • 1987–93 Family Allowance Supplement added for low-income families • 1993 Additional Family Payment replaced Family Allowance Supplement	• 1942 Means tested • 1989 Became part of Sole Parent Pension	• 1973 Sole Parent Pension – until youngest child is 18 years old (means tested) • 1988 Child Support Scheme • 1989 JET scheme introduced and SPP duration reduced (age of youngest child 16 years) • Renamed Sole Parent Benefit	• No statutory benefits • 1912–78 Universal maternity allowance • 1985 Multiple birth payment (employer-sponsored benefit) • 1996 Maternity allowance for all mothers at childbirth • 2004 Maternity allowance made universal, increased in value (tax-free)

Table 8.2 (*continued*)

Country	Family income Support	Child allowances	Widows pension	Benefit for lone mothers	Maternity/parental benefits
	• 1998: Parenting Payment (single and partnered) both means-tested • 2000: Partnered Benefit became Family Tax Benefit (means-tested)			• 1995 Converted to Parenting Allowance • 1998 Converted to Parenting Payment (single) • 2003: Lone parents asked to attend job-related interview once a year, and to seek at least 6 hours of paid work per week when youngest child reaches 12 years of age (down from 16)	
France	• 1913: Means tested benefit for large families • 1925 Illegitimate children excluded from income support • Revenu minimum d'insertion (RMI) for parents with dependent children • 1978 Improved tax benefits for larger families	• 1932–39 (Social insurance) • 1939–46 No allowance for 1st child but more for 3rd plus children • 1946–present Universal • Childcare allowance for employed mothers • 1978 Increased value of family allowance for 3rd child • 1985 Two child allowances combined into 'allocation de jeune enfant'	• Widow's benefit introduced in 1940s	• Allocation de parent isolé (API) introduced in 1976 (based on number of children and means-tested)	• 1909 Maternity leave • 1913 Maternity benefits • 1928 Part of social insurance with sickness benefits • 1984–5 Parental leave and parental education allowance • 1996 Income support during pregnancy and first 4 months after birth becomes income-tested

Table 8.2 (continued)

Country	Family income support	Child allowances	Widows pension	Benefit for lone mothers	Maternity/parental benefits
New Zealand	• 1938 Unemployment benefits (means-tested on household income)	• 1926 Means-tested • 1946–91 Universal • 1991 Income-tested tax credit	• 1911 Means-tested	• deserted wives 1936 (means-tested) • 1973 Domestic Purposes Benefit (means-tested) • 1997 National government tightened eligibility rules for DPB • 2002 Changed back by Labour government	• 2001 Flat-rate parental benefits for employees working for the same employer for 12 months
Sweden	• 1934 Unemployment benefits • 1956 Unemployment insurance • 1960 Equal pay legislation for men and women • 1994–5 Care allowance introduced by conservative government for mothers caring at home without childcare (rescinded by Social Democrats in 1995)	• 1947–present universal • 1992 Child allowance and supplementary benefit cut • 1998 Value of both benefits restored	• 1937 Universal	• 1937 Advanced alimony (universal)	• 1937 Maternity benefits (social insurance) • 1974 Converted to parental benefits (social insurance) • Compensation rate reduced in 1992 from 90% to 80% of previous wages, then 75% • 1998 restored to 80% and extended

Table 8.2 (*concluded*)

Country	Family income support	Child allowances	Widows pension	Benefit for lone mothers	Maternity/parental benefits
United Kingdom	• 1911 Unemployment insurance • 1934 Social assistance • 1988 Income Support • 1988 Family Credit (tops up income of low-wage parents)	• 1945–present Universal	• 1908	• 1977–97 One-parent benefit	• 1975 (Both social insurance and social assistance)
United States	• 1950–96 Aid to Families with Dependent Children (means-tested) • 1996 Temporary Assistance for Needy Families (means-tested)	• 1935–50 Aid to Children (means-tested) • No federal child allowance	• Varies by state	• 1950–96 Aid to Families with Dependent Children (means-tested) • 1996 Temporary Assistance for Needy Families (means-tested)	• No statutory payment at federal level (but several states offer paid parental benefits)

Source. Extracted from Lewis 1993; Wennemo 1994; Baker 1995; Baker and Tippin 1999; Kamerman and Kahn 2001; Leira 2002.

Throughout the 1980s, a number of Canadian provinces[3] initiated 'employability enhancement' programs that included life-skills and job-search counselling, information and education on employment training programs, help developing an employment plan, and partial reimbursement for transportation, supplies, and childcare. According to various assessments, these programs helped people return to work in the short term, but long-term effects were less encouraging. Many returned to welfare because they were laid off or quit or their temporary jobs came to an end (Evans 1988; Callahan et al. 1990).

Welfare-to-work initiatives are usually designed to reduce public expenditures and reinforce individual responsibility for well-being (Shragge 1997; Quaid 2002). 'Success' is typically measured by less time on income support rather than above-poverty incomes. Participants are encouraged to accept low-wage jobs. Consequently, these programs provide few prospects for the kind of upward mobility that could eventually lead participants out of poverty, especially those with sole responsibility for children (Evans 1996). They also do little to improve some people's position in the labour market and do not address other pressing concerns, such as finding affordable housing and childcare, improving people's long-term education and job prospects, and dealing with health problems. Nevertheless, provincial governments continued to build the idea of employability enhancement into welfare reform.

Throughout the 1990s, most Canadian provinces encouraged lone mothers on social assistance to enter paid work when their youngest child entered school (at five or six years of age). Yet there was always considerable provincial variation: Alberta (with a right-wing government) specified that mothers are 'employable' when their youngest child is six months old, while British Columbia (then with a left-leaning New Democratic Party government) considered welfare mothers to be 'employable' when their youngest child was twelve years old (National Council of Welfare 1995), although this was later reduced under a new government to six years and then more recently to three years. Conservative provincial governments reduced the maximum duration on welfare and also cut benefit levels. The government in Ontario, for example, reduced the absolute level of welfare benefits by 22 per cent in 1995, including income support for lone mothers (Evans 1996).

By the 1990s, most provinces had also tightened child support enforcement procedures, arguing that they were 'reducing child poverty'

---

3 Nova Scotia, New Brunswick, Quebec, Ontario, and British Columbia.

but also 'enforcing parental responsibility' (the media said they were 'catching dead-beat dads') (Baker 1998). In reality, these programs were designed to enforce private responsibility and to save public money. Unlike the Australia scheme, discussed later in this chapter, most Canadian provincial child support programs covered only welfare recipients, and none allowed custodial or resident mothers to keep any child support money paid by the father if the family was on welfare. This meant that although the state reduced its expenditures, women and children on income support were no better off financially and child poverty was not reduced when fathers paid child support (Baker 1998).

Welfare costs continued to rise with the increase in mother-led families and higher unemployment rates. The (Conservative) federal government expressed concern about the high and unpredictable cost of cost sharing but was unable to renegotiate their agreement until it ended in 1996. In 1990, the federal government curbed increases to three provinces[4] considered 'wealthy,' meaning that rising welfare expenditures were offloaded onto these provinces and that federal spending on welfare remained at 50 per cent in some provinces but fell to 20 to 30 per cent in others. The three provinces responded by tightening eligibility or reducing benefits, arguing that they could no longer afford such 'generous' benefits considering federal funding reductions (Mendelson 1995).

The Mulroney Conservative government restructured other social programs throughout the 1980s, saying that they were 'modernizing' them but also making them more 'efficient and cost-effective.' Eligibility for unemployment insurance was tightened and benefit duration shortened. Grants to the provinces for education and health care were curtailed. Tax concessions for children were gradually targeted to lower-income families 'to reduce child poverty.' Yet in 1987 the government raised childcare tax deductions for employed parents, which benefited mainly middle-class families with employed mothers (Baker 1995, 202). The universal Family Allowance was ended in 1993 and was replaced by the Child Tax Benefit, using money from the allowance and the child tax credits.[5] This new benefit was targeted to middle- and low-income families to 'reduce child poverty,' and an annual bonus of $500 was paid to the working poor as a 'work incentive.' The poorest families did

---

4 Alberta, British Columbia, and Ontario.
5. Quebec retained its own Family Allowance (established in the 1970s) and expanded the cash payments at childbirth that had been initiated in 1988.

not receive more money because the federal government surmised that their increases would be counteracted by reductions to (provincial) welfare benefits, such was the state of federal–provincial relations (Baker 1995).

By the 1993 federal election, concern about program cuts and high unemployment left the Conservatives with only two seats in the House of Commons. The Liberals won the election on a job-creation platform, but neoliberal ideas and practices continued. The Liberals immediately merged government departments, placing responsibility for income security in the same department as employment programs. They also began a social security review, emphasizing their intent to 'modernize' social programs (Government of Canada 1994), but this was soon truncated by severe budget cuts. The most consequential change affecting income support came in 1996 when CAP ended and was not renewed by the (Liberal) government. Instead, the government reduced provincial transfers[6] and began paying a block grant for social assistance, medicare, and tertiary education. This new program[7] removed most federal restrictions from welfare programs, allowing the provinces to introduce 'workfare' but forcing them to reduce social spending (Mendelson 1995).

Program cutbacks coincided with a rise in welfare caseloads. Separation and divorce rates had remained high since the 1980s, and less than half of lone mothers could support themselves through paid work. Unemployment rates had hovered around 10 per cent for several years, yet eligibility for unemployment insurance was tightened, forcing more people onto provincial benefits. At the same time, there was more public acknowledgment of the need for protection, counselling, and transitional housing for women and children from abusive homes.

The federal government announced further changes to the Child Tax Benefit in 1996 that were designed to 'reduce child poverty,' to 'provide work incentives' to low-wage parents, and 'to take children off welfare.' Beginning in July 1997, the working income supplement was increased and restructured to consider the number of children in the household. In 1998, the enriched supplement and the Child Tax Benefit were combined into one payment: the Canada Child Tax Benefit (CCTB). The CCTB provided more money for the first child than subsequent chil-

---

6 This amount was reduced from twenty-nine billion to twenty-five billion in two years, with more cuts expected in future years.
7 The Canada Health and Social Transfer (CHST).

dren, and offered maximum benefits to low-income families who were not receiving provincial social assistance. Families who did not claim the childcare expenses deduction received an additional amount for each child under seven, the same as they did under the previous version of the benefit. However, the working income supplement and the additional amount for larger families became less visible under the new system (NCW 1997, 6).

Critics argued that the 'new' money for the CCTB was actually the same money that was cut from federal transfers for provincial social assistance when the Canada Health and Social Transfer replaced the Canada Assistance Plan. Furthermore, this payment was based on the working status of parents rather than the financial needs of children, and the provinces could deduct the work incentive component from social assistance. This reinforced the old dichotomy between the deserving and undeserving poor, and the newer emphasis on employment. In addition, the lowest-income people could not claim the maximum supplement, which meant that many part-time or low-wage workers are penalized (Kitchen 1997; Pulkingham and Ternowetsky 1997). Although the government said that it was 'taking children off welfare,' we have already seen that children's poverty reflects their parents' economic circumstances.

The income tax deduction for childcare expenses[8] has always been considered an employment expense by the Canadian government. If this is viewed as a 'child benefit,' then the federal government provided more generous benefits to high-income families than to modest- and low-income families after this change (Kitchen 1997). Furthermore, the Liberal government spent less money on direct income support for families with children in 1996 than the Conservatives had in 1985, when the Mulroney government began restructuring child and family benefits (Kitchen 1997). The federal government's retreat from cost sharing since 1996 further reduced public resources for childcare and child welfare services (Doherty, Friendly, and Oloman 1998).

Quebec always retained its own child benefits, and for this reason they are worth noting. Since 1974, the Quebec government has supplemented the federal family allowance, and since the late 1980s has also paid parents two allowances: one for preschoolers and one for newborn children (Human Resources Development Canada [HRDC] 1994). The

---

8 Seven thousand dollars per preschool child and four thousand dollars for children aged seven to sixteen.

benefit for newborns was particularly controversial because it paid much more money for the third child than for the first and second children in a family, and was therefore seen to be pro-natalist. Furthermore, it was introduced with Québécois nationalist discourse by the Bourassa Liberal government (Baker 1994).

When the federal government targeted the Family Allowance, Quebec retained its own universal allowance. In 1997, however, the three provincial family-related programs were rolled into one targeted family allowance, based on household income and the number of children and parents in the family. This new allowance was then integrated with provincial social assistance (Government of Quebec 1997). The cash payment for newborns, which did not increase the francophone birth rate as intended, was quietly withdrawn despite its grand introduction in 1988 (Baker and Tippin 1999, 92). In 1997, however, the Parti Québécois government introduced a new childcare package that substantially reduced the cost to parents (Childcare Resource and Research Unit 2003).

Since 1997, the federal government has increased the money allocated for the Canada Child Tax Benefit, yet many families continue to live in poverty. The Child Poverty Action Group argues that Canadian public policy condemns women to poverty as either mothers or workers, and that the absence of strong family policies remains a major barrier to the social and economic equality of women. They further argue that the federal government needs to play a leadership role to ensure adequate and consistent standards of living for all children, women, and families across Canada. The CCTB offers some promise, partly because it involves greater coordination between federal and provincial governments. Yet this initiative narrowly focuses on welfare reform and low-wage work, and offers no long-term commitment to resolve child poverty (Freiler and Cerny 1998).

In 2004 the federal government divided the Canada Health and Social Transfer (created in 1996) into two separate funds. The creation of the Canada Social Transfer, responsible for funding provincial social assistance and social services, seemed to involve less public discussion than the Canada Health Transfer had. Political discourse was dominated by concerns about predictability and stability of funding for health care, increasing accountability and transparency of health expenditures, and reducing waiting lists for surgery and queues in emergency wards (Canadian Council on Social Development [CCSD] 2004). Welfare groups such as the CCSD pressured the federal government to further divide the Canada Social Transfer into a fund for social programs and another for post-secondary education. They also asked the government to restore funding to 1994–5 levels, to create common principles and objectives for social programs throughout the country, to measure national outcomes, and to share innovations among the provinces. The CCSD noted that the federal and provincial governments (except Quebec) had already signed the Social Union Framework Agreement (SUFA) in 1999, with some common objectives[9] for social programs. However, the provinces retain jurisdiction over income support and social services, making further cooperation difficult.

Recent changes in both provincial social assistance and federal child benefits place greater pressure on parents to alter their balance between paid work and care giving, as paid work and full citizenship rights are becoming increasingly linked. The federal government raised the value of child benefits when they cut transfer payments to the provinces in 1996. However, the amount of money allocated to resolve child poverty has been too little to counteract global labour market trends. Furthermore, state policies do little to prevent unemployment and especially underemployment.

Despite the restructuring of income support throughout the 1990s, public opposition has been relatively weak, for several reasons. Firstly, the federal government introduced major cuts while Canadians were preoccupied with national unity concerns. As in 1993 when the Family Allowance was abolished, Canada was in the midst of another national unity crisis when plans were made to abolish the Canada Assistance Plan. Canadian media and pressure groups were preoccupied with the 1995 sovereignty referendum in Quebec, allowing the federal government to push through what might otherwise have been unpopular changes.

Secondly, opposition parties focused on other agendas than preventing federal cutbacks. The Official Opposition in the mid-1990s was the separatist Bloc Québécois party, and although they supported stronger social programs, they also insisted on decentralization of powers to the provinces. In fact, federal cutbacks were used to further justify Quebec's need for sovereignty. The second opposition party of the time (the Reform Party) favoured decentralization, cuts in social spending, and

---

9 These include ensuring access to essential social programs and services of reasonably comparable quality, regardless of place of residence in Canada; providing assistance to those in need; and ensuring adequate, affordable, stable, and sustainable funding for social programs.

lower taxes. The political left, which traditionally supported strong national social programs, was seriously weakened in the 1993 federal election and held too few seats in Parliament to gain any real influence.

Thirdly, the more powerful provincial governments (Ontario, Quebec, and Alberta) also supported decentralization in the mid-1990s. Ultra-conservative governments in Ontario and Alberta favoured lower taxes and reduced social spending, and more provincial control over social programs allowed them to redesign programs and cut eligibility. The Quebec government supported greater sovereignty in all areas of jurisdiction.

Fourthly, neoliberal ideologies were pervasive throughout the 1990s even within political parties that previously supported the expansion of social programs. High government deficits reduced spending options, but the business lobby also encouraged voters to demand lower income taxes and public spending. On most issues the Canadian government listened more intently to the business lobby, economists, and conservative provincial governments than to anti-poverty, feminist, and social democratic groups. Yet groups supporting women's employment rights[10] were relatively successful in influencing public policy in the 1990s, as most female voters were employed and governments perceived that promoting two-earner families could be less costly than subsidizing one-earner families (without universal daycare).

Although neoliberal ideologies were also prevalent in Australia (Pusey 1991), the Australian government responded somewhat differently throughout the 1990s, especially with policies for low-income mothers.

Restructuring Income Support for Australian Families

Australian income support programs are funded and administered by the federal government, allowing for a comparable national living standard. Unlike in Canada, the unemployment benefit is financed through general revenue and is means-tested on household income. The supporting mother's benefit developed in 1973 continues to be based on the assumption that a woman who cares full time for young children should not be forced into the workforce because of the absence of a breadwinner, although there is political pressure to reduce the time mothers spend on this benefit. The universal family allowance became

---

[10] Such as the National Action Committee on the Status of Women and Women's Legal Education and Action Fund.

income-tested in 1987 (well before Canada's was targeted), and the Family Allowance Supplement (FAS) was established to provide additional income for low-income families (Bolderson and Mabbett 1991). FAS was indexed to rising costs, included rent assistance, and was paid directly to the mother, acknowledging her caring responsibilities (Cass 1989, 171). FAS later became assets-tested, indicating further targeting of family benefits (Bolderson and Mabbett 1991).

From the 1970s to the 1990s similar socio-economic conditions prevailed in Australia as in Canada. Inflation, higher unemployment rates, and acceptance of feminist ideologies encouraged more women to enter the workforce; but fewer Australian wives accepted paid work, especially full time. Divorce rates rose after the divorce law was liberalized in 1975, and lone parents as a percentage of all families with children increased from 9 per cent in 1974 to 18 per cent in 1994 (Australian Bureau of Statistics 1994). Australians also expressed concern about the 'feminization of poverty' and 'child poverty.' However, neoliberalism was less pronounced in Australia and was implemented differently (Castles 1996).

A Labor government was elected in 1983 and won the next four elections. Restructuring was then negotiated between this government and trade unions through quasi-corporatist arrangements and understandings known as 'the Accord,' which helped maintain job security and permitted modest wage increases. Instead of introducing a consumption tax[11] (as did Canada), the government reduced the highest tax rate but initiated a capital gains tax and progressive fringe-benefits tax on business expenses. This indicates that policy options are shaped by political alliances and institutions, rather than by economic forces alone (Castles 1996). The Hawke (Labor) government initiated a social security review in 1987, which expressed concern about 'dependency' and poverty among lone parents. Several policy changes arose from this report, including the Child Support Scheme (1988), Sole Parent Pension (1989), and Jobs, Education and Training programme (1989).

In 1975, the Family Law Act had introduced a 'no-fault' divorce based on one-year separation, whereas similar legislation was delayed until 1985 in Canada (Baker 2001b, 186). In the 1970s and 1980s, Australian judges retained some discretion in property and support decisions. Support awards tended to be small and non-compliance was consider-

---

11 Australia eventually did introduce a goods and services tax under conservative prime minister John Howard.

able, leading to concern about poverty in mother-led households (McDonald 1986). In 1988, a new Child Support Scheme was introduced, allegedly to reduce child poverty and public expenditures and to enforce parental responsibility (Millar and Whiteford 1993). Several years after implementation, the proportion of lone parents receiving child support had increased and awards were one-third higher (Harrison 1991). However, registration in the scheme did not guarantee support, as only 70 per cent of money due was collected. Evaluations acknowledged that substantial reductions in social assistance were not feasible because child support did not cover child-rearing costs even though mothers are allowed to keep some paternal support money without forfeiting their state benefits (Millar and Whiteford 1993).

In 1989, the Australian Sole Parent Pension (SPP) was introduced, combining the supporting parent benefit and the widows' pension, and reducing eligibility to the sixteenth (rather than eighteenth) birthday of the youngest child. To qualify, the parent had to be living outside a marital or *de facto* relationship, with low assets and income. A government survey indicated that 84 per cent of sole parents received at least some income from SPP (Australia, DSS 1996), much higher than the 44 per cent of Canadian lone parents on 'welfare' at that time (Dooley 1995). However, concern about costs and growing numbers of sole parents led to several employment initiatives.

In 1989 the government introduced the Jobs, Education and Training (JET) program, which integrated previous programs for income support and training, and provided employment counselling and access to improved childcare services. Priority was given to teenage lone parents, those at the end of eligibility, and parents with children over six who had been receiving the SPP for more than a year (Saunders and Matheson 1991). Restructuring continued when the unemployment benefit was abolished in 1991 and replaced by two employability programs (Lambert 1994). In addition, the government initiated a wage subsidy program for employers hiring people from targeted groups, including lone parents (Perry 1991).

Childcare spaces under JET increased by 47 per cent, but lack of spaces and permanent full-time jobs remained a problem for lone mothers attempting to return to work (McHugh 1996). Australian employment enhancement schemes were subject to similar scrutiny and criticisms as Canadian initiatives. Shaver (1993) reported that 40 per cent of female sole-parent pensioners who moved from government benefits to paid employment actually experienced a drop in income.

She also found that some women unable to locate jobs simply moved to unemployment benefits, which were more stigmatized than the SPP.

In 1993, the Basic Family Payment replaced the Family Allowance and the Additional Family Payment replaced the Family Allowance Supplement. This change in terminology removed any connotation of automatic entitlement or social rights. In 1994, the government released a White Paper entitled *Working Nation*, announcing changes to unemployment benefits. These included greater work incentives for unemployed people, additional training opportunities, and a Parenting Allowance for low-income parents caring for children under sixteen. The Parenting Allowance replaced the practice of paying a supplementary unemployment benefit to the husband at the 'married rate,' and spouses began to be treated as unemployed individuals rather than 'dependants' in 1995. If an unemployed husband found a low-paying job, the wife could still receive the Parenting Allowance. However, spouses who did not care for young children were encouraged to find paid work unless they were over forty and had little job experience, when they might be eligible for a Partner Allowance (Government of Australia 1994).

The (Keating) Labor government introduced the Home Child Care Allowance in September 1994, replacing the former tax rebate for a dependent spouse caring for a child. This new benefit, supported by the Liberal Democrats and the Australian Council of Social Services, allowed the carer herself to receive the payment rather than giving a tax benefit to her husband (Bittman and Pixley 1997). In 1995, the Partner Allowance and Home Child Care Allowances were rolled into the Parenting Allowance to simplify the benefit system. In 1996, a Maternity Allowance was established for mothers on the birth of their child (Bradbury 1996).[12] These benefits indicated Labor's support for family carers as well as their attempt to woo the female vote before the 1996 election (Bittman and Pixley 1997).

Throughout the 1990s, unemployment remained nearly as high in Australia as in Canada, and 'new right' critiques of welfare programs and social benefits were prevalent. They focused on widening the gap between the deserving and undeserving poor (Cass 1992) and reducing social security fraud. The 1993 Green Paper *(Restoring Full Employment)*

---

12 Although Canada never created a maternity allowance, the Quebec government introduced a birth allowance in 1988 in an attempt to increase fertility. The value of this benefit for the third child was eight thousand dollars.

and the 1994 White Paper (*Working Nation*) stated that Australian policies were being reformed to acknowledge labour force trends such as the increasing employment of married women, high youth unemployment, the expansion of non-standard work, and growing long-term unemployment. Yet reforms were also attempting to reduce government expenditures (Lambert 1994) and bring Australian social policies in line with those of other countries.

After the 1996 election, the Howard (conservative) government introduced the Family Tax Initiative for middle- and low-income families, to acknowledge 'the additional costs of bringing up children' and to give parents 'more choice in ordering their lives' (Moylan 1996; Thorp 1996). More federal government money was also added for 'special-needs childcare,' but daycare funding was cut for employed parents. There seemed to be little acknowledgment on the part of the Howard government that entering the workforce or staying at home with children was not just a matter of personal 'choice,' but was influenced by various social and economic constraints. These include the availability of suitable local jobs, the woman's earning capacity, the income of her partner, the number of children present, the availability of childcare, social expectations, and personal perceptions (Bradbury 1996; McHugh 1996).

The Howard government continued to restructure income support programs and family benefits. In March 1998, the Sole Parent Pension and the Parenting Allowance were rolled into one benefit called the Parenting Payment, providing income support to the primary caregiver of a dependent child (Government of Australia 2003). The payment had two streams: one for lone parents and the other for one parent in a couple. In 2000, a portion of the latter benefit became a part of the Family Tax Benefit Part B (discussed below). To qualify for the Parenting Payment a person must care for a child under the age of sixteen and have low assets and income. Reforms to Family Assistance, effective from 2000, reduced ten different payments to two (Family Tax Benefit, Parts A and B), and entitlement rules were made more consistent. Part A provides income support to families raising children up to twenty-one years old (or twenty-four if they are studying full time and not receiving Youth Allowance or another payment).[13] Family Tax Benefit

---

13 The maximum rate in 2003 was about $3,400 per year per child for families with incomes under $31,755, but it continues to be paid in part for families with incomes well over $100,000, especially if they have more than two children (Government of Australia 2003).

Part B[14] provides extra assistance for families with only one main earner, and is paid to families for children up to sixteen years old (or eighteen if they are studying full time) (Government of Australia 2003).

Australian parents may also be eligible for a one-off maternity allowance, assistance with child support from non-resident parents, a childcare benefit for employed parents to subsidize up to fifty hours a week of childcare, and an immunization allowance.[15] The introduction of statutory maternity benefits has been debated for several years but not passed into legislation, although new mothers have access to fifty-two weeks of unpaid leave (Allard 2002). Business organizations oppose any social insurance scheme that would ask them to finance such a program with payroll taxes, as in Canada.

By 2003, sole parents relying on income support were asked to attend a job-related interview once a year and then to seek at least six hours of paid work per week when their youngest child is over twelve years old, down from sixteen years previously. In addition, the Howard government introduced discussions about flattening tax rates and replacing the variety of social benefits with a single standard payment. The rationale behind these proposals was that the cost of benefits is increasing so fast that they will be unsustainable in ten to twenty years, but also that the current system is complex and difficult for applicants to understand (Garnaut 2003).

Family programs dominated the May 2004 budget in Australia. Referred to in the media as 'the mother of all spending sprees' (Dodson 2004), it included an increase in the Family Tax Benefit Part A, an increased maternity payment of three thousand dollars for working and stay-at-home mothers (with promises of future increases), and more subsidized childcare places. Showing the concern about fertility decline, the treasurer (Peter Costello) was quoted as saying: 'If you can have children, it's a good thing to do – you should have one for the father, one for the mother and one for the country, if you want to fix the ageing demographic.' The Howard government was hoping to remain in power in the 2005 election,[16] despite widespread criticism about

---

14 Family Tax Benefit Part B pays the maximum of about $2,900 per year for children under five years.
15 For low-income parents who have their children immunized before their second birthday.
16 The Howard government did win the 2005 election.

refugee policy and the prime minIster's alliance with the United States over the Iraq war.

In summary, the Howard government has continued state support for parenting at home but also reinforced the idea that beneficiaries must begin to see themselves as future employees earlier than before. At the same time, conservative politicians and advocacy groups have expressed concern about the declining birth rate. Fewer births and more retirements mean a higher percentage of the population outside the workforce. Despite the 2004 budget announcement about new childcare places, the Howard government has made little effort to assist middle-class mothers to combine earning and caring. The male breadwinner/female caregiver model of family is still widely accepted, and the government does not want to increase unemployment rates.

Comparing Canadian and Australian Reforms

Both countries continue to tighten eligibility and work incentives for income support, but Canada has been stricter in these requirements. Until recently, Australian low-income mothers with school-aged children were exempt from paid work requirements. Now the state continues to pay the Parenting Payment with no obligation for the parent to find paid work until the youngest child in a lone-parent family reaches the age of thirteen years, and even after that child reaches thirteen the obligation is only for six hours of paid work per week. Canada has no federal benefit for parenting or for lone mothers caring for children. Instead, provincial welfare programs provide support for low-income people with few assets, and families with young children are paid at a higher rate than childless individuals. In no Canadian province can a lone mother receive welfare without pressure to find a job when her children are over six years old or in school. Both countries pay social assistance to low-income households with few assets, but unemployment benefits differ considerably (Eardley et al. 1996). In Canada they are paid through social insurance involving individual contributions and entitlement, but in Australia they are means-tested to household income and assets. Consequently, the Australian system tends to disadvantage unemployed partners (often wives).

Policy similarities can be attributed to the fact that historically both countries were British colonies and, with the exception of the Canadian province of Quebec,[17] continue to share a common legal, cultural, and social policy tradition. Policy differences developed from the efforts of local lobby groups, variations in labour markets, and the ways that social benefits were institutionalized and modified over time. Australian trade unions were unusually powerful in the development of the welfare state. Unions pressured the government for the family wage, which was institutionalized by the Harvester Judgement in 1907 in a way that it never was in Canada (Baker and Robeson 1981; Armstrong and Armstrong 1984; Castles 1985).

Australian unions fought to incorporate the male-breadwinner family into social policy and kept men's wages higher than in most other countries (Castles 1996). They also excluded married women and mothers from the labour force, and restricted the immigration of non-white immigrants until the 1970s. The trade union movement was a stronger force in Australian public policy formulation, although the demise of central bargaining will gradually reduce this influence (O'Connor, Orloff, and Shaver 1999, 217). Furthermore, the alliance between the unions and the Labor Party was always more solid and effective than that between Canadian unions and the leftist New Democratic Party (NDP). The NDP never won a federal election, had few opportunities to influence policy directly, and after the 1993 election were further edged out as the Reform Party and the Bloc Québécois gained more parliamentary seats.

Strong union support for male earners discouraged Australian women's full-time employment and helped promote the public discourse that children 'need their mums.' Women's full-time employment rates were always higher in Canada, especially for mothers, and they remain so today. Although women's employment has increased in both countries, 41 per cent of employed women work part time in Australia compared to 28 per cent in Canada (OECD 2001, 37). Lower full-time employment rates for Australian women also coincide with higher total fertility rates: in 2000 Australian women had 1.8 children on average while Canadians had only 1.6 (see Table 2.1). Ironically, the Australian government seems more concerned about declining fertility than the Canadian government.

---

17 Quebec was a French colony until 1759, when the British conquered the French. After Confederation in 1867, Quebec retained its language, legal system, and religion within Canada.

Canadians rejected the policy option of paying low-income mothers a special benefit to care for their children at home because it was seen as more costly to the state than expecting women to be employed. Furthermore, no social benefit could be high enough to raise lone mothers out of poverty without substantially raising general taxes. Canadians also argued that payment would demean the relationship between family members by commodifying a 'labour of love.' More importantly, it could ghettoize women into a domestic role that further limits their long-term earnings and autonomy. And finally, politicians and policy makers have been concerned that payment for care might encourage more women to leave their husbands (Ursel 1992; Little 1998; Evans 1996). Despite these concerns, child poverty rates among lone-parent families[18] have been higher in Canada than in Australia (OECD 2003b, 53), whether parents are employed or not. Paying mothers to care for their own children is clearly a lifeline for many Australian sole mothers and their children. However, the benefit level cannot pull them much above poverty, and it discourages full-time participation of these mothers in the labour market.

The current focus on 'employability' in Australia still exempts mothers with children under twelve, as prevailing attitudes continue to embrace the idea that caring for young children is socially useful work that should be supported by the state and that group care is less desirable than maternal care. Research from the 1990s indicated that sole mothers about to lose the parenting benefit tended to see themselves as mothers first and employees second (Shaver et al. 1994). Although more lone mothers are now entering employment, Australians continue to express concerns about their children's supervisory needs (McHugh 1996; Chalmers 1999; Walter 2002). Yet payments for care deliberately remain below average wages in order to 'maintain work incentives' and keep taxes low. When Australian women enter the full-time workforce, however, they earn higher wages relative to men than do Canadian women, due to a legacy of centralized bargaining and the wage arbitration system.

In contrast, Canadian policies and legal reforms increasingly assume a two-earner family. Since 1971, employed mothers have been entitled to fifteen weeks' statutory maternity benefits through (un)employment insurance if they worked for the requisite time period. In 1990, ten

---

18 'Family poverty' is defined as households with incomes below 50 per cent of the median disposable income, adjusted for family size.

weeks of parental benefits were added for either father or mother, and this was expanded to thirty-five additional weeks in 2001 (Lawlor 2003). Federal childcare funding for low-income families was provided from 1966 to 1996 under the Canada Assistance Plan, and relatively generous income tax concessions[19] have been available since 1971 for employed parents with childcare receipts (Baker 1995). Although the need for affordable and high-quality care outstrips the availability, the prevailing Canadian discourse is that public childcare is a necessity for employed parents. Furthermore, the belief is widespread that group care enhances the social development of preschool children. The two-earner family model is also implicit within legislation such as the 1985 Divorce Act and provincial child and spousal maintenance laws (Baker 1997a).

Social policy in both countries has been driven largely by economic concerns for the last decade or more. The focus on work incentives, which tends to place the onus for unemployment on individuals, is being used by governments to divert attention from structural unemployment aggravated by global markets, which government policy cannot deal with effectively (or does not want to). Policies of decentralization have sometimes offloaded responsibility for service cuts to provincial and state governments and placed more burdens on family carers. In Canada, cuts in federal transfers have forced provincial governments to curb eligibility for income support and to encourage more recipients to enter paid work.

A stronger emphasis on paid work can be an effective strategy to raise household income, reduce child poverty, and promote gender equality when jobs are available. In Sweden, such policies have been successful because governments established public-sector jobs with statutory protections, developed lengthy family leave policies, ensured pay equity, established an extensive system of public childcare services, and actively promoted gender equality (Baker 1995; Daunne-Richard and Mahon 2003). In Canada and Australia, work incentives and employability programs are promoted within a context of private job creation, flexible labour markets, a lower percentage of full-time jobs with high wages and statutory protections, and a shortage of subsidized childcare services. Under these cirumstances, urging everyone into paid work,

---

19 In 2004, the lower income earner in the family could deduct seven thousand dollars per child from her taxable income with receipts for non-family childcare. This could substantially reduce her taxable income.

including low-income mothers with preschool children, is unlikely to reduce family poverty or promote gender equity in the workplace.

A stronger emphasis on paid work may reduce public expenditures, but it is unlikely to raise mothers out of poverty without additional supports and legislated protection. Instead, it could create an underclass of low-paid workers who are sporadically and marginally employed, and are unable to provide their children with an adequate living standard. Plenty of evidence indicates that children raised in poverty experience more social and health problems than those from higher-income families. Yet in the current climate of lower taxes and less state intervention, the creation of new full-time jobs with 'living wages,' increased statutory protections, and more affordable childcare is less likely. Nor are governments likely to bolster pay equity programs.

This comparison between Canadian and Australian policies suggests that family poverty and dependence will be resolved neither by paying mothers to care for their children at home nor by insisting on employment. Australian mothers have been allowed more 'choice' to care for their children at home (with poverty-level benefits) or to enter the workforce with higher wages but little childcare or statutory parental benefits. Australian policies have promoted part-time employment for mothers, which does not enable them to exit from poverty or become independent of the family or state.

Australian policies have avoided some of the pitfalls of expecting relatively unqualified people with family responsibilities to find jobs and childcare in a competitive and global labour market. Yet payments for care are costly to the state, even when paid at a low level, especially when most lone mothers receive some money from the Parenting Payment. These payments are also costly to the mothers who receive them. Long-term financial dependence on either husbands or government benefits means that future labour force participation is less likely to lead to financial autonomy. After ten or twenty years at home, few women can recover their lost earnings when they return to paid work. Yet high rates of relationship breakdown, insecure employment or underemployment for many males, and neoliberal practices require more mothers to contribute to their households while raising children.

The (Howard) Australian government was undoubtedly influenced by restructuring in New Zealand. In 1997, New Zealand lone mothers on social benefits were expected to look for a part-time job when their youngest child was seven years old and a full-time job when their youngest child was twelve years old, although this was relaxed by the subsequent Labour government. The (conservative) Australian government is now asking low-income mothers with younger children to return to paid work earlier than in the past, but not as early as in New Zealand. Yet in a rapidly changing labour market, lone mothers with young children have difficulty competing with men and childless women if the state does not provide some income support, statutory leave provisions, and affordable childcare services.

Conclusion

In this chapter, I have shown that most OECD countries have developed some kind of subsidized housing program for low-income families and that the contribution of affordable housing to family well-being is recognized. Higher housing subsidizes are always offered for families with more children, but most countries focus on low-income families. The exceptions are Norway, Sweden, and Denmark, which offer a housing benefit for all families with children (Bradshaw and Finch 2002, 68). However, some of the liberal welfare states used to ensure more affordable housing in the 1970s than they do now, as many sold off state houses in the 1980s and 1990s, leaving a dearth of social housing that now needs renewal.

Since the early 1990s, most liberal welfare states have targeted child benefits to moderate-or low-income families rather than paying a universal allowance to all parents with children. Universal benefits recognized the social contributions parents made to the country by raising children, but targeted benefits focus on household income as the defining criteria for state support. In addition, most liberal states now calculate and pay these benefits through the taxation system rather than the social welfare department, suggesting that taxpayers are more worthy of public support than beneficiaries. Eligibility for income support has also been tightened, placing more emphasis on employability initiatives. However, some governments have also increased entitlement and funding for employment leave at childbirth and for public childcare services, thereby strengthening the policy focus on the importance of paid work.

We have seen from the research discussed in this chapter that income support alone will not ensure the economic and social well-being of families with children, but it can help counteract the insecurity of reliance on labour market earnings or on marriage. Income support can also keep more children out of poverty. We have seen that mothers experience different challenges than fathers in making the transition from income support to paid work. However, we need to acknowledge that the social and economic circumstances of mothers also vary considerably, influencing their ability and opportunities to raise healthy and confident children.

Mothers with low education, several children, and no male partner face the most challenges when they try to become self-supporting while caring for children, but policy research indicates that those countries with the best outcomes for mother-led families do not focus on lone mothers. Instead, they offer a variety of social supports and focus on universal programs for enhancing income in all families. They also provide social housing, universal health services, preschool childcare, public education, state-enforced child support, job training, employment assistance, and family leave programs. Caring for children on a very low budget demands emotional strength, parenting skills, and considerable time, but most states now expect low-income parents to earn money to support their children as well as to supervise their upbringing.

Research suggests that the designers of employability programs need to be more cognizant of the interaction among low income, poor health, childcare problems, and the ability to find and retain paid work with adequate wages. Living in low-income and dangerous neighbourhoods augments parental concerns about child safety, and expecting lone mothers to become both earners and carers under these conditions often increases their stress levels. If parents appear to neglect their children or leave them unsupervised, even while they are working, truant officers and child protection authorities could step in and investigate, with the threat of fines or ultimately removing children from their parental home. Greater surveillance and higher risk of losing children to separated partners or state authorities is a concern for parents receiving income support, especially in liberal welfare states.

9 Divorce, Child Support, and International Migration

In this chapter, I examine some of the social and legal implications of relationship breakdown in a world where fewer people legally marry, relationships have become less stable, and more people travel internationally. Child custody after separation is sometimes divided between parents, but more divorced parents cross international borders to find work or start a new life. The first half of this chapter discusses the convergence in divorce trends, including laws related to marriage breakdown, child custody, and child support. The second half focuses on multilateral agreements that attempt to ensure that crossing international borders does not release parents from obligations to their children. This chapter indicates that family policies matter to the 'post-divorce family,' and that national governments are increasingly pressured by transnational organizations and other governments to provide comparable policies and consistent enforcement procedures.

Changing Attitudes to Divorce

The expansion of secular individualism as well as changing gender relations and more competitive labour markets have encouraged similar expectations about marriage and family life. Since the 1960s, public attitudes towards marriage and divorce have changed in OECD countries, and more people now view the legal termination of marriage as an acceptable conclusion to a relationship that has already broken down. However, cultural values are diverse, and attitudes towards divorce remain quite traditional in countries such as Ireland and Turkey. In most countries, people have come to appreciate that marital and relationship breakdown does not necessarily arise from the culpability of one partner but more probably stems from the complex interaction of personal, social, and economic factors (Baker 2001b, 206).

Marriage breakdown has become more prevalent with opportunities to live outside marriage and greater expectations of personal happiness and freedom of choice. In addition, more exogamy, or marriage outside one's social group, means that an increasing percentage of partners hold different ideas about what constitutes a good relationship and desirable lifestyle, which can lead to marital conflict. More people now postpone legal marriage until their late twenties or beyond, preferring to cohabit without a legal contract in order to avoid traditional ties and the possibility of legal divorce. As cohabiting partners are statistically more likely to separate than married partners, relationship instability in the larger society has increased with rising rates of cohabitation (Beck-Gernsheim 2002).

Reformed laws have made legal divorce easier and altered the relationship between the family and the state (Lloyd 1978). In most OECD countries, unhappily married couples can no longer be kept together by religious doctrine, legal enactments, or family pressure (Beck-Gernsheim 2002). The family courts, established in the 1980s as separate entities from the criminal courts, have made divorce cases less adversarial by focusing on conciliation, mediation, and counselling. Policy reforms are also apparent in spousal support, the division of matrimonial property, and the enforcement of child support, but these remain sources of contention in many jurisdictions.

Public debate continues about how to deal with the economic and social consequences of separation and divorce. There are several reasons for this. Firstly, the courts have been unable to compensate for the gendered nature of paid and unpaid work, which creates both economic and social inequalities between husbands and wives that continue after separation. Many mothers work part time in order to retain their family responsibilities, but in doing so they reduce their earnings compared to men and to childless women. When marriages end, mothers with young children more often than fathers need a transitional period of state income support, but this seldom pays above the minimum wage. Secondly, most children continue to live with their mother after separation even though laws have been made gender neutral and custody is based on the 'best interests of the child.' These mother-led households tend to experience a drop in income even when these mothers are working for pay, as families increasingly need two incomes and male incomes tend to be higher. Thirdly, many fathers fail to pay the required amount of child support and some lose contact with their children altogether. Most divorced men re-partner and produce additional children, but most fathers cannot earn enough to support two households.

As the nature of marriage changes, laws and policies need to be reformed to deal with the new realities. Most politicians publicly say that children should not have to live in poverty, but few welfare states have succeeded in bridging the poverty gap between two-parent and one-parent families. Furthermore, more parents now migrate for employment or remarriage, which means that the state needs to ensure that non-resident parents are guaranteed access to their child, unless there is a valid reason to restrict access. An additional controversy in the Netherlands and Belgium is the request for divorce among some of the same-sex couples who have been permitted to marry since 2001 (Arie 2003). Before these issues are discussed in more detail, some contextual information is needed. How do divorce rates vary cross-nationally, how have policies changed, and what does social research conclude about the impact of divorce on children?

Comparative Divorce Rates

All OECD countries compile official statistics on divorce and remarriage, which makes cross-national comparisons possible. However, divorce rates have become a less effective measure of relationship breakdown as more people cohabit; legal divorce rates record only a fraction of relationship breakdowns. Further insights about the impact of relationship insecurity can be gleaned from official statistics on marital status, remarriage rates, child custody and support, and income by family structure.

Whatever measure we use of marriage breakdown, and there are several, rates have increased substantially since the 1970s. Average divorce rates measured in comparison to marriages in the same year have tripled in OECD countries, from 14.3 per cent of marriages in 1970 to 41.2 per cent in 1998 (OECD 2001, 32). Table 9.1 compares the divorce rates in 1973 and 1998, using the crude divorce rate (or number of divorces per thousand population in a given year). This table shows an increase in most countries, but also the high rate in the United States and the low rate in Italy and Spain. Cross-national variations in divorce statistics are related to legal differences, high employment rates for women, differences in economic prosperity, cultural and religious fac-

Table 9.1
Crude divorce rates in selected OECD countries, 1973–98
(per 1,000 mid-year population)

Country	1973	1998
Australia	1.21	2.70
Canada	1.66	2.28
Denmark	2.52	2.48
Finland	1.89	2.67
France	0.98	2.00
Germany	1.46*	2.30
Ireland**	–	–
Italy	0.33	0.60
Netherlands	1.33	2.10
Portugal	0.07	1.50
Spain**	–	0.90
Sweden	2.00	2.30
United Kingdom	2.14	2.70
United States	4.36	4.20

* West Germany only
**Spain passed divorce legislation in 1981 and Ireland in 1996
Source: Lewis 2003, 25.

tors, and the average age of the population (as younger people are more likely to divorce) (OECD 2001, 32).

Jurisdictions with low divorce rates tend to make divorce legally difficult, to view marriage as a sacred bond that cannot be broken, and to emphasize duty and obligation to kin rather than personal satisfaction. Furthermore, individuals are socialized to tolerate or compensate for marital unhappiness in order to keep the marriage together and their family reputation intact. Wives are particularly encouraged to take greater responsibility than husbands for maintaining marital relationships and to accept the role of kin keepers (Nett 1988; Bittman and Pixley 1997). In addition, low-divorce jurisdictions often discourage full-time employment for middle-class wives and mothers but seldom provide adequate income support for low-income lone mothers. Financially and socially, women in these countries would find it difficult to establish autonomous households and support their children without a male earner in the household. In addition, husbands in these countries are deterred from initiating a divorce because it is difficult and expensive, and because their legal obligation to support their ex-wife usually continues until her remarriage or death. In some cases, husbands are encouraged to take a mistress before seeking a divorce, as long as they are discreet.

In contrast, jurisdictions with moderate to high divorce rates usually make divorce legally easier. Some American states, such as California, were permitting liberal access to divorce in the 1960s (Phillips 1988, 567), a decade before Australia or Canada made similar reforms, and two or three decades before some European countries even made divorce legally possible.[1] High-divorce jurisdictions publicly value lifestyle choice and emphasize individuality and self-fulfilment more than obligations to family or community. However, some patriarchal societies (such as those based on traditional Moslem laws) have granted men easy access to divorce but made it legally complicated and social unacceptable for women to divorce their husbands or to live outside marriage.

Divorce rates stabilized during the 1980s and 1990s in countries where legal marriage rates declined, but marriages do not last as long as a few decades ago. The mean duration of marriage varies crossnationally but is particularly low in the United States and Australia (OECD 2001, 33). Divorce has become easier, both legally and socially, especially among childless couples and those with smaller families. In countries such as Canada and New Zealand, only about half of divorces involve children under eighteen (Baker 2001b, 181), but both parents and the state must consider their emotional and economic well-being. Researchers and counsellors nevertheless argue that the perpetuation of an unhappy marriage can be more harmful than separation to both adults and children (Amato and Booth 1997; Pryor and Rodgers 2001, 239).

Separation, Divorce, and Children

The impact of divorce on children has become a popular research topic since the 1970s. Many policy initiatives have arisen from the disturbing research finding that children living in lone-parent households are more likely to suffer from a variety of negative outcomes than children living in 'intact' households. These outcomes include lower educational attainment, behavioural problems, delinquency, leaving home earlier, teenage pregnancy or parenthood, higher divorce rates when they marry, and

---

[1] Spain made divorce legally possible in 1981 (Phillips 1988, 562) and Ireland in 1997 (OECD 2001, 32).

many others (Pryor and Rodgers 2001). Researchers typically ask if these negative outcomes arise from the absence of a father in the household or from having lived (and perhaps still living) in a conflictual household. Less often, studies examine the socio-economic conditions prevalent in 'post-divorce families' as well as those prone to divorce or separation.

Firstly, it is important to emphasize that most children living with lone parents do not experience problems, but they are at *higher risk* than children from two-parent families. Furthermore, the incidence of negative outcomes declines but does not disappear when studies control for family income (Elliott and Richards 1991; Maclean and Kuh 1991; Kiernan 1997). The Canadian National Longitudinal Survey on Children and Youth found that about 19 per cent of children from low-income families headed by a lone mother experience a 'conduct disorder,' compared to 9 per cent of children from two-parent families. For those from higher-income families, this percentage drops to 13 per cent for lone-mother families and 8 per cent for two-parent families (Lipman, Offord, and Dooley 1996).

One finding that is seldom highlighted is that many lone-parent families experienced economic disadvantage *before* divorce as well as after, as people from lower socio-economic groups tend to have higher rates of bereavement, separation, and divorce (Pryor and Rodgers 2001). Social research also concludes that when children are raised in low-income households, regardless of family structure, they are more likely to suffer from certain socio-economic disadvantages that continue into adulthood. These include delayed school readiness, lower educational attainment, more trouble with school authorities and the law, more serious childhood illnesses, higher accident rates during childhood, premature death, high rates of depression, and high rates of smoking and alcohol abuse as young adults, to name only a few (National Longitudinal Survey of Children and Youth 1996; Kiernan 1997; Canadian Institute of Child Health 2002).

Contact and support from the father is also an important variable influencing the outcomes of children after parental separation. Children who live with their mothers often experience diminished contact with their father (especially if the parents are not legally married) and suffer distress from this loss (Furstenberg, Morgan, and Allison 1987; Cockett and Tripp 1994; Funder 1996). Many fathers fail to pay the required amount of child support, and about one-third lose contact with their children altogether (Smyth 2004). The quality of time with the father and the absence of conflict in these meetings are more important than the amount of time (Amato and Rezac 1994; Pryor and Rodgers 2001). Furthermore, whether or not the father continues to pay child support may influence both the children's adjustment and the socio-economic status of the lone-parent family.

Never-married mothers who become pregnant before their education is completed are particularly vulnerable to low income and children's behavioural problems (Dooley 1995). These mothers often re-partner within a few years of the child's birth, but the socio-economic disadvantages of bearing a child at a young age may linger. These children are most likely to spend their early years in one or more stepfamilies, which are not always harmonious (Marcil-Gratton 1998). These factors may partially account for higher rates of behavioural problems in the children of never-married mothers.

Research shows no direct relationship between parental separation and children's adjustment, although many studies find differences between children from two-parent families and those from separated families (Amato and Keith 1991; Burghes 1994). Parental separation adds stress to children's lives through changes in relationships, living situations, and parental resources, but few studies conclude that psychological disturbance is severe or prolonged (Emery 1994). It is difficult to determine whether problems that surface later in adult life are attributable to parental divorce or other factors.

Woodward, Fergusson, and Belsky (2000) analysed longitudinal data from the (New Zealand) Christchurch Health and Development Study. They found that exposure to parental separation was significantly associated with lower attachment to parents in adolescence and more negative perceptions of both maternal and paternal care and protection during childhood. The younger the child at the time of separation, the lower their subsequent parental attachment and the more likely they were to perceive their parents as less caring but overprotective. Furthermore, numerous studies suggest that having divorced parents raises the chances of ending one's own marriage in divorce (Beaujot 2000). This may result from poor relationship models in childhood, mistrust of the opposite sex learned from the resident parent, or personal knowledge of divorce procedures and their aftermath.

Lone Parenthood and Re-partnering

Although public discourse sometimes implies that lone parenthood is a permanent status, it is actually a temporary stage for most people.

British research from the National Child Development Study found that half of lone mothers re-partnered within three years if they had never married, at around five years if they had divorced, and at closer to eight years if they had separated or been widowed (McKay and Rowlingson 1998). These figures are similar to but slightly longer in duration than those of earlier studies from the United Kingdom and longer than those in American research. The duration of lone parenthood appears to be lengthening but is longer for mothers than fathers, for those living in social housing, and for men who are unemployed. Poor economic prospects, especially for young men, discourage marriage and remarriage among lone parents (McKay and Rowlingson 1998). There is no financial advantage for a lone mother to marry an unemployed man, as her economic hardship could increase and she could lose social benefits. This helps to explain the high prevalence of lone parenthood among certain cultural groups that share high unemployment rates, high fertility, and strong cultural values about the importance of family and children.[2]

Re-partnering typically means improved childcare and a more comfortable home environment for resident fathers and an economic and lifestyle improvement for resident mothers. However, research suggests that it does not necessarily improve children's emotional well-being or happiness. Numerous studies have found that stepfamilies experience more conflict than lone-parent families because they involve both resident and absent parents as well as children from different parents and backgrounds (Pryor and Rodgers 2001; Cartwright 2002). In addition, stepfamilies often live with financial problems, especially when fathers are supporting children in more than one household. These difficulties may lead to more general disputes about the fair allocation of resources, time, and attention.

Most children fare well in both stepfamilies and lone-parent households. Yet compared to children in lone-parent households, children living in stepfamilies have higher accident rates, higher levels of bedwetting, more contact with the police, and lower self-esteem and are more likely to leave school earlier without qualifications (Wadsworth et al. 1983; Ferri 1984; Elliott, Richards, and Warwick 1993). These experiences can be explained by the lower aspirations and expectations that stepparents have for their stepchildren than for their biological

---

2 Such as Afro-Americans, First Nations, and Caribbean peoples in Canada, and Maori in New Zealand.

children, as well as by family friction in these households (Pryor and Rodgers 2001). In stepfamilies, young children fare better than older children because adaptation is easier at an earlier age, before allegiances are developed to the absent parent. The role of stepmother appears to be more stressful than the role of stepfather, and mothers are more negative than fathers towards step-parenting (Cheal 1996).

Legal and Policy Issues

The Division of Family Assets and Spousal Support

Some cross-national convergence is apparent in divorce rates and family law, although legislation varies by jurisdiction. The English-speaking countries use variations of English common law, and the European countries (and the Canadian province of Quebec) use variations of civil law. Generally, common law relies more on precedents from judicial decisions and custom while civil law relies more on statutes and basic principles. Although individual spouses in common law jurisdictions are permitted to retain any property acquired before marriage, they are expected to share the income they earn and the possessions they acquire during marriage (such as marital home, furnishings, and the family car). However, the differences between these two types of family law may be diminishing in the case of marriage breakdown.

Civil law uses guiding principles for judicial decisions and written contracts regarding marital property. In Quebec, little judicial discretion used to be permitted in the division of matrimonial property (Baker 1997a). Couples signed a marriage contract either to keep their property separate during marriage (which meant that neither could claim the other's property upon divorce) or to share it equally under the control of the husband during the marriage. In 1989, Quebec passed a provincial law that required mandatory division of family assets when a marriage ended by divorce, annulment, separation, or death. The law also stated that the court may divide assets unequally if equal division would result in 'injustice,' and one spouse could be asked to provide a 'compensatory allowance' to repay the other for goods or services that enriched the other's property. Factors that are considered include the brevity of the marriage, waste of certain property by one spouse, and/or 'bad faith' by one spouse. This element of judicial discretion in Quebec's Civil Code brought it closer to the common law used in English Canada (Morton 1990).

In common-law countries, spousal maintenance used to be paid to full-time homemakers and mothers, or simply to assuage a husband's guilt (Harrison 1993). The court could ask former husbands to make these payments where it was 'proper'; where payers could afford to pay; where payees could not support themselves because of age, the care of children, disability, or illness; or for 'any other adequate reason' (46). By the late 1970s, these laws were viewed as too arbitrary. Some husbands felt that they were paying ex-wives too much, and many wives felt that their caring work and unpaid contributions to the home were undervalued.

After prolonged and controversial law reforms in the 1980s, the liberal welfare states now view divorce as a 'clean break' that terminates marital rights and obligations (but not obligations to support children). Legal reform has also enabled people to divorce their partner without their consent, which means that wives can no longer delay court proceedings in order to negotiate a better financial settlement. However, women's assets and earning capacity typically remain lower than men's, influenced by caring responsibilities, lack of career planning, and employment discrimination (Baker 2001b). Gendered patterns of paid and unpaid work contribute to the high poverty rates of mother-led families.

Guardianship, Custody, and Access to Children

Under both common law and civil law, the state used to label children born outside marriage as 'illegitimate,' which meant that they acquired no automatic right to their father's surname, his financial support, or any inheritance from him. Furthermore, the unmarried father had no legal right to decide how his children would be raised. By the 1990s, most countries had removed legal distinctions for children based on their parents' marital status, and laws now expect fathers to support their children regardless of whether they have ever lived with or married the child's mother (Kamerman and Kahn 1997). New ways have now been developed to establish paternity, and some countries (such as the United States) spend considerable public resources trying to identify fathers and force them to support their children. Welfare benefits are sometimes reduced or withheld from mothers who refuse to identify the child's father.

In terms of child custody and access, many countries assume that separating parents can decide these matters for themselves, and the courts intervene only in a small minority of cases when requested.

Before the 1970s, judges in common law countries used to award children's physical care and legal guardianship to only one parent, usually to the mother because she had been the primary caregiver during marriage. Judges assumed that it would be impractical to award legal rights to both parents or to have the child share two homes. Mothers could lose guardianship if they were found to be 'unfit mothers,' which historically meant that they had abandoned their children, engaged in 'immoral' behaviour, were alcoholics, or were mentally ill (Little 1998; McClure 1998). When fathers contested custody, which they rarely did, it was often granted for older and male children.

By the 1970s, laws and judicial practices rejected the implication that children could be the property of either parent. The (current) 1985 Canadian divorce law, for example, clearly states that either parent or both together could be granted custody after divorce, and that this decision should be based on the 'best interests of the child' rather than any notion of parental rights. Yet this concept continues to raise considerable debate, as professionals and parents often disagree about what is the best arrangement for a specific child. When consulted, different professionals also express different views, and children themselves are sometimes ambivalent, preferring to live with both parents even when it is no longer feasible.

Despite legal reform, about three-quarters of children involved in divorce cases continue to live with their mothers after separation and divorce (Baker 2001b, 193). Both parents typically decide that their children should live with the mother, the courts legalize these arrangements, and parents rarely contest these decisions in court. Joint custody was introduced in the 1980s in the common law countries, but this means joint *legal* responsibility rather than shared physical parenting. In Canada, the percentage of children involved in awards of joint custody increased from zero to 21 per cent in ten years, yet considerable variation in custody awards is apparent among provinces (Vanier Institute of the Family 2000, 69). Recent figures from Statistics Canada indicate that, among the thirty-five thousand custody cases that went to court in 2002, custody of only 49.5 per cent of the children went to the mother only, down from 75.8 per cent in 1988 (Pereira 2004). This shows a rapid trend towards joint legal custody in Canada, shared by other common law countries.

Separating and divorcing parents are usually expected to make a parenting plan for their children with the assistance of counselling, conciliation, and mediation. Although both parents now retain parenting responsibilities, mothers tend to remain the 'resident parent' and the main provider of daily care for young children after divorce. Fathers often become 'non-resident parents' because they visit their children but do not live with them most of the time. However, fathers have gained more access to their children and legal rights to make decisions about them after separation.

The main reason that fathers do not receive sole custody after divorce seems to be that they seldom ask for it (at least initially). Many fathers feel they cannot handle daily childcare while working full time. They also believe that their children are better off with their mother or that she should not be deprived of custody because it is important to her (Richardson 2001). Throughout marriage, mothers have been mediators between their husbands and their children, and most fathers have not developed as close a relationship with their children as their wives have (Dulac 1995). A small percentage of fathers believe that the courts will not give them custody and consequently do not ask for it. Some join fathers' rights groups and engage in political protest over fathers' alleged discrimination in custody cases.

In New Zealand, a high-profile custody case was discussed in the media in January 2005. A couple who had been residing in Wales brought their six-month old baby to New Zealand to visit the husband's family, and within two weeks the father applied for custody of his child, stating his desire to remain in his homeland of New Zealand (MacLennan 2005). The mother was forced to return to Wales but applied for the case to be heard under the Hague Convention, discussed later in this chapter, on the grounds that the child normally resided in Wales and that the custody dispute should be resolved there. The local New Zealand fathers' rights group used this case to argue that the legal system works against fathers.

After divorce, most fathers see their children and continue to support them. Research from several countries suggests that about one-third of non-resident fathers are highly involved in their children's lives and another third are disengaged but still maintain some contact. The final third have little or no contact (Smyth 2002; Amato 2004). 'Fading fathers' either enter the divorce with little interest in the children or become alienated from them after divorce, sometimes due to the perceived difficulties involved in visiting their children or the superficial nature of that kind of relationship (Furstenberg and Cherlin 1991; Amato 2004). Some fathers rekindle interest in their children after divorce and either become regular 'weekend parents' (Beck-Gernsheim 2002) or attempt to alter existing custody or access arrangements. When fathers contest custody or access in court, research suggests that they are as likely as mothers to be awarded it (Greenwood 1999, 127; Richardson 2001).

Awarding and Enforcing Child Support

All OECD countries require fathers to support their children, but enforcement procedures have often been lax, especially in the liberal welfare states. Before the 1990s, the children's mother was expected to take the father to court if he failed to provide financial support, which meant she had to prove he was the father, know where he lived, take him to court in the jurisdiction where he lived, and pay court expenses. These procedures were impractical and too expensive for most mothers.

As divorce rates soared in the 1970s and 1980s, policy makers and social service workers became concerned about the poverty in households where fathers were not paying. Government-sponsored research found that two-thirds to three-quarters of fathers failed to pay the full amount of court-awarded child support within a few years of the divorce (Trapski et al. 1994; Funder 1996; Richardson 2001). Consequently, most lone mothers had to rely on paid work, loans from friends or family, or state income support. As an inducement to paying child support, the Canadian government used to offer non-custodial parents (mainly fathers) an income tax deduction on support paid. Ironically, they also required custodial parents (mothers) to pay income tax on support money received (Baker 1995, 330). Yet this tax deduction proved to be an ineffective inducement for most men, and payment rates remained low (Richardson 1996; Boyd 2003).

The United States and Australia initiated major reforms in the assessment and enforcement of child support in the 1980s, and the other liberal welfare states followed. Child support agencies were established within the taxation offices, and these agencies collected support money to be paid directly to residential parents (mothers), often through welfare offices. The assessment of child support was taken out of the courts in some jurisdictions (such as Australia, Britain, and New Zealand) and placed in the hands of the child support agency. Calculation of support payable was based on the number of children and the non-residential parent's (father's) income. These schemes involved both married and unmarried parents and generally increased the proportion of lone mothers receiving child support as well as the amounts paid (Harrison 1993). Nevertheless, the state has been unable to collect the full amount from many fathers, especially those who are less affluent, unemployed, difficult to trace, never married, or no longer in contact with their children or who separated many years ago (Millar and Whiteford 1993; Jones 1996, 97).

Canadian child support schemes are designed and administered by the provinces and territories. All provinces have tightened their enforcement procedures since the 1980s but awards are still set by judges in court, based on national guidelines established in 1997 and amended in 2002. Some provinces focus their enforcement on families receiving income support while others have used the 'first default principle,' which means that the government scheme is activated only when parents make a complaint about unpaid child support. Since 1987, the federal government has provided the provinces with enforcement tools, including sharing information to locate and intercept defaulters, suspending or denying federal licences or passports, and operating an automated telephone information system (Canada, Department of Justice 2003).

While Canadian default rates decreased with the new enforcement systems, over half of cases were still in default, meaning less than the total amount was paid, the amount owing was not paid on time, or it was not paid at all. Considerable research has been done on the non-payment of child support. Studies find that the percentage of fathers who clearly refuse to pay is small. Most 'defaulters' say that they are temporarily unable to pay, are caught in administrative disputes, or are in the process of having the award adjusted in court (Lapointe and Richardson 1994).

In other jurisdictions, such as Australia and New Zealand, child support assessment has been removed from the courts, standardized, and indirectly paid in order to reduce continued contact between former spouses. However, contact generally continues anyway when fathers have access to their children or when parenting is shared. If fathers pay support, their children may be no better off financially if the household relies on income support: if the father's support money goes directly to the agency fund, it is usually used to offset social assistance expenditures; if it goes directly to the mother, it is treated as earned income and any welfare benefits she receives are subsequently reduced. This suggests that enforcement procedures are not designed to reduce 'child poverty,' as political discourse often suggests, but rather to save the government money and reinforce private responsibility for economic well-being (Baker and Tippin 1999, 108).

Improving the enforcement of child support has done little to resolve the high level of poverty among lone mothers in liberal welfare states because poverty is caused by many factors other than sporadic or low levels of paternal child support. Low household income is also influenced by mothers' part time employment, low-wage jobs, ungenerous income support, high housing costs, and childcare expenses. Yet conservative politicians and policy makers continue to search for more effective ways to enforce private child support, and spend considerable amounts of public money on surveillance and enforcement procedures.

International Agreements on the Enforcement of Child Support

In the past twenty years, most states have tightened child support enforcement procedures, including for parents who cross borders to evade their support obligations. International conventions on 'maintenance obligations' date back to 1956, with the United Nations Convention on the Recovery Abroad of Maintenance. More recent conventions include the 1968 Brussels Convention and the 1973 Hague Convention on the Recognition and Enforcement of Decisions Relating to Maintenance Obligations, which has been ratified by nineteen countries (UK Child Support Agency 2003). Governments also initiate bilateral agreements with individual countries. For example, the United Kingdom has agreements with over one hundred countries, Australia and New Zealand signed a bilateral agreement in April 2000, and Australia and the United States signed an agreement in June 2002 (Australia, Parliament 2003).

Before states can enter into international reciprocal agreements, they must develop procedures to establish paternity and support orders, to enforce support, and to collect and distribute payments. They must also be willing to provide administrative and legal assistant to the country seeking cooperation without additional cost to that country. And finally, a central authority is needed to facilitate the implementation of support enforcement (US Department of State 2003). An application to retrieve child support from someone living in another jurisdiction has to be processed according to the laws of that jurisdiction. In other words, effective reciprocal agreements require some convergence in laws, procedures, and practices.

The United States has made it a federal offence for people to travel interstate or internationally with the intent of evading child support obligations (US Department of State 2003). American enforcement agencies are also mandated to garnish federal or state income tax refunds, put liens on property, report unpaid support to credit agencies, suspend licences (such as drivers' licences), freeze bank accounts, and deny passports to parents in arrears. The United States has also signed agreements with other countries and Canadian provinces to apprehend defaulters and retrieve payments (US Department of Health and Human Services 2003; US Department of State 2003). Ironically, the United States spends considerable public money on this kind of enforcement but is also the most punitive in terms of providing income support to lone-mother families.

Child Custody, Domestic Violence, and the Hague Convention[3]

States have also signed multilateral agreements relating to child custody and access disputes. The following section provides an illustration of how one international treaty deals with incidents of 'child abduction' across international boundaries. The Hague Convention on the Civil Aspects of International Child Abduction is the primary international treaty dealing with child custody issues. It was opened for signatures in 1980, and by 2002 seventy states had signed, including New Zealand, Australia, United States, Canada, the United Kingdom, and members of the European Union (Crouch 2003).

The Hague Convention's provisions apply where one parent from a signatory country moves to another signatory country with a child under sixteen against the objections of the other parent. The primary goal is to reinstate the status quo, implying that the 'child's best interests' are served by being returned to his/her place of habitual residence as quickly as possible (Lowe 1994, 374). Speed is important in convention hearings (S. Armstrong 2002, 428) and an investigation into either parent's history or capabilities is discouraged, generally disallowing oral evidence by either party (Coester-Waltjen 2000).

The convention assumes that children's best interests are protected by the courts in their home country because these courts will be able to carry out a substantive hearing. Local courts will also be able to determine and enforce custody and access issues, or accept and abide by decisions made in other contracting states (Kaye 1999, 195). However, the operation of the Hague Convention depends upon the goodwill of

---

3 Thanks to Magdalena Harris, who compiled the research for this section.

the signatory countries, with no legally binding force to ensure state compliance.

Violence against women is a notable risk factor for parental abduction. In a study of parental abductions, at least half of these relationships were characterized by violence (Kaye 1999, 193). Women who try to leave violent partners are vulnerable to separation assault and may seek refuge in another country in order to escape from the violent partner. The majority of abduction cases concern primary caregivers returning to their former residences and taking the children with them. Coester-Waltjen (2000, 81) points out that if a parent retains child custody, she may not realize that crossing a border is unlawful, and argues that access decisions between separating persons should take into account the freedom of the primary caregiver to relocate.

A common judicial response to allegations of domestic violence is to issue the remiss parent with 'undertakings,' which are measures such as attending an anger management program or abiding by protective orders. These undertakings are likely to have limited effect in child abduction cases because they cannot be legally enforced in either of the countries concerned (Coester-Waltjen 2000, 68). Beaumont and McEleavy (1999, 260) recommended that undertakings be followed up by existing social services in the state in question.

Article 13(b) of the Hague Convention states that exceptions to a child's return are allowed if 'there is a grave risk that his or her return would expose the child to physical or psychological harm or otherwise place the child in an intolerable situation.' This exception is sometimes interpreted to include domestic violence, but the trend has been to not consider it as constituting a 'grave risk' (Kaye 1999; Jaffe, Lemon, and Poisson 2003, 62). It seems that the convention offers no protections against violence of the other parent or inhumane treatment by officials of the return state, nor any guarantee of a fair and impartial hearing in custody matters. Article 13 allows no room for the abducting parent's interests, especially where the abducting parent may suffer if expected to return to the habitual country with the child (Coester-Waltjen 2000, 66). Kaye (1999, 197–8) illustrated a number of cases in which the court minimized or overlooked the mother's fear of violence and portrayed her refusal to accompany the child back to its habitual residence as 'obstructive and manipulative.'

Kaye (1999) examined how the gendered nature of child abductions was ignored by convention protocol and argued that violence against the fleeing women by their intimate partners is prevalent. In her analysis of Hague Convention cases involving violence, Kaye identified four common themes: the depiction of the mother as hostile and manipulative, an unrealistic faith in the ability of the legal system to protect women and children from violence, an underestimation or dismissal of the harm caused to children by experiencing domestic violence, and the recognition that the presence of violence in relationships is so widespread that any 'special' consideration to the victims of violence would undermine the convention. Comments in a British hearing illustrate the unwillingness of courts hearing these cases to take domestic violence into account: 'The situation is undoubtedly sad, but so many of these cases are sad. However, to accede to an appeal and to accede to this application would, as my Lord has said, drive a coach and horses through the provisions of the Act and of the Convention to which the United Kingdom is a party' (*Re G* [*minors*] 1994, quoted in Kaye 1999, 195).

While the Hague Convention is a standard treaty, counties vary in their implementation and interpretation of its various clauses. One of these concerns the facilitation of voluntary return. The 1997 Special Commission of the Convention uncovered two different approaches to voluntary returns. France, Germany, the Netherlands, and Scotland stated that they immediately undertook to secure a voluntary return by writing to the abductor once the return application was filed. Austria, Cyprus, England, Wales, Israel, and New Zealand stated that judicial proceedings would be brought immediately, while concurrently attempts might be made to secure a voluntary return. Their concern was that entering into negotiations could delay proceedings and/or give the abductor a chance to further conceal the child (Beaumont and McEleavy 1999, 246). In 1999, between 10 and 46 per cent of applications to the former states went to court and 16 to 80 per cent resulted in a voluntary return, while in the latter states 58 to 78 per cent of applications went to court with no more than a 15 per cent voluntary return rate. In Australia, where there is a statutory obligation to seek a voluntary resolution, an order is given at the same time, preventing the abductor from further removing the child (Armstrong 2002, 431).

Child Custody, Domestic Violence, and Border Crossings in Specific Countries

Generalizations have been made about child custody and domestic violence, but policies and court decisions vary cross-nationally. This section illustrates that international treaties and laws can be interpreted and applied in different ways.

UNITED STATES

Several policy statements in the United States have addressed domestic violence as a child custody issue. There are no federal laws addressing this issue, as the legal system excludes family law from the federal courts (with the exception of international law), but Congressional Resolution number 172, passed in 1990, states in part: 'It is the sense of Congress that, for purposes of determining child custody, credible evidence of physical abuse of a spouse should create a statutory presumption that it is detrimental to the child to be placed in the custody of the abusive spouse' (Jaffe, 2003, 63). In 1994, the Model Code on Domestic and Family Violence (MCoDFV) was released; it had taken a national task force composed of judges, prosecutors, defence attorneys, legislators and domestic violence experts three years to develop it. Section 401 of this code states that in child custody dispute cases where domestic violence is evident, there can be a 'rebuttable presumption' that it would be detrimental to the child to be placed in the violent parent's custody (63).

By 1999, the Uniform Child Custody Jurisdiction and Enforcement Act (UCCJEA) was ratified in fourteen American states; it includes provisions for emergency jurisdiction in a new state if the parent and child flee there to escape abuse. The petitioning parent does not have to disclose the child's address for the last five years if there has been partner or child abuse.

By the end of 2000, forty-seven states plus Washington, D.C., and Puerto Rico had passed laws addressing custody and visitation decisions in which domestic violence had occurred. These laws either specifically allow courts to take domestic violence into account when making custody decisions, or mandate that they do so (64–5). Recent tends in custody disputes show a trend towards recognizing the importance of domestic violence as a factor. But 'approximately 70 per cent of contested custody cases [in the United States] that involve a history of domestic violence result in an award of joint or sole custody to the abuser' (90). Many of these decisions are reversed upon appeal.

Anomalies exist in American laws whereby battered parents can be charged with 'child abduction' if they flee or for 'failing to protect' their children if they stay with their abusive partner. Statutes often force battered women to stay in close physical proximity to the perpetrator to facilitate visitation because policies favour 'frequent and continuing contact' (72). The Model Code incorporates a presumption that the custodial parent should be allowed to relocate with the child if the parent feels that relocation is in the child's best interests, but no provision exists for cases in which the parent needs to flee before a custody order is issued. In most states, such sudden flight is seen as child abduction and may result in a criminal conviction and loss of custody. If the battered parent does not take immediate steps to protect the child, s/he may be seen as having 'failed to protect' the child and can be convicted of this charge and/or lose custody of her children. California is the only state to have legislation for such circumstances, providing a defence to criminal charges of child abduction if the parent or child has been subject to mistreatment or abuse (72–3).

If domestic violence victims cross state lines but remain within the United States, the case triggers the Uniform Child Custody Jurisdiction and Enforcement Act. If they cross international borders, the Hague Convention comes into play. Several American cases concluded that 'grave risk' must involve war, famine, or disease, and have rejected domestic violence as a reason to allow the child to stay in a new country. In other cases, courts take domestic violence seriously but attempt to arrange a safe way for the custody decision to be made in the home country, usually involving an undertaking that the violent party will abide by court-mandated conditions (98).

In 1995, the National Centre for Missing and Exploited Children assumed responsibility for all Hague Convention applications; the convention designates that a principal task of central authorities is to discover the whereabouts of the abducted child (Beaumont and McEleavy 1999, 244). This is seldom an issue yet seems to be associated with the stereotype that abduction is done by fathers. If the removal is carried out by the mother, she and her children usually return to live with relatives and are easily located. In the first three years of the Hague Convention's operation in the United States, the location of children was an issue in only 60 of 335 cases (Beaumont and McEleavy 1999, 244).

CANADA

In 1968, Canadian statutes first acknowledged domestic violence in divorce cases, recognizing both physical and mental cruelty as grounds for marriage dissolution. Currently both federal and provincial laws require custody and access disputes to be decided on the vague standard of the child's best interest (Jaffe, Lemon, and Poisson 2003, 78). Only in Newfoundland does legislation specifically address domestic violence as a custody or access issue (81). Federal law states that parents are equally entitled to custody of their children, with non-custodial parents receiving maximum provision for contact with the child. This comes under a 'friendly parent' provision (section 16[10], Federal Divorce Act), which ignores the existence of domestic violence and child abuse, assuming that contact with each parent is always in the best interests of the child. This may conflict with other policies such as the parental duty to protect the child from harm, which is required by provincial child welfare legislation. Also problematic is section 16(9) of the Divorce Act, in which the past conduct of parents is deemed irrelevant unless it affects their parenting ability. This can be and has been interpreted by judges to exclude evidence of domestic violence (Jaffe 79).

The response of the Canadian courts to allegations of domestic violence posing a 'grave risk' to the child has been mixed. The following two Hague Convention cases illustrate this point. In *RAH v. NJG* (1998), the British Columbia court heard a mother cite domestic violence as the reason for fleeing from Texas to Canada with her children. The court found that there was no grave risk, as the mother had exaggerated or fabricated the abuse. It also found that the children's wishes to remain with the mother were probably due to her influence and ordered their return to Texas. In *Pollastro v. Pollastro* (1999) the mother also fled to Canada from the United States to escape an abusive husband. Although the trial court ordered her to return her baby to the home jurisdiction for a custody trial, the appellate court took the father's violence and substance abuse seriously and reversed the decision (117).

AUSTRALIA

Historically, Australian law did not consider intimate partner violence when determining custody issues. The federal Family Law Act 1975 operated on the 'welfare of the child' premise, which allowed for consideration of child abuse but not the impact of adult abuse on the child. In 1994 the Australian Law Reform Commission addressed the issue of family law in the report *Equality Before the Law: Justice for Women*. This report recognized violence as an integral part of the inequality of women and advised an amendment to the Family Law Act to acknowledge the deleterious impact upon children of witnessing domestic violence (Jaffe, Lemon, and Poisson 2003, 83). In response, the act was reformed in 1995.

The Family Law Reform Act 1995 replaced the standard of the 'welfare of the child' with that of the 'best interests of the child.' The most significant change in the amended legislation was the new concept of shared parental responsibility. This meant that both parents must share responsibility for their child even when they are no longer living together, unless the court makes a specific order deeming only one parent responsible. The tensions arising from this clause reflect the conflicting interests of fathers' rights and feminist lobby groups. For example, the child's right of contact with both parents may conflict with section 68f(2), which states the need to protect the child from 'any family violence involving the child or a member of the child's family' (84). In 1997, commonwealth, state, and territorial governments signed an agreement called Partnerships on Domestic Violence (PADV) to reduce and prevent domestic and family violence in Australia (Queensland, State of 2000).

Five reported cases in Australia have used domestic violence to argue 'grave risk to the child,' and two trends are apparent in these cases. The first is the court's practice of relying only on affidavits rather than having an evidentiary hearing, which appears to arise from a strict interpretation of the Hague Convention's requirement for expeditious resolutions. However, courts in other countries do not come to this interpretation and often quickly hold evidentiary hearings (Jaffe, Lemon and Poisson 2003, 127). The second trend is the appellate court's refusal in every case to find that there was a grave risk of danger to the child if returned to the home country. These refusals occurred despite serious allegations of domestic violence and child abuse (Kaye 1999).

The rationale behind these refusals is that Australia focuses on the risk posed by the country as a whole and not on the qualities of an individual parent, trusting the courts and authorities of the return state to ensure the safety of the abused parent and child (Coester-Waltjen 2000, 65; Degeling 2000). An example of this policy is the case of *Murray* reported in Kaye (1999). In this case, the mother fled with her children from New Zealand to Australia to escape a husband who was a gang member of the Mongrel Mob and was extremely violent towards her in the presence of the children. Consequently, the mother could not safely reside in New Zealand. The trial judge ordered the return of this woman and her children, saying: 'It would be to denigrate the New Zealand Courts, and in particular the Family Court of New Zealand, to assert that the wife and children could not be protected from harm if the need arose' (199).

NEW ZEALAND

New Zealand has dealt with at least two cases under the Hague Convention: *Damiano v. Damiano* (1993) and *S v. S* (1999). In both cases, the court concluded that there was no grave risk to the children and ordered them to be returned to their home countries. *Damiano v. Damiano* involved a New Zealand mother and Canadian father who married and had three children in Canada. As a result of separate incidents in which the father threatened to kill the daughters and assaulted and threatened to kill the mother, the mother fled with the children back to New Zealand. The court made the return order conditional on several undertakings by the husband, including vacating the family home and having only supervised access with the children until the Canadian courts could make a determination (Jaffe, Lemon, and Poisson 2003, 111).

In *S v. S* the mother fled from Australia to New Zealand with her three children, and her husband petitioned the New Zealand court to order the wife and children to return to Australia. The Family Court found evidence of 'grave risk' based on the husband's long-term abuse of the wife, the children's exposure to violence, and the likelihood of future violence towards the children. However, this ruling was overturned by the Court of Appeal, which stated that it wanted to 'demonstrate to potential abductors that there is no future in interstate abductions.' The Court of Appeal stressed that the issue is not whether allowing custody or access to one parent would involve a grave risk to the child, but whether the legal system in the home country can be entrusted to safeguard the child's interests (112).

ENGLAND AND WALES

In 1989, the United Kingdom passed a new custody law, the Children's Act, which took effect at the beginning of 1992. This law emphasized the need for both parents to share equally in decision making about the children and for children to retain regular contact with both parents after separation. No exceptions were provided for domestic violence cases (Jaffe, Lemon, and Poisson 2003, 83). In 2001, guidelines were introduced for good practice on parental contact in cases involving domestic violence. The following year, the Adoption and Children Act 2002 extended the definition of 'significant harm' within the Children's Act 1989 to include 'impairment suffered from seeing or hearing the ill-treatment of another' (Women's Aid 2003a).

In 2003, a Women's Aid survey of 127 refuge organizations in England found that a significant proportion of contact decisions made within the family courts allow violent parents access to their children, at times unsupervised. According to this survey, these findings reflect the increased emphasis placed on enforcing family contact in family proceedings, instigated by the 2001 government consultation paper 'Making Contact Work' (Women's Aid Federation of England 2003a).

In England and Wales, one central authority deals with Hague Convention cases, and a high proportion of applications go to court. In 1999, 60 per cent of incoming cases to England and Wales went to court, compared with 29 per cent in the United States and 37 per cent in Germany (S. Armstrong 2002, 428). In terms of speed and number of applications, Sarah Armstrong suggested that 'England and Wales stands out as the model Convention country' (427). However, England and Wales may have neglected the convention obligation to seek the voluntary return of the child. Article 7(c) states that central authorities shall take all appropriate measures 'to secure the voluntary return of the child or to bring about an amicable resolution of the issues' (427). Armstrong argued that England and Wales should ensure a system for dealing with Hague Convention applications that incorporates the requirement to seek voluntary resolutions, by mandating either the child abduction unit or the solicitor in the case to seek a voluntary return. This would not delay proceedings significantly and might help ensure greater communication between parties, which is ultimately in the best interests of the child (435).

EUROPEAN COUNTRIES

In Europe, there are two agreements relating to child custody. The European Convention on Recognition and Enforcement of Decisions concerning Custody of Children was signed in 1980 in Luxembourg. It has also been implemented in the United Kingdom by Part 2 of the Child Abduction and Custody Act. The European Convention's primary aim is to enforce custody orders from one jurisdiction to another. Where either the Hague Convention or the European Convention can be utilized, the Hague Convention takes precedence (Davis, Rosenblatt, and Galbraith 1993, 34). Article 7 of the European Convention specifies that a decision relating to custody given in a contracting state must be recognized and enforced in every other contracting state. No specific reference to domestic violence is made in the convention but a possible avenue for addressing this could be in article 10(b), which states that recognition and enforcement of custody may be refused if circumstances change and are no longer in accordance with the welfare of the child (161).

Child custody and access decisions have increasingly reflected awareness of the detrimental impact domestic violence has on children, but countries implementing the Hague Convention still have a long way to go. Common interpretation of the convention is that the most expeditious way to deal with cases is to send children back home. This is viewed as returning the child to the care of the country rather than the individual abuser. The convention relies on the country of residence to adequately hear and enforce custody issues and to protect the child and parent from further domestic violence. Research suggests that this fatih is not always justifiable. The failure of court systems to protect women and children from domestic violence is evident in domestic homicide statistics. An internationally recognized convention that governs child abduction incidents should be beneficial, but the current interpretation and application of the Hague Convention seems to disadvantage victims of violence.

Conclusion

In the past three decades, most OECD countries have experienced similar trends relating to relationship breakdown, including higher separation and divorce rates, a greater percentage of mother-led families, and more children born outside marriage. Most jurisdictions have liberalized their divorce laws and developed gender-neutral laws relating to divorce and child custody. In deciding where the post-divorce child should live, many jurisdictions emphasize the 'best interests of the child' rather than parental rights, but at the same time have encouraged more contact between non-resident parents and their children without always considering the possibility of domestic violence. In addition, most states have established family court systems that include mediation and less adversarial practices than in the criminal courts.

With 'no-fault' divorce and a greater percentage of consensual unions, more women need to become self-supporting and to remain in the labour force throughout their adult lives. Nevertheless, mothers and fathers seldom have equal earning capacity, as we saw in chapter 6. Despite legal changes affecting the 'post-divorce family,' mothers tend to retain the daily care of their children after marriage breakdown. In the liberal welfare states, fathers have gained more legal rights to make decisions about their children's welfare since the 1980s, but child support enforcement laws have been unable to extract financial support from all fathers expected to pay, especially when they move to another jurisdiction.

Within countries, reliance on private enforcement of child support has proven less effective than state schemes that view the welfare of children as a public responsibility. These state programs guarantee the maintenance of all children regardless of their parents' marital status, income, or willingness to pay. International agreements to enforce custody and support rely heavily on international cooperation in locating parents who cross borders, depend on national courts for conflict resolution, and expert some convergence in legal practices. However, cross-national variations remain in the interpretation of international agreements as well as national laws and legal practices.

In the next chapter, all the factors discussed in previous chapters are brought together to develop some conclusions about the impact of various international and national trends on family life and family policy reform.

10 Strengthening and Reducing Family Support

In the previous five chapters of this book, a number of specific family issues have been discussed in order to illustrate and expand on the factors influencing family policy restructuring that were outlined in chapters 2 to 4. I argued that socio-demographic changes in family patterns tend to provide a strong impetus for national family policy reform but that politicians and interest groups interpret the meaning and potential outcomes of these trends in quite different ways. Within countries, these varying interpretations encourage controversy and negotiations among political parties and interest groups about policy solutions, leading to cross-national differences in social programs.

Historical and existing patterns of social provision also influence restructuring and often set the baseline for reform. I argue that similar welfare regimes tend to accept certain policy options while rejecting others, and acceptable policy options usually fit within prevailing ideas about the appropriate role of the state in family life, suitable levels of taxation and social support, and cultural notions of the ideal family. Within similar welfare regimes, national policy variations result from the negotiations between interest groups and political parties, as well as other political concerns influencing policy development and restructuring at the national level.

Finally, I showed that a variety of international organizations, especially the United Nations, the OECD, International Labour Organisation, and the European Union, pressure governments to harmonize employment practices, family policies, and social services for families. Attention to individual family policy issues is not uniform, as some areas receive a great deal of international attention while others do not. These organizations particularly focus on employment-related issues and try to ensure that new parents gain access to paid employment leave, mothers with infants are entitled to breastfeeding breaks from work, and childcare services are available for employed mothers, especially those with low incomes. Globalizing labour markets and more employed mothers and work-related migration encourage these organizations to strive for international standards in employment practices but also in income support, the enforcement of child support, and the legal recognition of relationships. Yet the success of their efforts is often limited because international rulings and conventions are seldom legally binding or truly enforceable at the national level. In addition, policy agendas are sometimes resisted by political parties or interest groups that view these international agendas as contravening local interests.

In this last chapter, I discuss the controversies involved in several family programs that have been strengthened in recent years and others that have been eroded. Although there are many other policies mentioned throughout this book, there is insufficient space in this chapter to discuss all of them. However, several more have been included in Table 10.1, which provides a quick visual summary.

Secondly, I identify some of the types of political parties and interest groups promoting specific family policy reforms. Although I acknowledge that terminology, and especially what it means to be politically 'left' and 'right,' varies in different jurisdictions, this categorization nevertheless provides some indication that politics matter. In other words, the ideologies of interest groups and the party in power, as well as local political circumstances, are important in explaining the restructuring of family policies.

Finally, I discuss the future of family policies, arguing that pressures for convergence will continue with freer trade and neoliberal restructuring. However, cross-national convergence will continue to be impeded by ideological differences, cultural preferences, and prioritizing of issues such as equity and cost containment. Historical precedents in institutional arrangements will also interfere with convergence, as will different perceptions of the state as a welfare provider. Furthermore, I argue that focusing only on 'at-risk' families will not provide the support that most parents need when earning a living and raising children in a globalizing economy.

Which Family Programs Have Been Strengthened?

The Expansion of Paid Parental Leave

As more women remain in paid work throughout their lives, most

OECD countries have either developed or further enhanced maternity or parental benefits for employees. However, several important concerns remain about the entitlement, delivery mechanisms, and funding of such benefits. Firstly, we need to reiterate that some states still offer employees *no* statutory right to paid maternity or parental benefits, while others have only recently introduced such programs. The United States is an example of a country that offers no statutory right at the federal level to paid employment leave at childbirth, although unpaid leave is available for 'medical reasons.' In addition, paid maternity/parental leave is provided by several American states (Baker 1997b). New Zealand is an example of a country that only recently introduced paid parental benefits. Twelve weeks of benefits were first offered in 2002 (later raised to fourteen), paid at a flat rate to employees who had worked continuously for the same employer for one year (later six months) before becoming parents. Before 2002, only unpaid leave was available to employees who became new parents.

The second policy concern is that even when statutory maternity/parental benefits are offered, many women workers remain ineligible because they have not worked long enough for the same employer to qualify. This means that the coverage rate is quite low in some jurisdictions. Parental benefits may be available only to those employees who have worked continuously for the same employer for a specified period and/or have worked for a specified number of hours per week. Some countries provide parental benefits to all employees giving birth or adopting children. Others offer payments to all pregnant women regardless of their labour force attachment, but these are usually set at a lower rate than for employment-related benefits.

The financing of maternity/parental benefits is also a controversial issue. These benefits are usually financed either through general revenue (from income taxes and government taxation) or from social insurance contributions (from employers, employees, and sometimes government) that form part of programs for employees who are sick, disabled, or unemployed. If parental benefits are financed from general revenue, the benefit level usually approximates the level of 'welfare' payments. If they are financed through social insurance and vary with earnings, payments are usually more generous, especially for those employees with higher pre-leave earnings, but fewer new parents will qualify. The replacement rate of previous wages varies considerably, from 100 per cent in European countries such as France, Germany, and Norway, to 55 per cent of previous earnings in Canada, to nothing in most of the United States. Where replacement rates are low, parents often take less than the maximum leave entitlement because they need their full earnings for economic survival.

The duration of benefits has also become contentious. As we saw in chapter 6, most OECD countries offer a relatively short period of parental benefits (about fourteen weeks), with the option of longer unpaid leave or extended leave at a lower rate. However, Sweden provides 480 days to either parent (but not both at once), while the Canadian government extended maternity/parental benefits to fifty weeks but continues to pay only 55 per cent of previous wages to a (modest) maximum, which seldom is enough to pay household bills. A short leave period that forces employees to return to work quickly after childbirth could encourage maternal or infant health problems, discourage breastfeeding, and lead to difficulties finding and paying for infant childcare.

Fathers seldom take extended parental leave even when it is paid, but mothers with another income in the household sometimes use extended unpaid leave instead of paying for infant childcare services. However, taking unpaid leave is only available to wealthier families and could also perpetuate a gendered division of labour in the household. In other words, both the duration and level of parental benefits could influence parental behaviour, the household division of labour, and women's employment patterns. In providing paid parental leave, policy makers often implicitly assume that employment patterns are the same for both women and men, yet women are far more likely to work part time, to work fewer hours per week, and to take time off paid work for child rearing.

Adding parental benefits to social insurance programs also changes the original understandings behind those benefits. For example, when maternity/parental benefits form part of unemployment insurance, this alters the age-old expectation that the unemployed worker is available for work. Where leave for childbirth or adoption forms part of disability or sickness benefits, childbirth and adoption are falsely portrayed as illnesses or disabilities. Providing gender-neutral leave programs that could be used by either males or females has sometimes dampened the opposition to contributing to such programs. Nevertheless, where the 'male' model of full-time year-round employment forms the basis of entitlement rules, many women lose access to paid maternity/parental benefits.

The Expansion of Childcare Services

The second area in which family policy has been strengthened in recent years is state funding for public childcare services. Most OECD countries now provide some subsidies for childcare, although many target these to low-income families, families receiving social benefits, or one-parent households. If subsidies are targeted only to low-income parents or beneficiaries, childcare provision is likely to be seen as a 'welfare issue' designed to make mothers more employable and to move them from 'welfare to work.' Some countries, such as Australia and New Zealand, have only recently extended the hours of childcare subsidized by the state to coincide with the hours of full-time work. These countries formerly subsidized only part-time childcare for low-income mothers because these mothers were expected to move from social benefits to paid work only when their youngest child attended school. Once mothers worked full time, the state assumed that they no longer needed childcare subsidies. Now more governments acknowledge that lone mothers are unlikely to be able to support themselves and their children from full-time employment if they must also pay for childcare on the open market. Consequently, entitlement to subsidized care has been expanded in some countries (such as the United Kingdom) to include a broader category of families.

Even when states subsidize childcare services, parents often continue to pay substantial fees because the subsidies pay only a fraction of the actual cost, as in New Zealand. This means that parents themselves are expected to pay the majority of the cost of care. Some are fortunate to have a relative or neighbour to care for their children while they work, but others are forced to reduce their work hours to coincide with school hours or the availability of unpaid care providers. In the Nordic countries, state subsidies pay for most of childcare expenses, and in France early childhood education is financed through the education system and paid for through taxation.

When subsidies are paid directly to parents, policy makers assume that childcare is available in the community, yet many families cannot find affordable and high-quality services close to home, especially if the parents work shifts. For this reason, some states now offer parents more choice in the type of care available for subsidies, extending them to family-based and employer-sponsored care as well as centre-based childcare. However, adding subsidies for more types of care may be accompanied by funding cuts to centre-based care (as in Australia). Governments usually subsidize care that is not-for-profit and regulated by local government, although some jurisdictions also subsidize commercial or franchised care centres. Although private preschools can offer high-quality care, commercial daycares often cut corners by using workers with lower qualifications and paying them less (Brennan 1998; Friendly 2001).

Other childcare policy options include extending both paid and unpaid parental leave entitlements to permit employed parents to care for their own infants or preschoolers at home. Extended employment leave can reduce the public shortage of infant daycare, which is expensive for both parents and the state because it requires a higher staff-child ratio and scrupulous hygiene practices to prevent the spread of disease. However, we already noted that this option requires another income in the household. Also, it is seldom chosen by fathers, although it satisfies the desire of some mothers to care for their children at home.

While most liberal welfare states target childcare subsidies to low-income families and to lone parents, some also provide tax deductions for parents requiring childcare services to maintain their employment. However, this type of government support for childcare provides more meaningful benefits to middle-income families because childcare tax deductions make a smaller reduction of income tax payable for high earners, and low-income families who pay no or little income tax cannot benefit as much from an income tax deduction.[1] Nevertheless, middle-income families clearly need assistance with childcare expenses. We have seen in previous chapters that lack of state support for childcare expenses tends to limit women's employment opportunities as well as their household incomes.

We also saw that those states paying income support to parents (mothers) caring for their children at home (such as Australia and New Zealand) generally have lower rates of full-time maternal employment than states that invest more in childcare subsidies or tax benefits. When children grow up and leave home, these mothers are often left with limited job experience and outmoded skills, and are particularly vulnerable to poverty if they no longer have a male earner in the household. Consequently, state support for childcare in *all* families regardless of household income remains important both to women's opportunities and to family well-being.

Child Benefits and Child Support

Most states provide some measure of income support for families with dependent children in order to encourage reproduction and to acknowl-

---

[1] They would benefit more from a refundable tax credit.

edge the high costs of raising children. However, many states now channel child benefits (but not 'welfare' payments) through the income tax system to enable governments to better target them to household income in the previous taxation year. For example, we saw in chapter 8 that the Canadian federal government combined the former universal family allowance and child tax credits into a targeted child tax benefit in 1993. Work incentives were added for low-earner families, and in recent years the value of this federal benefit has been enhanced.

The child benefit is no longer a universal payment in Canada, but it continues to be available to families with relatively high incomes. The threshold is also set relatively high in Australia, although it is much lower for the child benefit in New Zealand. (The child benefit remains universal in the United Kingdom, but no such benefit ever existed in the United States.) Targeting child benefits to parents who earn moderate or low incomes saves public money and conveys the message that governments expect parents to support their children through paid work. However, children's needs do not depend on their parents' earning activities. Paying a higher child benefit to the children of working parents than to children whose parents are out of the workforce has been seen as inequitable and unjustifiable by anti-poverty groups.

Most countries have also restructured their assessment and enforcement procedures for child support in recent years, acknowledging that former systems were ineffective. In some countries (such as the United States), considerable resources are spent on forcing 'welfare mothers' to name the father of their children, identifying 'dead-beat dads,' and enforcing paternal support. Child support is now enforced through the income tax system in many jurisdictions, which means that payments can be deducted at source along with income tax, and delivered directly to the children's resident parent or through social services departments. The trend to deliver these payments through the taxation department worries some centre-left critics because it removes social policy from people with social service training and places it in the hands of more conservative economists.

Many governments have also altered family taxation practices so that husbands and wives can file separate income tax returns as two individuals rather than as a family unit (Baker 1995). Individual claims benefit working wives and mothers whose earned incomes entitle them to childcare subsidies or other state benefits. Taxing the couple or family as a unit is usually more beneficial to husbands and fathers, who may be able to deduct their wife and children as dependants. This form of taxation may create 'horizontal equity' for families with similar incomes, with and without children, but provides disincentives for the employment of wives. Hence, perceiving 'the family' as a unit in which all members share similar interests may not always be beneficial to women.

Improvements to Child Welfare Practices

In recent years, most states have also made improvements to their child welfare practices, but many services remain under-resourced, especially in the liberal welfare states. Requiring professionals (and sometimes friends and neighbours) to report suspected incidents of child abuse and neglect has increased the detection of these problems but also dramatically raised the caseloads of child welfare workers. In addition, better record keeping about perpetrators and 'at-risk' children requires more surveillance by social service workers. Heavier sentences for convicted abusers also require more work by police, lawyers, social workers, probation officers, and prison officials.

Foster parents are now harder to find, as more women are employed and fewer foster parents can care for children on meagre government allowances. In most jurisdictions, legal adoption procedures have changed and now require stricter measures for gaining informed consent from the birth mother or father. This sometimes means that birth parents disagree about adoption or that birth mothers change their minds after the adoptive parents have bonded with their new child. Since the 1960s, fewer 'stranger' adoptions have taken place in OECD countries, and more now involve stepfamilies, where parents with sole custody share the legal responsibility of their children with their new partner. In addition, greater use is now being made of kin care rather than removing abused or neglected children from their homes and communities and placing them in institutions or with unknown foster parents. However, using kin care sometimes means that the child is left in an impoverished home where conflict or abuse can continue.

Laws or policies preventing the physical punishment of children by parents and teachers have been introduced in some jurisdictions, and the issue has been widely debated in many others. All these child welfare reforms remain controversial because they involve more state intervention in personal life but also more administrative work in detection and case management at a time when social service workforces are stretched to capacity. In addition, some new practices rely heavily on untrained supervisors or family members, whose participation may not improve circumstances for the child, while others require more state resources to become effective.

The quality of child welfare services continues to vary with levels of state funding and the nature of the welfare regime. In the liberal welfare states, more citizens have demanded better child protection services and rigorous law enforcement for perpetrators, including young offenders, but also lower taxes and smaller government. Social agencies acknowledge that many violent families live in poverty and experience multiple problems, but these agencies are forced to search for solutions involving minimal state funding. This means that child protection departments or agencies are either forced to rely more on voluntary organizations and family/community support to resolve these issues, or must attempt to better educate the state and voters on the actual costs of effective protection.

New Ways of Dealing with Violence against Women

Most OECD countries have also reformed the ways that social workers and police deal with violence against women in intimate relationships. Police are now more likely to press charges, and the courts more often punish or attempt to reform perpetrators. Abused women are helped to develop protection plans, are offered transitional housing, and are given income support if necessary. However, women's groups continue to argue that transition houses are underfunded and that too many scarce resources are allocated to programs for perpetrators rather than the women victims and their children. They also argue that international agreements and courts do not always give adequate credence to abused women's psychological, financial, and social circumstances. At the same time, some men's rights groups claim that women are using allegations of abuse as retribution against their former partners or to retain child custody. Politicians wishing to remain in office must deal with these contradictory points of view.

Relationship Rights for Same-Sex Couples

Some states have offered legal relationship rights and spousal benefits to same-sex couples, although this issue remains very controversial in most OECD countries. A number of countries have created a new legal arrangement for same-sex or cohabiting couples called a 'civil union,' as an attempt to avoid the religious opposition to redefining marriage. Civil unions may acquire some but not all of the legal rights of marriage and are often easier to dissolve. However, this policy solution creates two kinds of marriage and may complicate the legal system.

Jurisdictions that recently enabled same-sex marriage have not always allowed for the legal dissolution of these relationships, because the wording of divorce legislation focuses on heterosexual unions. This means that offering relationship rights to same-sex couples may require broader legal changes touching on a variety of family issues such as foster care, adoption, and access to fertility treatments as well as divorce.

Better Pay for Part-time Workers in Some Jurisdictions

The European Union has successfully pressed member states to offer equal hourly wages and prorated employment benefits to part-time workers. This agreement has benefited women more than men, as women are far more likely to work part time. Nevertheless, not all EU countries have signed the agreement, and part-time workers continue to receive lower wages than full-time workers in some member states. Furthermore, women's annual earnings remain even lower than men's because they tend to work shorter hours. In most of the liberal welfare states, part-time jobs are usually paid less than full-time jobs and the wage gap between men and women is particularly high, with larger percentages of women than men working in low-wage jobs without union protection. Consequently, women who work part time throughout their lives are economically disadvantaged. In Australia, the lifetime earnings of part-time women workers tend to remain stable over the years while those of full-time workers usually rise substantially with experience and seniority (Chalmers and Hill 2005).

These are only a few of the areas of family policy that have been improved, although each area retains policy problems and positive changes are not apparent in all jurisdictions. Table 10.1 provides some generalizations about family policies that have been expanded in recent years as well as those that have been eroded; the latter are discussed below.

Which Family Benefits Have Been Eroded?

Cuts to Income Support

In a number of countries, social programs have been restructured around neoliberal principles and practices, creating more stringent employability initiatives and curtailing entitlement to income support. Some juris-

Table 10.1
Overview of the erosion and strengthening of family policies*

Erosion	Strengthening
• Family allowances: universality removed in liberal states (except U.K.) when allowances were converted to tax benefits • Income support reduced to low-income families in many countries (duration reduced and eligibility tightened to tie it to employability) • Support for childcare centres in some places was reduced when family-based and employer-based care was expanded (i.e., Australia) • Direct public funding for contraception and abortion reduced in some jurisdictions (Canada, U.S., Poland) • Taxpayers can no longer claim wife and children as 'dependants' in some jurisdictions • Fathers can no longer receive a tax deduction for child support paid (Canada) • Adoption of children by unrelated families now discouraged • Education allowances cut for young adults living with parents • Social housing has been reduced in some jurisdictions (i.e., selling of state houses in New Zealand and council houses in U.K. in 1990s) • Labour force deregulated or laws made more lenient in some jurisdictions, reducing family income (New Zealand in 1990s)	• Many jurisdictions have raised the level of child benefits or allowances • Childcare subsidies increased for mothers in welfare-to-work programs (i.e., U.K., Australia, New Zealand) • More employer-based childcare and family-based services (U.S., Australia) • Income tax deductions raised for childcare expenses of employed parents (Canada) • Parental benefits improved (i.e., Canada, New Zealand) • Relationship rights to cohabiting and same-sex couples/civil unions (i.e., Belgium, Netherlands, Canada) • Better enforcement of child support after separation in most countries • Child welfare practices improved in most places: higher qualifications for child protection workers, new reporting procedures, informed consent required for adoption, rules against corporal punishment of children, etc. • More services for abused wives or former partners (but shortages of transition housing) • Social housing expanded in some jurisdictions (New Zealand after 2000) • Pay equity and prorated employment benefits for part-time workers (i.e., EU)

* Generalizations are difficult with considerable variation by country.

dictions within the liberal welfare states cut absolute benefit levels in the 1990s, and many limited both entitlement to and duration of benefits. For example, we noted that in 1996 the United States federal government required state governments using federal funds to limit their welfare payments to any individual recipient to two consecutive years or five years over a lifetime. These new rules also stipulate that no additional benefits should be provided for children born to welfare recipients, and expect lone mothers to seek employment but also to name their children's father or forfeit welfare benefits.

The liberal welfare states have attempted to strengthen work incentives for all categories of beneficiaries. Welfare-to-work programs sometimes include educational upgrading, skills training, résumé preparation, interview skills training, confidence building, and assistance with transportation costs and childcare services, which are all valuable services. However, some states urge their 'customers' (beneficiaries) to accept any paid job, and cut their benefits if they refuse. Welfare-to-work programs have been less effective in transforming lone mothers (as opposed to most other categories of beneficiary) into financially secure employees. Generally, those with little education or work experience, several children, and family or personal problems and who are seeking work in a competitive job market experience difficulty in the transition from welfare to work. They may find paid work but have trouble keeping it. Furthermore, the kinds of jobs they are able to find often pay low wages, are temporary, give them low status, and offer few employment benefits.

Most liberal welfare states have also placed greater expectations on middle-income parents to support their children even when those children become post-secondary students. Increasingly, parents are expected to contribute to the cost of tertiary education if their children live with them or if the children are under a specified age and live apart. Until recently, some of these students would have received student allowances even in the liberal states. In social democratic welfare regimes such as Denmark, the state continues to exempt students from tuition fees and also offers living allowances to a larger percentage of the student population.

Some countries also expect parents to support a pregnant teenage daughter if she is under eighteen years old. From the 1970s until recently, many jurisdictions would have offered this woman state income support, enabling her to maintain a dwelling separate from her parents. In addition, some countries are pressuring grandparents to accept the responsibility of custody or financial support for their grandchildren if parents are unable or unwilling to do so.

Reproductive Services

Some states have cut back on direct support for reproductive health services, refusing to provide or to pay the full cost of contraception, sterilization operations, or abortions. For example, the Polish government recently restricted access to abortion after lobbying pressure from the Catholic Church. In the United States, the anti-abortion lobby remains strong, backed by Catholics and fundamentalist Christians. State support for sex education in the schools also remains controversial in the United States, as well as in some other countries. Where the state is uninvolved or has retreated, voluntary organizations such as Planned Parenthood continue to offer sex education and reproductive services, but they depend on private donations or temporary grants from government.

Waiting Lists for Family Services

Although new protocols have been developed for child welfare interventions, these services often fail to meet the needs of families with serious problems. Most jurisdictions have experienced dramatic increases in allegations of child abuse and neglect, and investigating these allegations has created backlogs in systems that are already under-resourced. In addition, high turnover rates among child protection workers are widespread because the work has become even more bureaucratic, challenging, and stressful in recent years. To adequately deal with the rising reports of child abuse, many states outlaw physical punishment, train more nurses and social workers, and place them within the schools. Parents and young people need more effective income support, drug-and-alcohol-abuse programs, relationship counselling, and social housing. However, liberal welfare states continue to focus on families who have already come to the attention of authorities rather than spending more time and money on prevention programs that are more effective in the long term.

The same could be said for violence against women. Although most states seem to be taking this issue more seriously, non-government organizations continue to deliver many of the services to women, children, and perpetrators. This would not be a problem if their funding was secure, if counselling was readily available for all, and if safe social housing was available for homeless and abused women and children. However, many transition houses operate on the verge of closing from lack of resources, and their ability to carry out their mandate depends partly on their own fund-raising activities. This is not a new situation, but reports of violence are increasing faster than funding in some jurisdictions.

Changing Employment Protections

In many countries, working conditions have deteriorated since the 1970s. More people work part time or in temporary jobs, fewer are protected by trade union agreements, employers tend to expect higher qualifications, and wages have not always increased with rising living costs. Some governments have either deregulated the labour force or done little to ensure employment security or pay equity. These governments seemed to have listened more to interest groups representing employer concerns about 'compliance costs,' profit margins, or the need to remain competitive within global markets. In doing so, these governments have failed to improve leave for family responsibilities, statutory holiday entitlement, or childcare subsidies. At the same time that working conditions have deteriorated, more employees have direct responsibility for the care of children and other family members.

Although some governments and employers have introduced paid parental benefits and equity programs for female employees, global labour market changes have actually eroded some of these gains. For example, a number of multinational companies have moved to less developed parts of the world, where production and 'compliance costs' are lower. In other firms, policies to ensure family-related leave and work-life balance have been developed, but these have been counteracted by more competitive working environments that expect higher levels of commitment to paid work. Generally, the 'long-hours culture' discourages reproduction, breastfeeding, family leave, and prolonged employment leave for any reason unrelated to career development. So, even when 'family-friendly' policies are in place, employees may be reluctant to take full advantage of them if they believe that it could disadvantage their career prospects.

The picture that emerges from this review is that a number of employment-related benefits have been strengthened to accommodate the growth of dual-earner couples and more international migration. Children's rights have also been strengthened, as well as measures to protect vulnerable family members. At the same time, labour market changes and neoliberal principles within restructuring have encouraged longer working hours and lower public spending, especially on passive income support. This has meant that more family members are working in the labour market with less time for caring responsibilities.

Which Governments Best Protect Family Benefits?

It is difficult to draw cross-national conclusions about which governments are most supportive to family policies, for a number of reasons. Firstly, governments with similar labels vary considerably among countries and operate within different political, economic, and cultural environments. Secondly, new leaders, political challenges, and public expectations require changes in the platforms of political parties over the years. Thirdly, some governments favour programs for certain types of families but tend to neglect other types. Nevertheless, political ideology is important, and several broad trends are apparent in the family policy issues supported by certain political groups. A few are outlined below and also displayed in Table 10.2 in an oversimplified way but one that I believe is useful way for pedagogy.

Generally, social conservative or centre-right governments and interest groups strive to offer more social protection to the male breadwinner/female caregiver family than to families in which both partners are earners. Conservative governments often provide tax deductions or exemptions for the one-earner family, which usually is comprised of husbands supporting 'dependants' (both wives and children). Conservative governments might also tax the married couple as a unit, which means that when wives earn more than a minimal amount, their husbands must pay more income tax. If wives' employment increases their husband's tax liability, some husbands might dissuade their wives from seeking paid employment, which could encourage a more gendered division of labour at home and jeopardize women's financial security if the marriage dissolves.

Social conservative governments also tend to reinforce the male breadwinner/female caregiver family by promoting public discourse about the importance of mothering at home. In some cases, they might provide state income support for mothers caring for children (or frail elderly relatives) at home. Encouraging the male breadwinner family might also involve subsidizing early childhood education and development programs for several hours per day or week rather than subsidizing employment-related childcare all day, to enable full-time maternal employment. Although these policy approaches are most likely to be accepted by 'conservative' or 'right-of-centre' governments, the male breadwinner family has been the norm in some countries. In Australia, the United Kingdom, and the Netherlands, for example, all governments have granted considerable public support to the maternal care of children at home.

Table 10.2
Right/left views on selected family policies

Support for specific family policy issues	Social conservatives or political right	Social reformers/feminists or political left
1. Focus of family policies	• Male breadwinner/female caregiver family where couple is legally married	• Dual-earner family, regardless of legal status of relationship (all families should be equal in policy)
2. Declining fertility	• A serious problem for Society • Married couples should be encouraged to reproduce	• The state should not interfere with fertility decisions but some policy initiatives are needed to compensate
3. Contraception and abortion	• Sex education should take place at home and perhaps in schools • Contraception should be available within marriage • Abortion should be restricted (i.e., rape and incest) • Christian right says no sex before marriage	• Contraception and abortion should be available to those who need it, including teenagers and unmarried couples
4. Childbirth	• Some support cash grants to encourage fertility and compensate for higher household costs • Mothers should be encouraged to care for their children at home (if husbands can support them)	• Employed mothers and fathers should be given statutory employment leave, flexible working hours, and subsidized childcare services to help them earn a living while raising children
5. Family income support	• Should be available for poor but include strong work requirements • Universal allowances are too costly for taxpayers and unnecessary for the rich	• All families with children should be supported by state to show social support for reproduction and children • Universal child allowances should be paid directly to mothers
6. Childcare services	• Public childcare mainly a welfare issue, to give poor children a 'head start' and enable 'welfare mothers' to enter paid work • Private care for few hours	• Affordable daycare is important for women's employment equity and also for children's early development • Care that is subsidized and regulated by the state is more

Table 10.2 (*Concluded*)

Support for specific family policy issues	Social conservatives or political right	Social reformers/feminists or political left
	per week is beneficial for child development	affordable and guarantees quality
7. Pay equity for women (and others)	• Too costly and complicated for employers	• Important for social justice reasons and because mothers cannot always compete with other workers
8. Civil unions and gay marriage	• 'Marriage' is a heterosexual union blessed by God	• 'Marriage' is a partnership between couples making a public commitment to live together and support each other

Governments supported by Christian right groups tend to be conservative with respect to many aspects of family policy. For example, they are likely to support a gendered family model with a male breadwinner and female caregiver, and might also attempt to increase fertility by providing 'baby bonuses' or cash grants to parents at childbirth. These governments might try to curtail public spending on sex education and contraception and to limit access to abortion. They might attempt to maintain strict requirements for divorce and to preserve legal marriage as a heterosexual relationship. Governments supported by the Christian right might also place strict requirements on who can adopt or receive state funding for assisted conception, with priority given to heterosexual married couples in stable relationships.

In contrast, 'progressive,' 'social democratic,' or 'left-of-centre' governments usually offer more opportunities for both parents to become earners by providing paid maternity or parental leave and subsidizing childcare services that coincide with full-time or shift work. They also tend to be more supportive of pay equity and affirmative action programs to assist women (and other groups) to progress through the ranks. Centre-left governments are also more likely to extend relationship rights and family benefits to same-sex couples. However, all governments must extend some social benefits to male breadwinner families for reasons of fairness and equity, as well as to stay in power.

In recent years, neoliberal governments under conditions of market capitalism have given mixed messages to families. They have elevated the importance of paid employment, home ownership, and the acquisition of family assets, thereby devaluing childbearing and family work (Rudd 2003). They have expected fathers to support their children but have done little to ensure job security or 'fair' wages. Neo-liberal governments have pushed 'welfare mothers' into paid work with inadequate job training, childcare services, and public transportation, but at the same time blamed these mothers when their children seem to be neglected or misbehave. Ironically, neoliberal governments have expected both fathers and low-income mothers to work for a living but have applauded middle-class mothers who care for their children at home.

In some of the corporatist welfare states of western Europe, governments have expected women either to become full-time workers without acknowledging their family responsibilities or to remain at home as mothers. Especially in the southern European countries, women have reacted to this lack of state support by reducing their fertility, as fewer women seem to be prepared to choose large families over financial security. However, other continental European countries, such as Belgium and France, have ensured that extensive childcare services are available for employed mothers. Social democratic governments such as Sweden and Denmark have also provided extensive support for both caring and earning by focusing on universal services and guaranteed incomes.

This suggests that different ideologies about 'family,' parental responsibilities, and the role of the state in family life underlie the social programs developed by political parties. Yet these ideologies often remain implicit. Seldom is there a public debate about the advantages and disadvantages of various family policy options, such as the relative cost to the taxpayer of state income support for mothers caring for children at home compared to the cost of public childcare services. Governments seldom discuss in any open way the values that underlie their policies to support parents and children, although many political parties and interest groups *say* that they support 'family values.'

Family Policy and Future Convergence

As women increasingly remain in paid work throughout their lives, the prevalent model of family that underlies social policy has subtly changed from the male breadwinner/female caregiver model of the 1950s to the dual-earner family of the twenty-first century, which 'outsources' some of the care work and other household tasks. Yet men remain the primary family breadwinner in many countries even when the wife works for pay, and women remain the primary carer. Nevertheless, accommodating or encouraging paid work has become a priority when governments restructure their family policies. Most governments in OECD countries have expanded their employability programs and encouraged both men and women into paid work, but not all governments have successfully dealt with the consequences of more maternal employment, especially the problems of finding suitable care for children and older family members with disabilities.

One of the prevailing themes in welfare state research is the extent of convergence or divergence in social policies among 'advanced market democracies' since the Second World War (Kangas 1991; Jessop 1994; P. Pierson 1994; Mishra 1999). Convergence hypotheses have focused on such concepts as modernization, the logic of industrialism, post-industrialism, 'post-Fordism,' and globalization as driving forces that create similarities among economic institutions, national labour markets, and social rights (Flora 1986; Montanari 2001). Montanari used the term 'old convergence' when referring to hypotheses about modernization and the logic of industrialism and 'new convergence' to refer to hypotheses focusing on post-industrialism, post-Fordism, and globalization, and claimed that the old-convergence thinking predicts the emergence and expansion of welfare states along similar lines, while the new theories predict welfare state retrenchment.

Earlier studies of the convergence of social policies often relied on cross-sectional data that represented a snapshot in time and place. However, convergence is a process. Furthermore, it is difficult to determine which factors cause similarities when countries are at different stages of economic or political development (Monanari 2001). In addition, many quantitative studies have focused on social expenditure as an indicator of the development of social rights, but the levels and changes in social security expenditure often vary with business cycles, variations in unemployment, and demographic changes such as higher divorce rates and more one-parent families in the population. Consequently, they do not always measure social entitlements or social rights, although they may tell us something about political priorities within those countries (Korpi 1989; Esping-Andersen 1990).

Throughout this book, I have suggested that a strong political will to standardize social policies could lead to the adoption of minimum common standards around distinct approaches to family policy, especially within common markets such as the European Union. However, not all member states of these organizations have agreed to sign the relevant agreements or conventions, and some who have signed do not honour their commitment. Yet international pressure to harmonize legal practices and social policies presents national governments with specific policy options and encourages debate about these issues in political situations. Interest groups can also use the international standards to negotiate for reform with governments or to lobby for the status quo if domestic policies are considered to be more generous or effective than alternative proposals..

From the evidence in this book, I would argue that family policy issues will persist on government agendas, especially with continued anxieties about certain socio-demographic trends and with continued pressure for neoliberal restructuring. For example, concerns about population aging and potential labour force shortages will force governments to address a number of family policy concerns. Women's increased presence in paid work, high rates of separation and divorce, and the high poverty rates among lone mothers will continue to require state support (Gauthier 1996). However, especially in the liberal welfare states, government intervention will be restricted by budget constraints, ideologies of non-intervention and individual self-support, and a shift in focus towards concerns about the elderly rather than families with young children. From the evidence presented in chapters 5 to 9, I argue that state support for families will remain a major political issue during the next decades but with budget constraints severely limiting government action.

Future trends in family policy are also likely to focus on targeted tax benefits, reconciliation between family and employment responsibilities, more employer involvement as labour market pressures grow, and better coordination among the different elements of state support. However, cross-national convergence in family programs will continue to be impeded by differences in ideology, cultural preferences, and giving of priority to issues such as public responsibility, equity, and cost containment. Dissimilar institutional arrangements will also interfere with convergence, as will historical precedents and legacies and different perceptions of the state as a welfare provider (Gauthier 1996).

The research findings discussed in this book clearly indicate that the focus of state support for families with children, delivery mechanisms, and levels of funding vary considerably among OECD countries. These variations are influenced by the pace of demographic change, labour market differences, political ideologies, and the relative power and effectiveness of different interest groups within each country. Variations are also influenced by existing institutional structures that reflect the national history of social program delivery in each country as well as vested interests created by these structures. In addition, negotiations among international organizations, governments in power, and interest groups lead to different policy outcomes.

Throughout this book, we have seen that state income support alone cannot ensure the economic and social well-being of families with children, but it can help counteract labour market insecurity and keep more families out of poverty. In addition, I argue that governments need to provide and enhance a variety of social services for families with children. Those countries that view children as a collective responsibility tend to show more positive indicators of family well-being than those who leave child-rearing and childcare to individual parents and their extended families. In addition, governments that maintain some control over job creation, wages, and employment conditions are better able to control family poverty rates than those who permit the market to prevail. Policy makers also need to keep in mind that mothers caring for young children continue to face different challenges than fathers in earning a living, and therefore need special legislation and services in order to create a 'level playing field' in terms of direct caring responsibilities. However, the social and economic circumstances of mothers vary considerably, influencing their opportunities to raise healthy and confident children.

We have seen that those countries with the best outcomes for families offer a variety of social supports. For example, they provide universal income support programs for families with children, universal health services, affordable childcare for both preschool and school-age children, public education, guaranteed child support after separation or divorce, job training and employment assistance, family leave programs, and social housing. These social programs are becoming increasingly important as global markets reduce economic security for some families while improving the financial situation of others. This situation suggests that focusing only on 'at-risk' families will not provide the support that most parents need when earning a living and raising children in a globalizing economy.

Works Cited

Adair, Vivienne, and Christine Rogan. 1998. 'Infertility and Parenting: The Story So Far.' In *The Family in Aotearoa New Zealand*, ed. by V. Adair and R. Dixon, 260–83. Auckland: Addison Wesley Longman.
Adams, Julia, and Tasteem Padamsee. 2001. 'Signs and Regimes: Rereading Feminist Work on Welfare States.' *Social Politics* 8 (1): 1–23.
Akyeampong, Ernest B. 1998. 'Work Absences: New Data, New Insights,' *Perspectives on Labour and Income* 9 (1): 9–17.
Albanese, Patrizia. 2004. 'Abortion and Reproductive Rights under Nationalist Regimes in Twentieth Century Europe.' *Women's Health and Urban Life* 3 (1): 8–33.
– 2005. 'Ethnic Families.' In *Families: Changing Trends in Canada*, ed. M. Baker, 121–42. 5th ed. Toronto: McGraw-Hill Ryerson.
Albury, Rebecca M. 1999. *The Politics of Reproduction: Beyond the Slogans*. Sydney: Allen and Unwin.
Allard, Tom. 2002. 'PM Polishes His Plan for Families,' *Sydney Morning Herald* (online), 18 July. http://www.smh.com.au.
Allen, M., and N. Burrell. 1996. 'Comparing the Impact of Homosexual and Heterosexual Parents of Children: Meta-Analysis of Existing Research.' *Journal of Homosexuality* 32 (2): 19–35.
Amato, Paul., 2004. 'Parenting through Family Transitions.' *Social Policy Journal of New Zealand* 23 (December): 31–44.
Amato, P., and A. Booth. 1997. *A Generation at Risk: Growing Up in an Era of Family Upheaval*. Cambridge, Mass.: Harvard University Press.
Amato, P., and B. Keith. 1991. 'Parental Divorce and the Well-being of Children: A Meta-analysis.' *Psychological Bulletin* 110 (1): 26–46.
Amato, P.R., and S.J. Rezac. 1994. 'Contact with Nonresident Parents, Interparental Conflict, and Children's Behavior.' *Journal of Family Issues* 15 (2): 191–207.

Anttonen, A., and J. Sipalä. 1996. 'European Social Care Services: Is It Possible to Identify Models?' *Journal of European Social Policy* 6 (2): 87–100.

Arai, A. Bruce. 2000. 'Self-Employment as a Response to the Double Day for Women and Men in Canada.' *Canadian Review of Sociology and Anthropology* 37 (2): 125–42.

Arie, Sophie. 2003. 'EU Goes Dutch on Gay Rights.' *The Guardian* 26 September. http://www.guardian.co.uk.

Armstrong, Pat. 1996. 'The Feminization of the Labour Force: Harmonizing Down in a Global Economy.' In *Rethinking Restructuring: Gender and Change in Canada*, ed. by Isabella Bakker, 29–54. Toronto: University of Toronto Press.

Armstrong, P., C. Amaratunga, J. Bernier, K. Grant, A. Pederson, and K. Willson. 2002. *Exposing Privatization: Women and Health Care Reform in Canada*. Toronto: Garamond.

Armstrong, Pat, and Hugh Armstrong. 1984. *The Double Ghetto: Canadian Women and Their Segregated Work*. 2nd ed. Toronto: McClelland and Stewart.

Armstrong, Sarah. 2002. 'Is the Jurisdiction of England and Wales Correctly Applying the 1980 Hague Convention on the Civil Aspects of International Child Abduction?' *International and Comparative Law Quarterly* 51 (April): 427–35.

Atasoy, Yildiz, and William Carroll. 2003. *Global Shaping and Its Alternatives*. Toronto: Garamond.

Australia. Department of Social Security. 1996. *Basic Pension Survey*. Canberra. Department of Social Security.Australia. Parliament. 2000. 'Joint Standing Committee on Treaties.' 13 March. http://wipi.aph.gov.au/search/ParlInfo.ASP.

– 2002. 'Joint Standing Committee on Treaties.' 12 July. http://wipi.aph.gov.au/search/ParlInfo.ASP.

– 2003. Official website. http://www.aph.gov.au.

Australian Bureau of Statistics. 1994. *Labour Force Status and Other Characteristics of Families*. Canberra: Australian Bureau of Statistics.

– 1995. *Australian Social Trends 1995*. Catalogue no. 4012.0. Canberra: Australian Bureau of Statistics.

– 1999. *Australian Social Trends 1999*. Catalogue no. 4102.0. Canberra: Australian Bureau of Statistics.

– 2002. *Births Australia 2001*, Catalogue no. 3301.0. Canberra: Australian Bureau of Statistics.

Ayusawa, Iwao F. 1966. *A History of Labor in Modern Japan*. Honolulu: East-West Centre Press.

Badgley, Robin (Chair). 1984. *Sexual Offences against Children*. Report of the

Parliamentary Committee on Sexual Offences against Children and Youth. Ottawa: Minister of Supply and Services.
Baird, P. 1997. 'Individual Interests, Societal Interests, and Reproductive Technologies' *Perspectives in Biology and Medicine* 40 (3): 440–52.
Baker, Maureen. 1990. 'The Perpetuation of Misleading Family Models in Social Policy: Implications for Women.' *Canadian Social Work Review* 7 (2): 169–82.
– 1994. 'Family and Population Policy in Quebec: Implications for Women.' *Canadian Journal of Women and the Law* 7 (1): 116–32.
– 1995. *Canadian Family Policies: Cross-national Comparisons.* Toronto: University of Toronto Press.
– 1996. 'Social Assistance and the Employability of Mothers: Two Models from Cross-National Research.' *Canadian Journal of Sociology* 21 (4): 483–503.
– 1997. 'Parental Benefit Policies and the Gendered Division of Labour.' *Social Service Review* 71 (1): 51–71.
– 1998. 'Poverty, Ideology and Employability.' *Australian Journal of Social Issues* 33 (4): 355–77.
– 2001a. 'Child Care Policy and Family Policy: Cross-national Examples of Integration and Inconsistency,' In *Our Children's Future: Child Care Policy in Canada*, ed. G. Cleveland and M. Krashinsky, 275–295. Toronto: University of Toronto Press.
– 2001b. *Families, Labour and Love: Family Diversity in a Changing World*. Sydney: Allen and Unwin/Vancouver: University of British Columbia Press.
– 2002a. 'Child Poverty, Maternal Health and Social Benefits,' *Current Sociology* 50 (6): 827–42.
– 2002b. 'Poor Health, Lone Mothers and Welfare Reform: Competing Visions of Employability.' *Women's Health and Urban Life* 1 (2): 4–25.
– 2004a. 'Devaluing Mothering at Home: Welfare Restructuring and "Motherwork."' *Atlantis* 28 (2): 51–60.
– 2004b. 'The Elusive Pregnancy: Choice and Empowerment in Medically Assisted Conception.' *Women's Health and Urban Life* 3 (1): 34–55.
– 2005. 'Families, the State and Family Policies.' In *Families: Changing Trends in Canada*, ed. M. Baker, 258–76. 5th ed. Toronto: McGraw-Hill Ryerson.
Baker, Maureen, and Shelley Phipps. 1997. 'Canada.' In *Family Change and Family Policies in Great Britain, Canada, New Zealand and the United States*, ed. S.B. Kamerman and A.J. Kahn, 103–206. Oxford: Clarendon Press.
Baker, Maureen, and Mary-Anne Robeson. 1981. 'Trade Union Reactions to Women Workers and Their Concerns.' *Canadian Journal of Sociology* 6 (1): 19–31.

Baker, Maureen, and David Tippin. 1999. *Poverty, Social Assistance and the Employability of Mothers: Restructuring Welfare States.* Toronto: University of Toronto Press.
– 2002. 'When Flexibility Meets Rigidity: Sole Mothers' Experience in the Transition from Welfare to Work,' *Journal of Sociology* 38 (4): 345–60.
– 2004. 'More than Just Another Obstacle: Health, Domestic Purposes Beneficiaries, and the Transition to Paid Work.' *Social Policy Journal of New Zealand* 21 (March): 98–120.
Balakrishnan, T.R., Evelyne Lapierre-Adamcyk, and Karol J. Krotki. 1993. *Family and Childbearing in Canada: A Demographic Analysis.* Toronto: University of Toronto Press.
Banting, Keith G., and Charles M. Beach, eds. 1995. *Labour Market Polarization and Social Policy Reform.* Kingston, Ont.: Queen's University, School of Policy Studies.
Barber, J.S., and W.G. Axinn. 1998. 'Gender Differences in the Impact of Parental Pressure for Grandchildren on Young People's Entry into Cohabitation and Marriage,' *Population Studies* 52 (2): 129–44.
Bashevkin, Sylvia. 2002a. *Welfare Hot Buttons: Women, Work, and Social Policy Reform.* Toronto: University of Toronto Press.
– ed. 2002b. *Women's Work Is Never Done: Comparative Studies in Care-Giving, Employment, and Social Policy Reform.* New York: Routledge.
Baxter, Janeen. 1994. *Work at Home: The Domestic Division of Labour.* St. Lucia: University of Queensland Press.
Baxter, Janeen, and Michael Bittman. 1995. 'Measuring Time Spent on Housework: A Comparison of Two Approaches.' *Australian Journal of Social Research* 1 (1): 21–46.
Beaudry, Paul, and David Green. 1997. 'Cohort Patterns in Canadian Earnings.' Working Paper no. 96. Toronto: Canadian Institute for Advanced Research.
– 2000. *Earning and Caring in Canadian Families.* Peterborough: Broadview Press.
Beaujot, Roderic, and Jianye Liu. 2002. 'Children, Social Assistance and Outcomes: Cross-national Comparisons.' Luxembourg Income Study Working Paper no. 304 (unpublished). Syracuse.
Beaumont, Paul, and Peter McEleavy. 1999. *The Hague Convention on International Child Abduction.* Oxford: Oxford University Press.
Beck-Gernsheim, Elisabeth. 2002. *Reinventing the Family: In Search of New Lifestyles.* Cambridge: Polity.
Béland, Daniel. 2005. 'Ideas and Social Policy: An Institutionalist Perspective.' *Social Policy and Administration* 39 (1): 1–18.

Bélanger, Alain, Yves Carrière, and Stéphane Gilbert. 2001. *Report on the Demographic Situation in Canada 2000.* Statistics Canada catalogue no. 91-209-XPE. Ottawa: Minister of Industry.

Benoit, Cecilia, Dena Carroll, and Alison Millar. 2002. 'But Is It Good for Non-urban Women's Health? Regionalizing Maternity Care Services in British Columbia.' *Canadian Review of Sociology and Anthropology* 39 (4): 373–96.

Bergart, Ann M. 2000. 'The Experience of Women in Unsuccessful Infertility Treatment: What Do Patients Need When Medical Intervention Fails?' *Social Work in Health Care* 30 (4): 45–69.

Bernard, Paul, and Sébastien Saint-Arnaud. 2004. 'Du pareil au meme? La position des quatre principales provinces canadiennes dans l'univers des regimes providentiels.' *Canadian Journal of Sociology* 29 (2): 209–39.

Bharadwaj, A. 2000. 'How Some Indian Baby Makers Are Made: Media Narratives and Assisted Conception in India.' *Anthropology and Medicine* 17: 63–78.

Bianchi, Suzanne M., Lynne M. Casper, and Pia K. Peltola. 1999. 'A Cross-national Look at Married Women's Earnings Dependency.' *Gender Issues* 17 (3): 3–33.

Bibby, Reginald W. 2004–5. 'Future Families: Surveying Our Hopes, Dreams, and Realities.' *Transition* 34 (4): 3–14.

Bittman, Michael. 1991. *Juggling Time.* Canberra: Australian Bureau of Statistics.

– 1995. *Recent Changes in Unpaid Work.* Catalogue no. 4154.0. Canberra: Australian Bureau of Statistics.

– 1998. 'The Land of the Lost Long Weekend? Trends in Free Time among Working Age Australians.' Social Policy Research Centre Discussion Paper no. 83. Sydney: University of New South Wales.

– 2004. 'Sunday Working and Family Time.' Paper presented to the conference Work-Life Balance across the Lifecourse, University of Edinburgh.

Bittman, Michael, and Jocelyn Pixley. 1997. *The Double Life of the Family: Myth, Hope and Experience.* Sydney: Allen and Unwin.

Bittman, Michael and James Rice. 1999. 'Is the End of the Second Shift in Sight? The Role of Income, Bargaining Power, Domestic Technology, and Market Substitutes.' Paper presented at Annual Meeting of the Australian Sociologists Association (TASA), Monash University, Melbourne.

Bock, Gisela, and Pat Thane, eds. 1991. *Maternity and Gender Policies: Women and the Rise of European Welfare States 1880s–1950s.* London: Routledge.

Bolderson, Helen, and Deborah Mabbett. 1991. *Social Policy and Social Security in Australia, Britain and the USA.* Aldershot, UK: Avebury.

Borchorst, Anette. 1994. 'Welfare State Regimes, Women's Interests and the EC.' In *Gendering Welfare States,* ed. D. Sainsbury, 26–44. London: Sage.

Bosch, Xavier. 1998. 'Spanish Doctors Criticised for High Tech Births.' *British Medical Journal* 317 (7170): 1406.

Boyd, Susan B. 2003. *Child Custody, Law, and Women's Work*. Toronto: Oxford University Press.

Bradbury, Bruce. 1996. *Income Support for Parents and Other Carers*. Sydney: University of New South Wales, Social Policy Research Centre.

Bradshaw, Jonathan. 2003. 'How Has the Notion of Social Exclusion Developed in the European Discourse?' Keynote address to the Australian Social Policy Conference, University of New South Wales, Sydney.

Bradshaw, Jonathan, and Naomi Finch. 2002. *A Comparison of Child Benefit Packages in 22 Countries*. UK Department for Work and Pensions Research Report no. 174. Leeds: Corporate Document Services.

Brennan, Deborah. 1998. *The Politics of Australian Child Care: Philanthropy to Feminism and Beyond*. Melbourne: Cambridge University Press.

Briar-Lawson, Katherine, Hal Lawson, Charles Hennon, and Alan Jones. 2001. *Family-Centred Policies and Practices: International Implications*. New York: Columbia University Press.

Brodie, Janine. 1996. 'Restructuring and the New Citizenship.' In *Rethinking Restructuring: Gender and Change in Canada*, ed. Isabella Bakker, 126–40. Toronto: University of Toronto Press.

Brooks, Bradley, Jennifer Jarman, and Robert M. Blackburn. 2003. 'Occupational Gender Segregation in Canada, 1981–1996: Overall, Vertical and Horizontal Segregation', *Canadian Review of Sociology and Anthropology* 40 (2): 197–213.

Brush, Lisa D. 2002. 'Changing the Subject: Gender and Welfare State Regime Studies', *Social Politics* 9 (2): 161–86.

Bryson, Lois. 1992. *Welfare and the State*. London: Macmillan.

Bryson, Lois, and P. Warner-Smith. 1998. 'Employment and Women's Health.' *Just Policy* 14: 3–14.

Burghes, L. 1994. *Lone Parenthood and Family Disruption*. Occasional Paper no. 18. London: Family Policy Studies Centre.

Callahan, M., et al. 1990. 'Workfare in British Columbia: Social Development Alternatives.' *Canadian Review of Social Policy* 26: 15–25.

Callan, Victor J. 1982. 'Australian, Greek and Italian Parents: Differentials in the Value and Cost of Children.' *Journal of Comparative Family Studies* 13 (1): 49–61.

– 1987. 'The Personal and Marital Adjustment of Mothers and of Voluntarily and Involuntarily Childless Wives.' *Journal of Marriage and the Family* 49 (November): 847–56.

Cameron, Jan. 1990. *Why Have Children? A New Zealand Case Study.* Christchurch: Canterbury University Press.
– 1997. *Without Issue: New Zealanders Who Choose Not to Have Children.* Christchurch: Canterbury University Press.
Canada. Department of Justice. 2003. 'Child Support.' http://canada.justice.gc.ca/en/ps/sup/index.html.
Canadian Council on Social Development. 1996. 'Presentation to the Parliamentary Standing Committee on Human Resources Development on UI.' Ottawa: CCSD.
– 2004. 'What Kind of Canada? A Call for a National Debate on the Canada Social Transfer.' Ottawa: CCSD.
Canadian Institute of Child Health. 2002. *The Health of Canada's Children.* 3rd ed. Ottawa: CIH.
Cancian, M., R. Haveman, T. Kaplan, D. Meyer, and B. Wolfe. 1999. 'Work, Earnings and Well-being after Welfare: What Do We Do?' In *Economic Conditions and Welfare Reform: What Are the Early Lessons?* ed. S. Danziger. Kalamazoo, Mich.: Upjohn Institute.
Cantillon, Bea, and Karel Van den Bosch. 2002. *Social Policy Strategies to Combat Income Poverty of Children and Families in Europe.* Luxembourg Income Study Working Paper no. 336. http://www.lisproject.org
Carling, Alan. 2002. 'Family Policy, Social Theory and the State.' In *Analysing Families: Morality and Rationality in Policy and Practice,* ed. Alan Carling, Simon Duncan, and Rosalind Edwards, 3–20. London: Routledge.
Cartwright, Claire. 2002. *Parent–Child Relationships in Families of Remarriage: What Hurts? What Helps?* Doctoral diss. University of Auckland.
Cass, Bettina. 1989. 'Children's Poverty and Labour Market Issues.' In *Child Poverty,* ed. D. Edgar, D. Keane, and P. McDonald, 146–72. Sydney: Allen and Unwin.
– 1992. 'Fightback: The Politics of Work and Welfare in the 1990s.' *Australian Quarterly* 64 (2): 140–61.
Castles, Francis G. 1985. *The Working Class and Welfare: Reflections on the Political Development of the Welfare State in Australia and New Zealand, 1890–1980.* Sydney: Allen and Unwin.
– 1996. 'Needs-Based Strategies of Social Protection in Australia and New Zealand.' In *Welfare States in Transition: National Adaptations in Global Economies,* ed. G. Esping-Andersen, 88–115. London: Sage.
– 2002. 'Three Facts about Fertility: Cross-National Lessons for the Current Debate.' *Family Matters* 63 (Spring/Summer): 22–7.

Castles, Francis G., and Christopher Pierson. 1995. 'New Convergence? Recent Policy Developments in the United Kingdom, Australia and New Zealand,' *Policy and Politics* 24 (3): 233–45.

Castles, Francis G., and Ian F. Shirley. 1996. 'Labour and Social Policy: Gravediggers or Refurbishers of the Welfare State?' In *The Great Experiment: Labour Parties and Public Policy Transformation in Australia and New Zealand*, ed. F. Castles, R. Gerritsen, and J. Vowles, 88–106. Auckland: Auckland University Press.

Centre for Reproductive Rights. 2004. *Women of the World: Laws and Policies Affecting Their Reproductive Lives.* Available at http://www.crlp.org (accessed 4 February 2004).

Centre of Reproductive Rights and Policy. 2003. *Abortion and Human Rights.* Available at http://www.crrp.org (accessed on 27 November 2003).

Chalmers, Jenny. 1999. *Sole Parent Exit Study: Final Report.* Sydney: University of New South Wales, Social Policy Research Centre.

Chalmers, Jenny, and Trish Hill. 2005. 'Part-Time Work and Women's Careers: Advancing or Retreating?' Paper presented to the Australian Social Policy Conference, University of New South Wales, Sydney.

Chaykowski, Richard P., and Lisa M. Powell, eds. 1999. *Women and Work.* Kingston, Ont.: Queen's University, John Deutsch Institute for the Study of Economic Policy.

Cheal, David. 1996. 'Stories about Step-families.' In *Growing Up in Canada: National Longitudinal Survey of Children and Youth*, Ottawa: 93–101. Ottawa: Human Resources Development Canada and Statistics Canada.

Chesnais, J.C. 1992. *The Demographic Transition: Stages, Patterns, and Economic Implications.* Oxford: Clarendon.

Cheyne, Christine, Mike O'Brien, and Michael Belgrave. 2000. *Social Policy in Aotearoa New Zealand.* 2nd ed. Auckland: Oxford University Press.

Childcare Resource and Research Unit. 2003. 'Childcare in the News.' 11 December. http://www.childcarecanada.org

Christopher, Karen. 2002. 'Welfare State Regimes and Mothers' Poverty.' *Social Politics* 9 (1): 60–86.

Christopher, K., P. England, S. McLanahan, K. Ross, and T.M. Smeeding, 2001. 'Gender Inequality in Affluent Nations: The Role of Single Motherhood and the State.' In *Child Wellbeing, Child Poverty and Child Policy in Modern Nations*, ed. K. Vleminckx and T.M. Smeeding, 199–220. Bristol: Policy Press.

Clark, J. 1995. *Kinship Foster Care: An Overview of Research Findings and Policy-Related Issues.* Unpublished report, Department of Human Development and Families Studies, Pennsylvania State University.

Cleveland, Gordon, and Michael Krashinsky. 2003. *Fact and Fantasy: Eight Myths about Early Childhood Education and Care.* Monograph published by the Childcare Resource and Research Unit, University of Toronto.

Coester-Waltjen, Dogmar. 2000. 'The Future of the Hague Child Abduction Convention: The Rise of Domestic and International Tensions – The European Perspective.' *International Law and Politics* 33: 59–82.

Coney, Sandra, & Else, Anne. 1999. *Protecting Our Future: The Case for Greater Regulation of Assisted Reproductive Technology.* Auckland: Women's Health Action Trust with the New Zealand Law Foundation.

Connolly, Marie. 2003. *Kinship Care: A Selected Literature Review.* Unpublished paper prepared for the Department of Child Youth and Family Services. Wellington: New Zealand.

Cook, Kay, Kim Raine, and Deanna Williamson. 2001. 'The Health Implications of Working for Welfare Benefits: The Experiences of Single Mothers in Alberta, Canada.' *Health Promotion Journal of Australia* 11 (1): 20–6.

Council of Europe. 1950. *Convention for the Protection of Human Rights and Fundamental Freedoms.* Available at http://www.echr.coe.int (accessed on 15 December 2003).

– 1961. *European Social Charter.* Available at http://www.coe.int (accessed on 14 December 2003).

– 1996. *European Social Charter (revised).* Available at http://www.coe.int (accessed on 14 December 2003).

Crompton, Rosemary. 2004. 'Women's Employment and Work/Life Balance in Britain and Europe.' Plenary address at the conference Work/Life Balance across the Life Course, University of Edinburgh.

Crouch, John. 2003. 'The Hague Convention on the Civil Aspects of International Child Abduction.' http://patriot.net/~crouch/flnc/hague.html.

Curtis, Lori J. 2001. 'Lone Motherhood and Health Status.' *Canadian Public Policy* 27 (3): 335–56.

Dalto, G.C. 1989. 'A Structural Approach to Women's Hometime and Experience-Earnings Profile: Maternity Leave and Public Policy.' *Population Research and Policy Review* 8: 246–66.

Daly, Mary, and Katherine Rake. 2003. *Gender and the Welfare State.* Cambridge: Polity.

Daune-Richard, Manne-Marie, and Rianne Mahon. 2003. 'Sweden: Models in Crisis.' In *Who Cares? Women's Work, Childcare, and Welfare State Redesign,* ed. Jane Jenson and Mariette Sineau, 146–76. Toronto: University of Toronto Press.

Davies, Lorraine, and Patricia Jane Carrier. 1999. 'The Importance of Power

Relations for the Division of Household Labour.' *Canadian Journal of Sociology* 24 (1): 35–51.
Davis, Sandra, Jeremy Rosenblatt, and Tanya Galbraith. 1993. *International Child Abduction*. London: Sweet and Maxwell.
Degeling, Jennifer, ed. 2000. *International Child Abduction News*, No. 19 (December). http://www.law.gov.au/childabduction.
Dempsey, K. 1997. *Inequalities in Work and Marriage: Australia and Beyond*. Melbourne: Oxford University Press.
– 1999. 'Resistance and Change: Trying to Get Husbands to Do More Housework.' Paper presented to TASA Annual Meetings, Monash University. Melbourne.
Dickson, Janet, D. Ball, J. Edmeades, S. Hanson, and I. Pool. 1997. *Recent Trends in Reproduction and Family Structures*. Waikato, NZ: University of Waikato, Population Studies Centre.
Dodson, Louise. 2004. 'The Mother of All Spending Sprees.' *Sydney Morning Herald*, 5 December. http://www.smh.com.au.
Doherty, Gillian, Martha Friendly, and Mab Oloman. 1998. *Women's Support, Women's Work: Child Care in an Era of Deficit Reduction, Devolution, Downsizing and Deregulation*. Ottawa: Status of Women Canada.
Dooley, Martin. 1995. 'Lone-Mother Families and Social Assistance Policy in Canada.' In *Family Matters: New Policies for Divorce, Lone Mothers, and Child Poverty*, ed. M. Dooley et al. Toronto: C.D. Howe Institute.
Dorsett, Richard, and Alan Marsh. 1998. *The Health Trap: Poverty, Smoking and Lone Parenthood*. London: Policy Studies Institute.
Doyal, L. 1995. *What Makes Women Sick: Gender and the Political Economy of Health*. New Brunswick, N.J.: Rutgers University Press.
Drolet, Marie, and René Morissette. 1997. 'Working More? What Do Workers Prefer?' *Perspectives on Labour and Income* 9 (4): 32–8.
Drover, Glenn, and Patrick Kerans, eds. 1993. *New Approaches to Welfare Theory*. Aldershot, UK: Edward Elgar.
Duffy, Ann. 1997. 'The Part-Time Solution: Toward Entrapment or Empowerment.' In *Good Jobs, Bad Jobs, No Jobs*, ed. A. Duffy, D. Glenday, and N. Pupo. Toronto: Harcourt Brace.
Duffy, Ann, and Norene Pupo. 1992. *Part-Time Paradox: Connecting Gender, Work and Family*. Toronto: McClelland and Stewart.
Dulac, Germain. 1995. 'Rupture d'union et deconstruction du lien père-enfant.' *Prisme* 5 (3): 300–12.
Eardley, Tony, Jonathon Bradshaw, John Ditch, Ian Gough, and Peter Whiteford. 1996. *Social Assistance in OECD Countries: Country Reports*. Department of Social Security Research Report no. 47. London: HMSO.

Edin, Kathryn. 2003. 'Work Is Not Enough.' Plenary speech to Australian Social Policy Conference, University of New South Wales, Sydney.
Edin, Kathryn, and Laura Lein. 1997. *Making Ends Meet: How Single Mothers Survive Welfare and Low-Wage Work*. New York: Russell Sage Foundation.
Edwards, Anne, and Susan Magarey, eds. 1995. *Women in a Restructuring Australia: Work and Welfare*. Sydney: Allen and Unwin.
Eichler, Margrit. 1996. 'The Impact of New Reproductive and Genetic Technologies on Families.' In *Families: Changing Trends in Canada*, ed. M. Baker, 104–118. 3rd ed. Toronto: McGraw-Hill Ryerson.
– 1997. *Family Shifts: Families, Policies, and Gender Equality*. Toronto: Oxford University Press.
Eichler, Margrit. 2005. 'Biases in Family Literature.' In *Families: Changing Trends in Canada*, ed. M. Baker, 52–68. 5th ed. Toronto: McGraw-Hill Ryerson.
Elizabeth, Vivienne. 2000. 'Cohabitation, Marriage, and the Unruly Consequences of "Difference"', *Gender and Society* 14 (1): 87–100.
Elliott, J., and M. Richards. 1991. 'Parental Divorce and the Life Chances of Children.' *Family Law*: 481–4.
Emery, R. 1994. 'Psychological Research on Children, Parents, and Divorce.' In *Renegotiating Family Relationships: Divorce, Child Custody, and Mediation*, ed. R. Emery, 194–217. New York: Guildford:
Esping-Andersen, Gøsta. 1990. *The Three Worlds of Welfare Capitalism*. Cambridge: Polity.
– ed. 1996. *Welfare States in Transition: National Adaptations in Global Economies*. London: Sage.
– 2002. 'A Child-Centred Social Investment Strategy.' In *Why We Need a New Welfare State*, ed. G. Esping Andersen with D. Gallie, A. Hemerijck, and J. Myles, 26–67. Oxford: Oxford University Press.
European Parliament. 2002. *Report on Sexual Health and Rights*. Committee on Women's Rights and Equal Opportunities. Final Session Document A5-0223/2002. Available at http://www.europarl.eu.int (accessed on 12 December 2003).
European Union. 1992. *Treaty on European Union*. Available http://www.europa.eu.int (accessed on 12 December 2003).
Evans, Patricia. 1988. 'Work Incentives and the Single Mother: Dilemmas of Reform.' *Canadian Public Policy* 14 (2): 125–36.
– 1996. 'Single Mothers and Ontario's Welfare Policy: Restructuring the Debate.' In *Women in Canadian Public Policy*, ed. Janine Brodie, 151–71. Toronto: Harcourt Brace.
Everingham, Christine. 1994. *Motherhood and Modernity*. Sydney: Allen and Unwin.

Exley, Catherine, and Gayle Letherby. 2001. 'Managing a Disrupted Lifecourse: Issues of Identity and Emotional Work.' *Health* 5 (1): 112–32.

Fast, Janet, and Moreno Da Pont. 1997. 'Changes in Women's Work Continuity.' *Canadian Social Trends* 46: 2–7.

Ferri, E. 1984. *Step Children: A National Study*. Windsor, UK: NFER-Nelson.

Finkle, Jason L., and C. Alison McIntosh. 2002. 'United Nations Population Conferences: Shaping the Policy Agenda for the Twenty-first Century.' *Studies in Family Planning* 33 (1): 11–23.

Flaquer, Lluís. 2000. 'Is There a Southern European Model of Family Policy?' In *Families and Family Policies in Europe: Comparative Perspectives*, ed. A. Pfenning and T. Bahle, 15–33. Frankfort: Peter Lang.

Flora, Peter, ed. 1986. *Growth to Limits: The Western European Welfare States since World War II*. Berlin: Walter De Gruyter.

Fooks, Cathy, and Bob Gardner. 1986. The Implementation of Midwifery in Ontario. Current Issue Paper no. 50. Toronto: Ontario Legislative Library.

Ford, J., N. Nassar, E. Sullivan G. Chambers, and P. Lancaster. 2003. *Reproductive Health Indicators, Australia, 2002*. Sydney: Australian Institute of Health and Welfare.

Franklin, S. 1995. 'Postmodern Procreation: A Cultural Account of Assisted Reproduction.' In *Conceiving the New World Order: The Global Politics of Reproduction*, ed. F. Ginsburg and R. Rapp. Los Angeles: University of California Press.

Friedan, Betty. 1963. *The Feminine Mystique*. New York: W.W. Norton.

Freiler, Christa, and Judy Cerny. 1998. *Benefiting Canada's Children: Perspectives on Gender and Social Responsibility*. Ottawa: Status of Women Canada.

Friedman, Milton. 1962. *Capitalism and Freedom*. Chicago: University of Chicago Press.

Friendly, Martha. 2001. 'Child Care and Canadian Federalism in the 1990s: Canary in a Coal Mine.' In *Our Children's Future: Child Care Policy in Canada*, ed. G. Cleveland and M. Krashinsky, 25–61. Toronto: University of Toronto Press:

Funder, Kathleen. 1996. *Remaking Families: Adaptation of Parents and Children to Divorce*. Melbourne: Australian Institute of Family Studies.

Furstenberg, Frank, and Andrew J. Cherlin. 1991. *Divided Families: What Happens to Children when Parents Part*. Cambridge: Harvard University Press.

Furstenberg, F., F. Morgan, and P. Allison. 1987. 'Paternal Participation and Children's Well-Being after Marital Dissolution.' *American Sociological Review* 52: 695–701.

Gallie, Duncan. 1998. 'Unemployment and Social Exclusion in the European

Union.' Paper presented to Canada in International Perspective 1998 conference, at Queen's University.

Galtry, Judith. 2003. 'The Impact of Breastfeeding on Labour Market Policy and Practice in Ireland, Sweden and the USA.' *Social Science and Medicine* 57 (1): 167–77.

Garnaut, John. 2003. 'PM Backs Abbott's Radical "Maxi" Welfare Reforms.' *Sydney Morning Herald*, 13 January http://www.smh.com.au.

Gauthier, Anne Hélène. 1996. *The State and the Family: A Comparative Analysis of Family Policies in Industrialized Countries*. Oxford: Clarendon.

– 2001. 'Family Policies and Families' Well-being: An International Comparison.' In *Our Children's Future: Child Care Policy in Canada*, ed. Gordon Cleveland and Michael Krashinsky, 251–74. Toronto: University of Toronto Press.

Gazso-Windle, Amber, and Julie Ann McMullin. 2003. 'Doing Domestic Labour: Strategising in a Gendered Domain.' *Canadian Journal of Sociology* 28 (3): 341–66.

Gemmel, David James. 2003. *Association of Temporal Variations and Hospital Ownership with Cesarean Sections*. Unpublished doctoral diss., University of Michigan.

Gershuny, Jonathan, and Oriel Sullivan. 2003. 'Time Use, Gender, and Public Policy Regimes.' *Social Politics* 10 (2): 205–28.

Giddens, Anthony. 1992. *The Transformation of Intimacy: Sexuality, Love and Eroticism in Modern Societies*. Cambridge: Polity.

Gillespie, R. 1999. 'Voluntary Childlessness in the United Kingdom.' *Reproductive Health Matters* 7 (3): 43–53.

Gillett, W., and J. Peek. 1997. *Access to Infertility Services: Development of Priority Criteria*. Wellington: National Health Committee.

Girvin, Brian. 1996. 'Ireland and the European Union: The Impact of Integration and Social Change on Abortion Policy.' In *Abortion Politics: Public Policy in Cross Cultural Perspective*, ed. M. Githens and D. McBride Stetson, 165–184. New York: Routledge.

Goldscheider, Frances, and Gayle Kaufman. 1996. 'Fertility and Commitment: Bringing Men Back In.' *Population and Development Review* 22 (Supplement): 87–92.

González-López, Maria José. 2002. 'A Portrait of Western Families: New Modes of Intimate Relationships and the Timing of Life Events.' In *Analysing Families: Morality and Rationality in Policy and Practice*, ed. A. Carling, S. Duncan, and R. Edwards 21–48. London: Routledge.

Goode, William. 1963. *World Revolution and Family Patterns*. New York: Free Press.

Goodnow, J.J. 1989. 'Work in Households: An Overview and Three Studies.' In *Households Work*, ed. D. Ironmonger. Sydney: Allen and Unwin.

Goodnow, J.J., and D. Susan. 1989. 'Children's Household Work: Task Differences, Styles of Assigment, and Links to Family Relationships.' *Journal of Applied Developmental Psychology* 10: 209–26.

Gornick, Janet C. 2000. 'Family Policy and Mothers' Employment: Cross-national Variations.' In *Gender, Welfare State and the Market: Towards a New Division of Labour*, ed. T. Boje and A. Leira, 111–32. London: Routledge:

Gough, Ian. 2000. *Global Capital, Human Needs and Social Policies*. Houndmills, UK: Palgrave.

Government of Canada. 1994. *Improving Social Security in Canada*. Ottawa: Human Resources Development Canada.

Government of Australia. Committee on Employment Opportunities. 1994. *Working Nation*. White Paper. Canberra: Australian Government Publishing Service.

– 2003. The Family Assistance Office website. 18 September. http://www.familyassist.gov.au.

Government of Quebec. 1997. 'La Nouvelle allocation familiale.' Pamphlet.

Graham-Bermann, Sandra, and Jeffrey Edleson. 2001. 'Introduction.' In *Domestic Violence in the Lives of Children: The Future of Research, Intervention and Social Policy*, ed. S. Graham-Bermann and J. Edleson. Washington, D.C.: American Psychological Association.

Greenwood, Gaye A. 1999. Dissolution of Marriage: Public Policy and 'The Family-Apart.' Unpublished master's thesis, Massey University.

Guardian. 2004. 'Pope Has Warning on Role of Women.' Reprinted in *Sunday Star-Times* (New Zealand), 1 August.

Guest, Dennis. 1997. *The Emergence of Social Security in Canada*. 3rd edition. Vancouver: UBC Press.

Haas, Linda. 1990. 'Gender Equality and Social Policy: Implications of a Study of Parental Leave in Sweden.' *Journal of Family Issues* 11 (4): 401–23.

Hague Conference on Private International Law. 1980 'Convention on the Civil Aspects of International Child Abduction.' 25 October. (Contains full text of Convention no. 28.) http://www.hcch.net/e/conventions/text28e.html.

Hakim, C. 2000. *Work-Lifestyle Choices in the 21st Century*. Oxford: Oxford University Press.

Haney, Lynne. 2003. 'Welfare Reform with a Familial Face: Reconstituting State and Domestic Relations in Post-Socialist Eastern Europe.' In *Families of a New World: Gender, Politics and State Development in a Global Context*, ed. L. Haney and L. Pollard, 159–78. New York: Routledge.

Hantrais, Linda, and M.-T. Letablier. 1996. *Families and Family Policies in Europe*. London: Longman.
– 2000. *Social Policy in the European Union*. 2nd ed. Houndmills, UK: Macmillan.
– 2004. *Family Policy Matters: Responding to Family Change in Europe*. Bristol: Policy.
Harris, K.M. 1996. 'Life after Welfare: Women, Work and Repeat Dependency.' *American Sociological Review* 61: 407–26.
Harrison, Margaret. 1991. 'The Reformed Australian Child Support Scheme: An International Policy Comment.' *Australian Journal of Social Issues* 12 (4): 430–49.
– 1993. 'Patterns of Maintenance over Time.' In *Settling Down: Pathways of Parents After Divorce*, ed. K. Funder, M. Harrison, and R. Weston, 116–34. Melbourne: Australian Institute of Family Studies.
Hartmann, H.I. 1981. 'The Family as the Locus of Gender, Class and Political Struggle: The Example of Housework.' *Signs* 6 (3): 366–94.
Hayek, F. 1948. *Individualism and Economic Order*. Chicago: University of Chicago Press.
Health Canada 2000. *Canadian Perinatal Health Report 2000*. Ottawa: Minister of Health. Available at http://www.hc-sc.gc.ca (accessed 16 December 2003).
– 2003. *Canadian Perinatal Health Report 2003*. Ottawa: Minister of Health.
Heitlinger, Alena. 1993. *Women's Equality, Demography, and Public Policy: A Comparative Perspective*. London: Macmillan.
Held, David, and Anthony McGrew. 2002. *Globalization/Antiglobalization*. Cambridge: Polity.
Henshaw, Stanley, Susheela Singh, and Taylor Haas. 1999. 'Recent Trends in Abortion Rates Worldwide.' *Family Planning Perspectives* 25 (1). http://www.agi-usa.org/pubs/journals/2504499.html.
Hernes, Helga Maria. 1987. *Welfare State and Woman Power: Essays in State Feminism*. Oslo: Norwegian University Press.
Hettne, Bjorn, Andras Inotai, and Osvaldo Sunkel (eds). 1999. *Globalism and the New Regionalism*. vol. 1. Basingstoke: Macmillan.
Hinsliff, Gaby. 2004. 'Emergency Childcare for Working Mothers.' *The Guardian*, 1 August. online. http://www.guardian.co.uk
Hobcraft, John, and Kathleen Kiernan. 2001. 'Childhood Poverty, Early Motherhood and Adult Social Exclusion.' *British Journal of Sociology* 52 (3): 495–517.
Hochschild, Arlie Russell. 1989. *The Second Shift: Working Parents and the Revolution at Home*. New York: Viking Penguin.

Hulse, Carl. 2004. 'Senators Block Initiatives to Band [sic] Same-Sex Unions.' *The New York Times*. http://www.nytimes.com/2004/07/15.

Human Fertilisation and Embryology Authority. 1997. *Sixth Annual Report*. London: HFEA.

Human Resources Development Canada. 1994. *Basic Facts on Social Programs*. Ottawa: Minister of Supply and Services.

Hunsley, Terrance. 1997. *Lone Parent Incomes and Social Policy Outcomes: Canada in International Perspective*. Kingston, Ont.: Queen's University, School of Policy Studies.

Hunt, J. 2003. *Family and Friends Carers*. Report prepared for the UK Department of Health. http://www.doh.gov.uk/carers/familyandfriends.htm.

Immervol, Herwig, Holly Sutherland, and Klaas de Vos. 2001. 'Reducing Child Poverty in the European Union: The Role of Child Benefits.' In *Child Well-Being, Child Poverty and Child Policy in Modern Nations: What Do We Know?* ed. K. Vleminckx and T. Smeeding, 407–32. Bristol: Policy.

International Baby Food Action Network. 2000. 'Maternity Protection Coalition Press Release, 5th June 2000, Hard Bargaining at the ILO.' http://www.ibfan.org (accessed on 5 January 2004).

International Labour Organisation. 2000a. 'International Labour Conference, 88th Session, 30 May–15 June 2000.' Geneva: International Labour Office.

– 2000b. 'International Labour Standards on Maternity Protection.' http://www.ilo.org (accessed on 10 February 2004).

Jackson, A., and P. Roberts. 2001. 'Physical Housing Conditions and the Well-Being of Children.' Background paper on housing prepared for the report *The Progress of Canada's Children 2001*. Ottawa: Canadian Council on Social Development.

Jackson, Andrew, and Matthew Sanger. 2003. *When Worlds Collide: Implications of International Trade and Investment Agreements for Non-Profit Social Services*. Ottawa: Canadian Council on Social Development.

Jaffe, Peter, Nancy Lemon, and Samantha Poisson. 2003. *Child Custody and Domestic Violence: A Call for Safety and Accountability*. Thousand Oaks, Calif.: Sage.

Jaffe, Peter, Marlies Suderman, and Robert Geffner. 2000. 'Emerging Issues for Children Exposed to Domestic Violence.' In *Children Exposed to Domestic Violence: Current Issues in Research, Intervention, Prevention, and Policy Development*, ed. Peter Jaffe, Marlies Suderman, and Robert Geffner. New York: Haworth.

Jamieson, Lynn. 1998. *Intimacy: Personal Relationships in Modern Societies*. Cambridge: Polity Press.

Jansson, J., and M. Gahler. 1997. 'Family Dissolution, Family Reconstruction, and Children's Educational Careers: Recent Evidence from Sweden.' *Demography* 34 (2): 277–93.

Jeandidier, Bruno, and Etienne Albiser. 2001. *To What Extent Do Family Policy and Social Assistance Transfers Equitably Reduce the Intensity of Child Poverty? A Comparison between the US, France, Great Britain and Luxembourg.* Luxembourg Income Study Working Paper no. 255 (unpublished). http://www.lisproject.org.

Jenson, Jane. 2004. 'Changing the Paradigm: Family Responsibility or Investing in Children.' *Canadian Journal of Sociology* 29 (2): 169–92.

– 1996. 'Introduction: Some Consequences of Economic and Political Restructuring and Readjustment.' *Social Politics* 3 (1): 1–11.

Jenson, Jane, and Mariette Sineau. 2001a. 'The Care Dimensions in Welfare State Design.' In *Who Cares?* ed. J. Jenson and M. Sineau, 3–18. Toronto: University of Toronto Press:

– 2001b. *Who Cares? Women's Work, Childcare, and Welfare State Design.* Toronto: University of Toronto Press.

Jessop, B. 1994. 'The Transition to Post-Fordism and the Schumpeterian Workfare State.' In *Towards a Post-Fordist Welfare State?* ed. R. Burrows and L. Loader. London: Routledge.

Jezioranski, Lisa. 1987. 'Towards a New Status for the Midwifery Profession in Ontario.' *McGill Law Journal* 33 (1): 90–136.

Jones, Michael. 1996. *The Australian Welfare State: Evaluating Social Policy.* Sydney: Allen and Unwin.

Jones, R.J.B. 1995. *Globalization and Interdependence in the International Political Economy.* London: Pinter.

Kahn, Alfred J., and Sheila B. Kamerman. 1983. *Income Transfers for Families with Children: An Eight-Country Study.* Philadelphia: Temple University Press.

– eds. 1988. *Child Support: From Debt Collection to Social Policy.* Newbury Park, Calif.: Sage.

Kamerman, Sheila B., and Alfred J. Kahn. 1978. *Government and Families in Fourteen Countries.* New York: Columbia University Press.

– 1981. *Child Care, Family Benefits, and Working Parents.* New York: Columbia University Press.

– 1989. 'Family Policy: Has the United States Learned from Europe?' *Policy Studies Review* 8 (3): 581–98.

– eds. 1997. *Family Change and Family Policies in Great Britain, Canada, New Zealand and the United States.* Oxford: Clarendon.

– 2001. 'Child and Family Policies in an Era of Social Policy Retrenchment and Restructuring.' In *Child Well-Being, Child Poverty and Child Policy in*

Modern Nations: What Do We Know? ed. K. Vleminckx and T. Smeeding, 501–24. Bristol: Policy.

Kangas, Olli. 1991. *The Politics of Social Rights: Studies on the Dimensions of Sickness Insurance in OECD Countries.* Swedish Institute of Social Research Dissertation Series no. 19. Stockholm: SISR.

Kangas, Olli, and Joakim Palme. 1992–3. 'Statism Eroded? Labor-Market Benefits and Challenges to the Scandinavian Welfare States.' *International Journal of Sociology* 22 (4): 3–24.

Kay, Tess. 2000. 'Leisure, Gender and the Family: The Influence of Social Policy,' *Leisure Studies* 19 (4): 247–65.

Kaye, Miranda. 1999. 'The Hague Convention and the Flight from Domestic Violence: How Women Are Being Returned by Coach and Four.' *International Journal of Law, Policy and the Family* 13 (2): 191–212.

Keane, Conor. 2004. 'Workers Would Quit for Better Child Care.' *Irish Examiner*, 4 August. Available at http://www.childcarecanada.org.

Kedgley, Sue. 1996. *Mum's the Word: The Untold Story of Motherhood in New Zealand.* Auckland: Random House.

Kelsey, Jane. 1995. *Economic Fundamentalism.* London: Pluto.

– 1999. *Reclaiming the Future: New Zealand and the Global Economy.* Wellington: Bridget Williams.

Kiernan, Kathleen. 1997. *The Legacy of Parental Divorce: Social, Economic, and Demographic Experiences in Adulthood.* London: Centre for Analysis of Social Exclusion.

Kingfisher, Catherine, ed. 2002. *Western Welfare in Decline: Globalization and Women's Poverty.* Philadelphia: University of Pennsylvania Press.

Kitchen, Brigitte. 1997. 'The New Child Benefit: Much Ado About Nothing.' *Canadian Review of Social Policy* 39 (Spring): 65–74.

Korpi, Walter. 1983. *The Democratic Class Struggle.* London: Routledge and Kegan Paul.

– 1989. 'Power, Politics, and State Autonomy in the Development of Citizenship.' *American Sociological Review* 54: 309–28.

– 2000. 'Faces of Inequality: Gender, Class, and Patterns of Inequalities in Different Types of Welfare States.' *Social Politics* 7 (2): 127–91.

Krane, Julia. 2003. *What's Mother Got to Do with It? Protecting Children from Sexual Abuse.* Toronto: University of Toronto Press.

Krug, E., L. Dahlberg, J. Mercy, A. Zwi, and R. Lozano, eds. 2002. *World Report on Violence and Health.* Geneva: World Health Organisation.

Lamb, Michael, ed. 1976. *The Role of Father in Child Development.* New York: Wiley.

Lambert, Suzanne. 1994. 'Sole Parent Income Support: Cause or Cure of Sole Parent Poverty?' *Australian Journal of Social Issues* 29 (1): 75–97.

Lapointe, Rita Eva, and C. James Richardson. 1994. *Evaluation of the New Brunswick Family Support Orders Service.* Fredericton: New Brunswick Department of Justice.
Latten, J., and A. de Graaf. 1997. *Fertility and Family Surveys in Countries of the ECE Region.* Standard Country Report 10b: The Netherlands. New York: UN Economic Commission for Europe / UN Population Fund.
Lawlor, Allison. 2003. 'Births on the Rise.' *The Globe and Mail*, 12 August. http://www.globeandmail.com.
Lefebvre, Sophie. 2003. 'Housing: An Income Issues.' *Canadian Social Trends* 68 (Spring): 15–18.
Leira, Arnlaug. 2002. *Working Parents and the Welfare State: Family Change and Policy Reform in Scandinavia.* Cambridge: Cambridge University Press.
Lewis, Jane. 1992. 'Gender and the Development of Welfare State Regimes.' *Journal of European Social Policy* 2 (3): 159–73.
– 1997. *Lone Mothers and Welfare Regimes.* London: Jessica Kingsley.
– 2003. *Should We Worry about Family Change?* Toronto: University of Toronto Press.
Lightman, Ernie S. 1995. '"You Can Lead a Horse to Water, but ...": The Case against Workfare in Canada.' In *Helping the Poor: A Qualified Case for 'Workfare,'* ed. John Richards and William G. Watson, 151–83. Ottawa: C.D. Howe Institute.
– 1997. '"It's Not a Walk in the Park": Workfare in Ontario.' In *Workfare: Ideology for a New Under-Class*, ed. E. Shragge, 85–107. Toronto: Garamond.
Lipman, Ellen L., David R. Offord, and Martin D. Dooley. 1996. 'What Do We Know about Children from Single-Parent Families? Questions and Answers from the National Longitudinal Survey on Children.' In *Growing Up in Canada: National Longitudinal Survey on Children and Youth*, 83–92. Ottawa: Human Resources Development Canada.
Lister, Ruth. 1997. *Feminist Perspectives.* London: Macmillan.
Little, Margaret. 1998. *No Car, No Radio, No Liquor Permit: The Moral Regulation of Single Mothers in Ontario, 1920-1997.* Toronto: Oxford University Press.
Lopata, Helena. 1971. *Occupation: Housewife.* New York: Oxford University Press.
Lord, Stella. 1994. 'Social Assistance and "Employability" for Single Mothers in Nova Scotia.' In *Continuities and Discontinuities: The Political Economy of Social Welfare and Labour Market Policy in Canada*, ed. A.F. Johnson, S. McBride, and P.J. Smith, 191–206. Toronto: University of Toronto Press.
Lowe, Nigel. 1994. 'Problems Relating to Access Disputes under the Hague Convention on International Child Abduction.' *International Journal of Law and the Family* 8: 374–85.

Lloyd, Jacky. 1978. 'Marital Breakdown.' In *Families in New Zealand Society*, ed. Peggy Koopman-Boyden, 138–58. Wellington: Methuen.

Luxton, Meg. 1980. *More Than a Labour of Love*. Toronto: Women's Education Press.

– 2005. 'Conceptualizing "Families": Theoretical Frameworks and Family Research.' In *Families: Changing Trends in Canada*, ed. M. Baker, 29–51. 5th ed. Toronto: McGraw-Hill Ryerson.

Maclean, M., and D. Kuh. 1991. 'The Long Term Effects for Girls of Parental Divorce.' In *Women's Issues in Social Policy*, ed. M. Maclean and D. Groves, 161–178. London: Routledge.

MacLennan, C. 2005. 'Acting for the Sake of the Children.' *New Zealand Herald*, 20 January.

Macpherson, Cluny. 2000. 'The Children of Samoan Migrants in New Zealand.' In *We Are a People: Narrative and Multiplicity in Constructing Ethnic Identity*, ed. P. Spickard and W.J. Burroughs, 70–81. Philadephia: Temple University Press.

Mahon, Evelyn. 2001. 'Abortion Debates in Ireland: An Ongoing Issue.' In *Abortion Politics, Women's Movements, and the Democratic State: A Comparative Study of State Feminism*, ed. D. McBride Stetson, 157–79. New York: Oxford University Press.

Mahon, Rianne. 2001. 'Theorizing Welfare Regimes: Toward a Dialogue?' *Social Politics* 8 (1): 24–35.

Marcil-Gratton, Nicole. 1998. *Growing Up with Mom and Dad? The Intricate Family Life Courses of Canadian Children*. Ottawa: Ministry of Industry.

Marsh, Alan. 2001. 'Helping British Lone Parents Get and Keep Paid Work.' *Lone Parents, Employment and Social Policy: Cross-National Comparisons*. ed. J. Millar and K. Rowlingson, 11–36. Bristol: The Policy Press.

Marshall, Katherine. 1994. 'Balancing Work and Family Responsibilities.' *Perspectives on Labour and Income*, 6, (1): 26–30.

– 'Couples Working Shifts.' *Perspectives on Labour and Income* 10 (3): 9–14.

May, Elaine C. 1995. *Barren in the Promised Land: Childless Americans and the Pursuit of Happiness*. New York: Basic Books.

– 1997. *The Discovery of Early Childhood*. Auckland: Auckland University Press/Bridget William Books with the New Zealand Council for Educational Research.

McClure, Margaret. 1998. *A Civilised Community: A History of Social Security in New Zealand 1898–1998*. Auckland: Auckland University Press.

McDaniel, Susan A. 2002. 'Women's Changing Relations to the State and Citizenship: Caring and Intergenerational Relations in Globalizing Western Democracies.' *Canadian Review of Sociology and Anthropology* 39 (2): 125–50.

McDaniel, Susan A., and Lorne Tepperman. 2000. *Close Relations: An Introduction to the Sociology of the Families.* 1st ed. Toronto: Prentice Hall Allyn and Bacon Canada.
– 2004. *Close Relations: An Introduction to the Sociology of the Families.* 2nd ed. Toronto: Pearson / Prentice Hall.
McDonald, Peter, ed. 1986. *Settling Up: Property and Income Distribution on Divorce in Australia.* Melbourne and Sydney: Australian Institute of Family Studies / Prentice-Hall.
– 2000. 'Gender Equity in Theories of Fertility Transition.' *Population and Development Review* 26 (3): 427–39.
McGilly, Frank. 1998. *An Introduction to Canada's Public Social Services: Understanding Income and Health Programs.* 2nd ed. Toronto: Oxford.
McGlynn, Clare. 2001. 'European Union Family Values: Ideologies of "Family" and "Motherhood" in European Union Law.' *Social Politics* 8 (3): 325–50.
McHugh, Marilyn. 1996. 'Sole Mothers in Australia: Supporting Mothers to Seek Work.' Paper presented at the Australian Institute of Family Studies 5th Family Research Conference, Brisbane, 22–9 November.
McIvor, Tina. 2004. 'Civil Union Cloaks New Attack on "Relationship in the Nature of Marriage"' (NZ). Newsletter of the Women's Studies Association, no. 25 (1).
McKay, S., and K. Rowlingson. 1998. 'Choosing Lone Parenthood? The Dynamics of Family Change.' In *Private Lives and Public Responses: Lone Parenthood and Future Policy in the UK,* ed. R. Ford and J. Millar, 42–57. London: Policy Studies Institute.
McKeen, Wendy. 2004. *Money in Their Own Name: The Feminist Voice in Poverty Debate in Canada 1970–1995.* Toronto: University of Toronto Press.
McLaren, Angus. 1999. *Twentieth-Century Sexuality: A History.* Oxford: Blackwell.
McMahon, A. 1999. *Taking Care of Men.* Cambridge: Cambridge University Press.
McNair, Ruth, Deborah Dempsey, Sarah Wise, and Amaryll Perlesz. 2002. 'Lesbian Parenting: Issues, Strengths and Challenges.' *Family Matters* 63 (Spring/Summer): 40–9.
McRae, Susan. 1999. *Changing Britain: Families and Households in the 1990s.* Oxford: Oxford University Press.
Mendelson, Michael. 1995. *Looking for Mr. Good-Transfer: A Guide to the CHST Negotiations.* Ottawa: Caledon Institute of Social Policy.
Mikhailovich, K., S. Martin, and S. Lawton. 2001. 'Lesbian and Gay Parents: Their Experiences of Children's Health Care in Australia.' *International Journal of Sexuality and Gender Studies* 6 (3): 181–91.

- 2001. 'Work-Related Activity Requirements and Labour Market Programmes for Lone Parents.' In *Lone Parents, Employment and Social Policy: Cross-national Perspectives*. 189–210. Bristol: Policy.
Millar, Jane, and Karen Rowlingson, eds. 2001. *Lone Parents, Employment and Social Policy: Cross-National Comparisons*. Bristol: Policy.
Millar, Jane, and A. Warman, eds. 1995. *Defining Family Obligations in Europe*. Social Policy Papers no. 23. Bath: University of Bath.
Millar, Jane, and Peter Whiteford. 1993. 'Child Support in Lone-Parent Families: Policies in Australia and the UK.' *Policy and Politics* 21 (1): 59–72.
Millbank, J. 2002. 'Meet the Parents: A Review of the Research on Gay and Lesbian Families.' Gay and Lesbian Rights Lobby (New South Wales). http://www.glrl.org.au.
Mink, Gwendolyn. 1998. *Welfare's End*. Ithaca: Cornell University Press.
- 2002. 'Violating Women: Rights Abuses in the American Welfare Police State.' In *Women's Work Is Never Done*, ed. Sylvia Bashevkin, 141–64. New York: Routledge.
Mirchandani, Kiran. 1999. 'Legitimizing Work: Telework and the Gendered Reification of the Work-Nonwork Dichotomy.' *Canadian Review of Sociology and Anthropology* 36 (1): 86–107.
Mishra, Ramesh. 1977. *Society and Social Policy*. London: Macmillan.
- 1984. *The Welfare State in Crisis*. Brighton: Wheatsheaf Books.
- 1990. *The Welfare State in Capitalist Society*. Toronto: University of Toronto Press.
- 1999. *Globalization and the Welfare State*. Cheltenham, UK: Edward Elgar.
Mitchell, Deborah. 1995. 'Women's Incomes.' In *Women in a Restructuring Australia: Work and Welfare*, ed. A. Edwards and S. Magarey, 79–94. Sydney: Allen and Unwin.
Montanari, Ingalill. 1995. 'Harmonization of Social Policies and Social Regulation in the European Community.' *European Journal of Political Research* 27 (1): 21–45.
- 2001. 'Modernization, Globalization and the Welfare State: A Comparative Analysis of Old and New Convergence of Social Insurance since 1930.' *British Journal of Sociology* 52 (3): 469–94.
Moore, Oliver. 2003. 'Bush Wants to "Codify"Heterosexual Unions.' *The Globe and Mail*, 31 July. http://www.theglobeandmail.com.
Morell, Carolyn M. 1994. *Unwomanly Conduct: The Challenges of Intentional Childlessness*. New York: Routledge.
Morissens, Ann. 1999. 'Solo Mothers and Poverty: Do Policies Matter? A Comparative Case Study of Sweden and Belgium.' LIS Working Paper no. 210 and master's thesis, Stockholm University.

Morton, Mildred. 1990. 'Controversies within Family Law.' *Families: Changing Trends in Canada*, ed. M. Baker, 211–40. 2nd ed. Toronto: McGraw-Hill Ryerson:

Moylan, Judi. 1996. 'Strengthening Families.' Statement by the Minister for Family Services, 20 August, Canberra.

Murdock, George. 1949. *Social Structure*. New York: Macmillan.

Murphy, J.J., and S. Boggess. 1998. 'Increased Condom Use Among Teenage Males, 1988–1995: The Role of Attitudes.' *Family Planning Perspectives* 30 (6). 276–80.

Myles, John. 1996. 'When Markets Fail: Social Welfare in Canada and the United States.' In *Welfare States in Transition: National Adaptatons in Global Economies*, ed. G. Esping-Andersen, 116–40. London: Sage.

National Longitudinal Survey of Children and Youth. 1996. *Growing Up in Canada*. Ottawa: Human Resources Development Canada / Statistics Canada.

Nett, Emily. 1988. *Canadian Families Past and Present*. Toronto: Butterworths.

New Zealand, Ministry of Health. 1990. *Nurses Amendment Act 1990*. Wellington: Department of Health.

– 2003. *Report on Maternity 2000 and 2001*. Available at www.moh.govt.nz (accessed 24 January 2004).

Neysmith, Sheila, and Xiaobei Chen. 2002. 'Understanding How Globalisation and Restructuring Affect Women's Lives: Implications for Comparative Policy Analysis.' *International Journal of Social Welfare* 11 (3): 243–53.

Oakley, Ann. 1974. *The Sociology of Housework*. Oxford: Martin Robertson.

O'Connor, Julia S., and Gregg M. Olsen. 1998. *Power Resources Theory and the Welfare State: A Critical Approach*. Toronto: University of Toronto Press.

O'Connor, Julia S., Ann Shola Orloff, and Sheila Shaver. 1999. *States, Markets, Families: Gender Liberalism and Social Policy in Australia, Canada, Great Britain and the United States*. Cambridge: Cambridge University Press.

Oinonen, Eriikka. 2000. 'Finnish and Spanish Family Institutions: Similarities and Differences.' In *Families and Family Policies in Europe: Comparative Perspectives*, ed. A. Pfenning and T. Bahle, 141–61. Frankfort: Peter Lang.

Organisation for Economic Co-operation and Development 2001. *Society at a Glance: OECD Social Indicators 2001*. Paris: OECD.

– 2002. *OECD Employment Outlook July 2002*. Paris: OECD.

– 2003a. *OECD Employment Outlook: Towards More and Better Jobs 2003*. Paris: OECD.

– 2003b. *Society at a Glance: OECD Indicators 2002*. Paris: OECD.

– 2005. *Society at a Glance: OECD Social Indicators*. Paris: OECD.

Orloff, Ann Shola. 1993. 'Gender and the Social Rights of Citizenship: The

Comparative Analysis of Gender Relations and Welfare States.' *American Sociological Review* 58: 303–28.
– 2003. 'Markets Not States?: The Weakness of State Social Provision for Breadwinning Men in the United States.' In *Families of a New World: Gender, Politics and State Development in a Global Context*, ed. L. Haney and L. Pollard, 217–43. New York: Routledge.
Pampel, Fred C., and Paul Adams. 2002. 'The Effects of Demographic Change and Political Structure on Family Allowance Expenditures.' *Social Service Review* 66 (4): 524–46.
Papps, Elaine, and Mark Olssen. 1997. *Doctoring Childbirth and Regulating Midwifery in New Zealand: A Foucauldian Perspective*. Palmerston North, NZ: Dunmore.
Parsons, Talcott, and Robert Bales. 1955. *Family Socialization and Interaction Process*. New York: Free Press.
Patterson, C.J. 2000. 'Family Relationships of Lesbian and Gay Parents.' *Journal of Marriage and the Family* 62: 1052–69.
Peck, Jamie. 2001. *Workfare States*. New York: Guildford.
– 2004. 'Going after Neoliberalism.' Keynote address to the conference Beyond Neoliberalism? New Forms of Governance in Aotearoa New Zealand, University of Auckland.
Pedersen, Susan. 1993. *Family, Dependence, and the Origins of the Welfare State: Britain and France. 1914–1945*. Cambridge: Cambridge University Press.
Pereira, Diana. 2004. 'Number of Divorces Declining: Statscan.' *The Globe and Mail*, 5 May. www.theglobeandmail.com.
Perry, Julia. 1991. *Breadwinners or Childrearers: The Dilemma for Lone Mothers*. Canberra: OECD Working Party on Social Policy.
Petrella, R. 1996. 'Globalization and Internationalization: The Dynamics of the Emerging World Order.' In *States against Markets: The Limits of Globalization*, ed. R. Boyer and D. Drache. London: Routledge.
Phillips, Roderick. 1988. *Putting Asunder: A History of Divorce in Western Society*. Cambridge: Cambridge University Press.
Phipps, Shelley. 2000. 'Maternity and Parental Benefits in Canada: Are there Behavioural Implications?' *Canadian Public Policy* 26 (4): 415–36.
Pierson, Paul. 1994. *Dismantling the Welfare State? Reagan, Thatcher, and the Politics of Retrenchment*. Cambridge: Cambridge University Press.
– 2000. 'Increasing Returns, Path Dependence, and the Study of Politics.' *American Political Science Review* 94: 251–67.
Pierson, Ruth. 1977. 'Women's Emancipation and the Recruitment of Women into the Labour Force in World War II.' In *The Neglected Majority: Essays in*

Canadian Women's History, ed. S.M. Trofimenkoff and A. Prentice. Toronto: McClelland and Stewart.
Polakow, Valerie. 1997. 'Family Policy, Welfare, and Single Motherhood in the United States and Denmark: A Cross-National Analysis of Discourse and Practice.' *Early Education and Development* 8 (3): 245–64.
Presser, Harriet. 1998. 'Toward a 24 Hour Economy: The U.S. Experience and Implications for the Family.' In *Challenges for Work and Family in the Twenty First Century*, ed. D. Vannoy and P.J. Dubeck. New York: Aldine de Gruyter.
Pryor, Jan, and Bryan Rodgers. 2001. *Children in Changing Families: Life After Parental Separation*. Oxford: Blackwell.
Pudrovska, Tetyana, and Myra Marx Ferree. 2004. 'Global Activism in "Virtual Space": The European Women's Lobby in the Network of Transnational Women's NGOs on the Web.' *Social Politics* 11 (1): 117–43.
Pulkingham, Jane, and Gordon Ternowetsky. 1997. 'The New Canada Child Tax Benefit: Discriminating between the "Deserving" and "Undeserving" Poor Families with Children.' In *Child and Family Policies: Struggles, Strategies and Options*, ed. J. Pulkingham and G. Ternowetsky. 204–8. Halifax: Fernwood.
Pusey, Michael. 1991. *Economic Rationalism in Canberra: A Nation-Building State Changes Its Mind*. Cambridge: Cambridge University Press.
– 1993. 'Reclaiming the Middle Ground ... From New Right Economic Rationalism.' Discussion paper no. 31. Public Sector Research Centre, University of New South Wales.
Quaid, Maeve. 2002. *Workfare: Why Good Social Policy Ideas Go Bad*. Toronto: University of Toronto Press.
Radford, Lorraine, and Marianne Hester. 2001. 'Overcoming Mother Blaming? Future Directions for Research on Mothering and Domestic Violence.' In *Domestic Violence in the Lives of Children: The Future of Research, Intervention and Social Policy*, ed. S. Graham-Bermann and J. Edleson. Washington, D.C.: American Psychological Association.
Rahman, Anika, Laura Katzive, and Stanley K. Henshaw. 1998. 'A Global Review of Laws on Induced Abortion, 1985–1997.' *International Family Planning Perspectives* 24 (2): 56–64.
Ram, Bali. 1990. *New Trends in the Family*. Statistics Canada, Catalogue 91–535E. Ottawa: Ministry of Supply and Services.
Ranson, Gillian. 1998. 'Education, Work and Family Decision Making: Finding the "Right Time" to Have a Baby.' *Canadian Review of Sociology and Anthropology* 35 (4): 517–34.
Riccio, J., and Freedman, S. 1999. *Can They All Work? A Study of the Employ-*

ment Potential of Welfare Recipients in a Welfare-to-Work Program. New York: Manpower Demonstration Research Corporation.

Richardson, C. James. 1996. 'Divorce and Remarriage.' *Families: Changing Trends in Canada,* ed. M. Baker, 215–48. 3rd ed. Toronto: McGraw-Hill Ryerson.

– 2001. 'Divorce and Remarriage.' In *Families: Changing Trends in Canada,* ed. M. Baker, 206–38. 4th ed. Toronto: McGraw-Hill Ryerson.

Ricks, Shirley. 1985. 'Father-Infant Interactions: A Review of Empirical Research.' *Family Relations* 34 (October): 505–11.

Roberts C.L., S. Tracy, and B. Peat. 2000. 'Rates for Obstetric Intervention among Private and Public Patients in Australia: A Population Based Descriptive Study.' *British Medical Journal* 321: 137–41.

Roberts, Helen. 1997. 'Children, Inequalities and Health.' *British Medical Journal* 314 (12 April) (#7087): 1122.

Ross, David, K. Scott, and M. Kelly. 1996. *Child Poverty: What Are the Consequences?* Ottawa: Canadian Council on Social Development.

Ross, George. 2001. 'Europe: An Actor without a Role.' In *Who Cares? Women's Work, Childcare, and Welfare State Redesign,* ed. J. Jenson and M. Sineau, 177–213. Toronto: University of Toronto Press.

Rudd, Elisabeth C. 2003. 'They Say, "Oh God, I Don't Want to Live Like Her!": The Marginalization of Mothering in German Post-Socialism.' In *Families of a New World: Gender, Politics and State Development in a Global Context,* ed. L. Haney and L. Pollard, 179–95. New York: Routledge.

Rugman, A. 2001. *The End of Globalization.* New York: Random House.

Sainsbury, Diane. 1993. 'Dual Welfare and Sex Segregation of Access to Social Benefits: Income Maintenance Policies in the UK, the US, the Netherlands and Sweden.' *Journal of Social Policy* 22 (1): 69–98.

– ed. 1994. *Gendering Welfare States.* London: Sage.

– 1996. *Gender, Equality and Welfare States.* Cambridge: Cambridge University Press.

– 2001. 'Gender and the Making of Welfare States.' *Social Politics* 8 (1): 113–43.

Sarfati, Diana, and Kate Scott. 2001. 'The Health of Lone Mothers in New Zealand.' *The New Zealand Medical Journal* 114 (1133): 257–60.

Saunders, Peter, 1994. *Welfare and Inequality: National and International Perspectives on the Australian Welfare State.* Cambridge: Cambridge University Press.

Saunders, Peter, and G. Matheson. 1991. 'Sole Parent Families in Australia.' *International Social Security Review* 34 (3): 51–75.

Sev'er, Aysan. 1992. *Women and Divorce in Canada: A Sociological Analysis.* Toronto: Canadian Scholars' Press.

- 2002. *Fleeing the House of Horrors: Women Who Have Left Abusive Partners.* Toronto: University of Toronto Press.
Shaver, Sheila. 1993. 'Citizenship, Gender and the Life Cycle Transition: Sole Parents Whose Youngest Child is Turning 16.' In *Gender, Citizenship and the Labour Market: The Australian and Canadian Welfare States*, ed. S. Shaver. Sydney: University of New South Wales. Social Policy Research Centre.
- 2002. 'Gender, Welfare Regimes, and Agency.' *Social Politics* 9 (2): 203–11.
Shaver, Sheila, and Jonathan Bradshaw. 1995. 'The Recognition of Wifely Labour by Welfare States.' *Social Policy and Administration* 29 (1): 10–25.
Shaver, Sheila, Anthony King, Marilyn McHugh, and Toni Payne. 1994. *At the End of Eligibility: Female Sole Parents Whose Youngest Child Turns 16.* Report no. 117. Sydney: University of New South Wales, Social Policy Research Centre.
Shelton, B.A., and D. John. 1996. 'The Division of Household Labor.' *Annual Review of Sociology* 22: 299–322.
Shragge, Eric (ed). 1997. *Workfare: Ideology for a New Under-Class.* Toronto: Garamonde.
Skene, Loane. 2002. 'Genetics and Artificial Procreation in Australia.' In *Biomedicine, The Family and Human Rights*, ed. M.-T. Meulders-Klein, R. Deech, and P. Vlaardingerbroek. The Hague: Kluwer.
Smart, Carol, and Bren Neale. 1999. *Family Fragments?* Cambridge: Polity Press.
Smeeding, Timothy. 2002. 'Globalisation, Inequality, and the Rich Countries of the G-20: Evidence from the Luxembourg Income Study (LIS).' In *Globalisation, Living Standards, and Inequality: Recent Progress and Continuing Challenges*, ed. D. Gruen, T. O'Brien, and J. Lawson, 179–206. Australia: J.S. Macmillan Printing Group.
Smeeding, Timothy M., Katherine Ross, Paula England, Karen Christopher, and Sara S. McLanahan. 1998. *Poverty and Parenthood across Modern Nations: Findings from the Luxembourg Income Study.* Working Paper No. 194. Luxembourg Income Study. Available at http://www.lisproject.org.
Smyth, Bruce. 2002. 'Research into Parent-Child Contact after Separation.' *Family Matters* 62 (Winter): 33–7.
- ed. 2004. *Parent-Child Contact and Post-Separation Parenting Arrangements.* Research Report no. 9. Melbourne: Australian Institute of Family Studies.
Speirs, Carol, and Maureen Baker. 1994. 'Eligibility to Adopt: Models of "Suitable" Families in Legislation and Practice.' *Canadian Social Work Review* 11 (1): 89–102.
State of Queensland. (Office for Women). 2000. 'Partnerships on Domestic Violence. http://www.qldwoman.qld.gov.au/about/padv.html.

Statistics Canada. 2002a. '2001 Census: Marital Status, Common-Law Status, Families and Households.' *The Daily*, 22 October.
– 2002b. 'Changing Conjugal Life in Canada.' *The Daily*, 11 July.
Statistics New Zealand. 1998. *New Zealand Now: Families and Households*. Wellington: Statistics New Zealand.
– 2002. *New Zealand Official Yearbook 2002*. Wellington: Statistics New Zealand.
Stephansson, O., P.W. Dickman, A.L.V. Johansson, H. Kieler, and S. Cnattingius. 2003. 'Time and Risk of Intrapartum and Early Neonatal Death.' *Epidemiology* 14 (2): 218–22.
Stephens, John D. 1996. 'The Scandinavian Welfare States: Achievements, Crisis, and Prospects.' In *Welfare States in Transition*, ed. G. Esping-Andersen, 32–65. London: Sage.
Stratigaki, Maria. 2004. 'The Cooptation of Gender Concepts in EU Policies: The Case of "Reconciliation of Work and Family."' *Social Politics* 11 (1): 30–56.
Sullivan, Oriel. 2000. 'The Division of Domestic Labour: 20 Years of Change?' *Sociology* 34 (3): 437–56.
Sullivan, Robert. 2003. 'Roe No More.' *Vogue*, October, 162–68.
Swank, Duane. 2002. *Global Capital, Political Institutions, and Policy Change in Developed Welfare States*. Cambridge: Cambridge University Press.
Swift, Karen. 1995. *Manufacturing 'Bad Mothers'? A Critical Perspective on Child Neglect*. Toronto: University of Toronto Press.
Taylor-Gooby, Peter (editor). 2004. *New Risks, New Welfare: The Transformation of the European Welfare State*. Oxford: Oxford University Press.
Teeple, Gary. 1995. *Globalization and the Decline of Social Reform: Into the Twenty-First Century*. Humanities Press / Toronto: Garamond Press.
Tew, Marjorie. 1998. *Safer Childbirth? A Critical History of Maternity Care*. 3rd ed. London: Free Association Books.
Timpson, Annis May. 2001. *Driven Apart: Women's Employment Equality and Child Care in Canadian Public Policy*. Vancouver: University of British Columbia Press.
Titmuss, Richard M. 1974. *Social Policy: An Introduction*. London: Allen and Unwin.
Thorp, Diana. 1996. 'Howard Launches Tax Cuts.' *The Australian* 17 December.
Torjman, Sherri. 1996. *Workfare: A Poor Law*. Ottawa: Caledon Institute of Social Policy.
Torjman, Sherri, and Ken Battle. 1999. *Good Work: Getting It and Keeping It*. Toronto: Caledon Institute of Social Policy.

Townsend, P. 1993. *The International Analysis of Poverty*. Hemel Hempstead: Harvester Wheatsheaf.
Trapski, Judge, P.J. 1994. *The Child Support Review*. Wellington: New Zealand Parliament.
Ulrich, M., and A. Weatherall. 2000. 'Motherhood and Infertility: Viewing Motherhood through the Lens of Infertility.' *Feminism and Psychology* 10: 323–36.
United Kingdom. Government for Statistical Service. 2003. *NHS Maternity Statistics, England: 2001–02*. Available www.doh.gov.uk (accessed 22 January 2004).
– Office for National Statistics. 2002. 'Births: By Place of Delivery, 1961 to 1997: Social Trends 30.' Available at www.statistics.gov.uk. (accesssed 3 January 2004).
– Office for National Statistics. 2004. *Social Trends 30*. www.statistics.gov.uk.
United Nations. 1966. *International Covenant on Economic, Social and Cultural Rights*, New York, 16 December. Available at http://www.un.org (accessed 12 December 2003).
– 1979. *Convention on the Elimination of All Forms of Discrimination against Women*, New York, 18 December 1979. Available at http://www.un.org (accessed 12 December 2003).
– 1994. *Report of the International Conference on Population and Development*, Cairo, 5–13 September. Available at http://www.un.org.
– 1995. *Fourth World Conference on Women: Action for Equality, Development and Peace, Beijing Declaration and Platform for Action*, Beijing, 4–15 September. Available at http://www.un.org.
– 1996. *Reproductive Rights and Reproductive Health: A Concise Report*. New York: UN.
– 2000a. *The World's Women: Trends and Statistics*. New York: UN.
– 2000b. *World Population Prospects: The 2000 Revision: Highlights and Tables*. Available at http://www.un.org/esa/population/publications (accessed 2 Febuary 2004).
– 2001a. *Abortion Policies: A Global Review*, Vol. 1: *Afghanistan to France*. New York: UN.
– 2001b. *Abortion Policies: A Global Review*, Vol. 2, *Gabon to Norway*. New York: UN.
– 2002a. *Abortion Policies: A Global Review*, Vol. 3, *Oman to Zimbabwe*. New York: UN.
– 2003. *Fertility, Contraception and Population Policies*. New York: UN.
United Nations Children's Fund (UNICEF). 2000. *A League Table of Child Poverty in Rich Nations*. Florence: Innocenti Research Centre.

- 2003. *A League Table of Child Maltreatment Deaths in Rich Nations*. Florence: Innocenti Research Centre.
- 2004. 'The Baby-Friendly Hospital Initiative.' Available at www.unicef.org (accessed 9 February 2004).
- 2005. *Child Poverty in Rich Nations*. Florence: Innocenti Research Centre.

United States Department of Health and Human Services. 2003. *Handbook on Child Support Enforcement.* http://www.pueblo.gsa.gov/cic_text/children.
- Department of Health and Human Services. 2002. 'Births: Final Data for 2001.' *National Vital Statistics Reports* 51 (2): 1–103.
- Department of Health and Human Services. 2003. 'Births: Final Data for 2002.' *National Vital Statistics Reports* 52 (10): 1–114.
- Department of State, Office of Children's Issues. 2003. 'Child Support Enforcement Abroad.' http://travel.state.gov/child_support.html.

Ursel, Jane. 1992. *Private Lives, Public Policy: 100 Years of State Intervention in the Family*. Toronto: Women's Press.

Van den Berg, Axel, and Joseph Smucker. eds. 1997. *The Sociology of Labour Markets: Efficiency, Equity, Security*. Toronto: Prentice Hall Allyn / Bacon Canada.

Van Dyck, J. 1995. *Manufacturing Babies and Public Consent: Debating the New Reproductive Technologies*. London: Macmillan.

Vanier Institute of the Family. 2000. *Profiling Canadian Families 2*. Ottawa: VIF.
- 2004. *Profiling Canadian Families 3*. Ottawa: VIF.

Veevers, Jean E. 1980. *Childless by Choice*. Toronto: Butterworths.

Vosko, Leah F. 2000. *Temporary Work: The Gendered Rise of a Precarious Employment Relationship*. Toronto: University of Toronto Press.

Wadsworth, J., I. Burnell, B. Taylor, and N. Butler. 1983. 'Family Type and Accidents in Preschool Children.' *Journal of Epidemiology and Community Health* 37: 100–4.

Walby, Sylvia. 2004. 'The European Union and Gender Equality: Emergent Varieties of Gender Regime.' *Social Politics* 11 (1): 4–29.

Walker, Ruth, Deborah Turnbull, and Chris Wilkinson. 2002. 'Strategies to Address Global Caesarean Section Rates: A Review of the Evidence.' *Birth* 29 (1 March), 28–39.

Walter, Maggie. 2002. 'Working Their Way Out of Poverty? Sole Motherhood, Work, Welfare and Material Well-being.' *Journal of Sociology* 38 (4): 361–80.

Warner-Smith, Penny, and Carla Imbruglia. 2001. 'Motherhood, Employment and Health: Is There a Deepening Divide between Women?' *Just Policy* 24 (December): 24–32.

Webb, Steve, Martin Kemp, and Jane Millar. 1996. 'The Changing Face of Low Pay in Britain.' *Policy Studies* 17 (4): 255–71.

Weeks, J., C. Donovan, and B. Heaphy. 1998. 'Everyday Experiments: Narratives of Non-Heterosexual Relationships.' In *The New Family?* ed. E. Silva and C. Smart. London: Sage.

Weiss, Doris. 2000. 'The European Union and the Family.' In *Families and Family Policies in Europe: Comparative Perspectives*, ed. A. Pfenning and T. Bahle, 127–40. Frankfort: Peter Lang.

Wennemo, Irene. 1994. *Sharing the Cost of Children*. Stockholm: Swedish Institute for Social Research.

Westlander, Gunnela, and Jeanne Mager Stellman. 1988. *Government Policy and Women's Health Care: The Swedish Alternative*. New York: Haworth.

Weston, Ruth, and Robyn Parker. 2002. 'Why Is the Fertility Rate Falling? A Discussion of the Literature.' *Family Matters* 63 (Spring/Summer): 6–13.

White, Linda. 2001. 'Child Care, Women's Labour Market Participation and Labour Market Policy Effectiveness in Canada.' *Canadian Public Policy* 27 (4): 385–406.

Whitehead, Margaret, Bo Burström, and Finn Diderichsen. 2000. 'Social Policies and the Pathways to Inequalities in Health: A Comparative Analysis of Lone Mothers in Britain and Sweden.' *Social Science and Medicine* 50 (2): 255–70.

Wilson, Elizabeth. 1977. *Women and the Welfare State*. London: Tavistock.

Winfield, Nicole. 2003. 'Vatican Campaign.' *Montreal Gazette*, 29 December.

Wolcott, Ilene, and H. Glezer. 1995. *Work and Family Life: Achieving Integration*. Melbourne: Australian Institute of Family Studies.

Women's Aid Federation of England. 2003a. 'Domestic Violence Statistical Factsheet – 2002.' http://www.womensaid.org.uk/dv/dvfactsh2002.htm.

Woodward, Lianne, David M. Fergusson, and Jay Belsky. 2000. 'Timing of Parental Separation and Attachment to Parents in Adolescence: Results of a Prospective Study from Birth to Age 16.' *Journal of Marriage and the Family* 62 (February): 162–74.

World Health Organisation. 1981. *International Code of Marketing of Breast-Milk Substitutes*. Geneva: WHO.

– 1994. *Indicators to Monitor Maternal Health Goals: Report of a Technical Working Group, Geneva, 8–12 November 1993*. Geneva: WHO.

– 1998. *Life in the Twenty-First Century: A Vision for All*. The World Health Report 1998. Geneva: WHO.

WHO and Joint United Nations Programme on HIV/AIDS. 2003. *Aids Epidemic Update December 2000*. http://www.who.int (accessed 5 February 2004).

WHO and UNICEF. 1990. *Innocenti Declaration on the Protection, Promotion and*

Support of Breastfeeding. Available at http://www.unicef.org (accessed 8 February 2004).
WHO, UNICEF, and United Nations Population Fund. 1997. *Guidelines for Monitoring the Availability and Use of Obstetric Services.* 2nd ed. New York: UNICEF.
Wu, Zheng. 2000. *Cohabitation: An Alternative Form of Family Living.* Toronto: Oxford University Press.
Yeates, Nicola. 2001. *Globalization and Social Policy.* London: Sage.
Ziguras, Stephen. 2003. 'Welfare Reform: The Road to Nowhere?' *Just Policy* 30 (July): 14–23.

Index

abduction of children 74, 224–33
abuse, mandatory reporting of children's 242
abortion: access 91–5, 251; conscientious objectors to 93; and gestational age limits 93; laws in Poland 94, 247, 250; and Medicaid (US) 93; rates 92, 109
'access' to children 218
Accord, the (Australia) 197
adoption 155–6, 242; closed 156; and international agreements 157; open 157
advertising, and children/youth 36
advocacy groups 40. *See also* Christian right; fathers' rights groups; feminist advocacy groups; political left/right; trade unions
Afro-Americans 102, 216
Alberta 190, 196
anger management programs 225
Armstrong, Sarah 232
artificial insemination 37
asylum seekers 71, 73
'at risk': children 143, 175, 236, 242, 255; mothers 111
Australia: and centralized bargaining 115; and child support 221–2; and declining fertility 97; and Hague Convention 229. *See also* centralized bargaining; Parenting Allowance; Sole Parent Pension
Australian Law Reform Commission 229
autonomous households 49, 212

Baker, Maureen 57, 108, 174, 178
Baker and Tippin, 52, 222
Beaujot, Roderic 29, 97, 116
Beijing Conference (UN) 89, 93
benefits, means-tested 44
'best interests of the child' 159, 210, 219, 224, 228–30, 233
birth: at home 98, 102; low birth weight 86; rates 30, 32, 33; rates outside marriage 29, 33; rates of 'visible minorities' 32; teen birth rate 32; vaginal 100–3
Bloc Québécois 195, 203
Bock and Thane 48
border crossings 74, 223–232
Bradshaw and Finch 58–9, 148, 166
breastfeeding 104–6
Briar-Lawson et al. 80

bride price 39
British Columbia 99, 190
Brush, Lisa 50–1
Bryson, Lois 54

Caesarean births 99–104
Cairo Conference (UN) 88, 93
California 213
Canada: and childcare 124; and child support 222; and Hague Convention 228; maternity/parental benefits 130, 204; social housing 182; social programs 47
Canada Assistance Plan 146, 185, 192, 205
Canada Health and Social Transfer 192, 193, 194
Canada Pension Plan 172
care work 53, 143, 218; out-of-school care 149; and outsourcing 252
Castles, Francis 30, 47
centralized bargaining 47, 115
childbirth: laissez-faire policies for 130; 'medicalization' of 99; practices 97, 99, 111
childcare 76, 121, 144, 147, 149, 152–3, 238–40, 249, 250; advocacy groups 150; in Belgium 252; expenses deduction (Canada) 193; in France 147, 252; 'guarantee' 149; in Quebec 47, 147–8; regulation of 145; in U.K. 152
child minders (sitters) 149
children: abduction of 74, 224–33; abuse of 160–4, 163, 228, 233, 247; 'access' to 218; adoption of 155–6, 242; advertising and 36; 'at risk' 143, 175, 236, 242, 255; attachment to parents 215; benefits 184, 186–9, 191–2, 194, 240–2 (*see also* family allowance); 'best interests of the child' 159, 210, 219, 224, 228–30, 233; cost of 241; custody and access 218, 220, 223–32; 'illegitimate' 87, 155, 218; investing in 179; mortality rates of 95; maltreatment rates of 163; mandatory reporting of abuse of 242; neonatal mortality rates of 101; physical punishment of 242; and pornography 161; protection services 158, 160, 243, 247; and poverty 46, 55, 61, 76, 155, 169, 171–2, 177, 197, 204, 211, 214, 218, 223, 240; rights of 160, 248; as social capital 12, 176, 179; special-needs 150–1, 200; support 198, 214, 221–6, 234, 240–1, 252; welfare of 143, 163, 242
Child Poverty Action Group 180, 194, 241
Child Tax Benefit 191–2, 194
Children's Act (UK) 231
choice 38, 106, 111, 122, 200, 239
Christchurch Health and Development Study (NZ) 215
Christian right 27, 89, 247, 251
Christopher, Karen 55
civil law 217–18
civil unions 4, 26, 76, 250; in New Zealand 4, 27
'clean break' (and divorce) 218
Coester-Waltjen 225
cohabitation 24–8, 210–11; gay and lesbian 26–8
cohort difference 36
common law 217–18
comparative research 8
compensatory allowance 217

'compliance costs' 17, 83, 248
conception, medically assisted 37, 106–9. *See also* fertility
conduct disorder 214
conflict 216–17
confinement 103
Connolly, Marie 159–60
conscientious objectors to abortion 93
consensual unions 24. *See also* cohabitation
conservative welfare regimes 44
contraception 87–9, 247, 250
Convention on the Elimination of All Forms of Discrimination Against Women 87
Convention on the Rights of the Child
convergence: of social/family policies 5, 110, 223, 233, 235, 252–4; of socio-demographic patterns 6, 110, 233
corporatist welfare regimes 44
courtship 37
custody 218, 220, 223–32; joint 219

'daddy days' 139
Daly and Rake 48, 53, 139, 142
'dead-beat dads' 191, 241
decentralization 205
de-commodification' 46
'de-familialization' 49
default rates (child support) 222
Dempsey, Ken 137
Denmark 246
'dependency' 49, 52, 61
deregulation of labour force 248
'deserving poor' 44
discourse. *See* political discourse
divorce: attitudes to 209; and children 213–15; in Ireland 152, 209, 213; law reform and 39, 197, 213, 228, 229; no-fault 233; rates of 211, 212; in Spain 213
Domestic Purposes Benefit 60, 144
domestic: violence 164, 227 (*see also* violence against women); work 136 (*see also* care work; childcare)
'double day' 117, 120
double standard of sexual behaviour 86
dual welfare state 54
dual-earner family 51, 122, 250

education, compulsory 30
'economically active' 66–7, 114
economy, twenty-four-hour 69
egalitarian family 51, 52, 250
egg donation 109
employment 114: earnings 70, 115; maternal 117–22; programs 190, 204, 239; 246; protections 247; standard/non-standard 35, 72, 113; rates 113–14, 133
Employment Insurance (Canada) 204
England and Wales: and child poverty 170; and Hague Convention 231; and home births 98
episiotomies 99
equality: of opportunity 126; of outcome 126
Esping-Andersen, Gösta 43–4, 55, 62
Europe, and Hague Convention 232
European Convention on Recognition and Enforcement of Decisions concerning Custody of Children 232
European Court 76, 78

European Economic Commission 125
European Free Trade Association 79
European Parliament 94
European Union 3, 26, 53, 66, 73–9, 94, 148, 244, 253
European Women's Lobby 73
exogamy 210

'fading fathers' 220
'failing to protect' 227–8
familialism 50
families, definition of 13, 71, 73
family: allowance 183, 195, 197, 199, 250; assets 217, 251; courts 210, 230, 231, 233; demography 34; extended 14; dual-earner 51, 250; ideologies of 61, 235, 242, 252; models of 6, 249; narratives of 50; nuclear 14; policies (table) 245; policy, definition of 15; 'post-divorce' 214, 233; preservation 159; re-unification of 71; support 58, 244–8, 236–44 (*see also* children: benefits; children: protection services; family: allowance); values 5, 252; well-being 180
Family Tax Benefit (Australia) 200
fatherhood 121, 130, 139, 157, 191, 214, 216, 218, 219, 220–1, 228, 233, 238, 252
father's rights groups 95, 218, 220, 230, 243
feminism: advocacy groups 88, 132, 156, 196, 218, 230, 243; critiques of welfare regimes 48; liberal 126
fertility 90, 106; declining 29–34, 40, 96, 201, 250; rates 30, 33, 88, 128 (*see also* birth rates); total fertility rate 29, 30
fertilization: *in vitro* 107

'first default principle' 222
First Nations (Canada) 160, 216. *See also* 'visible minorities'
foetal: rights 93, 95; monitoring 99
'flexible' workplace 34, 120
foreigners 70–5. *See also* migration
foster care 158, 242
France 147, 239, 252
free trade 79
Free Trade of the Americas Agreement 79
'friendly parent' provision 229

Gauthier, Anne 40, 52, 254
gay marriage 26. *See also* civil unions, same-sex couples
gender: differentiation of family by 51, 57; gender mainstreaming 78, 125; gender-neutral benefits 129, 134–5; and welfare regimes 48–51, 54; and work 68, 116–17, 136, 210, 238
genital mutilation 88
gestational age limits, and abortion 93
globalization: 17–21, 70, 81–2, 236, 248, 253, 255; and culture 39; and restructuring 18
'grave risk' (Hague Convention) 225, 230, 231
grandparents 150, 246
guardianship 218, 219

Hague Convention 76, 164, 220, 223–32
Haney, Lynne 50
Hantrais, Linda 52, 53, 77
harmonization of policies 5, 235, 253–4. *See also* convergence: of social/family policies

Head Start 143, 144
health 85
Held and McGrew 19, 21
HIV 91
home births 98, 102
Home Child Care Allowance (Australia) 199
home ownership 47, 183, 251
homicides 233. *See also* children: maltreatment rates of
housework 136, 137
housing 180, 207
Howard government (Australia) 200–2

ideal types 46
ideologies of family 61, 235, 242, 252
immigration 71, 74
in vitro fertilization 107
incest 92
income support 169, 184, 221, 240, 244, 246, 250; in Australia 196; in Canada 185; in U.S. 224
indigenous children 160. *See also* First Nations; Maori
induced labour 99, 100
Industrial Relations Act (Australia, 1994) 116
infant mortality rate 101
Innocenti Report 171. *See also* UNICEF
international agreements 74–9, 223–32, 236, 244, 254; and adoption 157; and child support enforcement 223–33. *See also under* names of specific agreements
International Labour Organisation 76, 105, 125, 128
International Monetary Fund 75

international organizations 12, 74, 75
internationalization 65; of labour markets 65; and communication 70. *See also* globalization
Internet 73
Ireland, divorce in 152, 209, 213

Jenson and Sineau 165
JET (Australia) 197
judicial discretion 217, 222

Kamerman and Kahn 56
Kaye, Miranda 225, 230
Keynes, John Maynard 17
kin care 159, 160, 242
kindergarten 145
kin-keeping 132, 212
Korpi, Walter 57–8

labour force, polarization of 68–9
LAT relationships 28
leave policies 131
Leira, Arnlaug 51
level playing field 118, 255
Lewis, Jane 24, 51
liberal: feminists 126; welfare regimes 43
liberalism, market 17
life: chances 32; expectancy 85, 109; right to 93, 95
lone parents 215, 153–4, 178, 214–16, 239, 246; in Australia 197, 202; in Canada 202; in UK and Sweden 178
long-hours culture 68, 248
Luxembourg Income Study 55, 81

Maastricht Treaty 77, 94, 95
maintenance (spousal) 218
male-breadwinner/female caregiver

family 51, 123, 249. *See also* ideologies of family
male model of work 238
Maori (NZ) 101, 106, 150, 175, 216
marriage 76, 212, 213, 216, 243–4, 250–1; age of 106, 216; arranged 39; and contracts 217; cross-cultural 74; gay 26; separation of sex and 37; shot-gun 155
maternal: care at home 249; employment 117–22
maternity: benefits 126, 127, 128, 237, 238; care 97, 99, 103; care in British Columbia 99; care in Netherlands 103; homes 156
Maternity Protection Convention (ILO) 105
McDaniel, Susan 80
McKeen, Wendy 54
means-tested benefits 44
mediation 210, 218, 233
Medicaid (US), and abortion 93
methodology 7
midwives 98, 102, 111
migration 47, 70–5, 211, 236
Mishra, Ramesh 20
Model Code on Domestic and Family Violence (US) 227–8
models of family 6, 249. *See also* dual-earner family; male-breadwinner/female caregiver family
Montanari, Ingallil 253
moral right 84. *See also* Christian right; political: left/right
morality 111
Moslem laws 213
mother blaming 166, 252
motherhood 49, 175. *See also* ideologies of family; lone parents; maternal: employment; mother blaming; violence against women

mothering: 'good' 49, 175; 'unfit' mothers 219
multilateral agreements. *See* international agreements

narratives of the family 50
National Centre for Missing and Exploited Children (US) 228
National Child Development Study (UK) 216
National Longitudinal Survey of Children and Youth (Canada) 180, 214
national politics and restructuring 59–62, 184–206
National Strategy on Child Care (Canada) 146
neoliberalism 17, 141; and restructuring 79–81, 141, 244–5, 254
neonatal mortality rate 101
Netherlands 99, 249
never-married mothers 215
Newfoundland 229
New Democratic Party (Canada) 203
New Zealand: and civil unions 4; and Caesarean births 100; and child support 222; and equity program 175; and family model 123; *in vitro* fertilization 107; and Hague Convention 220, 231; and lone mothers 206; and midwives 103; parental benefits 123, 134, 237; and restructuring 60; and social housing 181
Neysmith and Chen 80
North American Free Trade Agreement 66, 79

obstetricians 99, 102, 104, 111
occupational segregation 115

Ontario 190, 196
Orloff, Ann 56

Pampel and Adams 56
parental: leave and benefits 126–35, 204, 236–238, 240; rights 219
parenthood: and employment 113, 122; and maturity 109; and 'normality' 96; parenting plan 219; shared parenting 219, 230; weekend parents (fathers) 220
Parenting Allowance (Australia) 144, 199
Partnerships on Domestic Violence (Australia) 230
part-time work 66–8, 121, 122, 174, 203, 244
papal warning 3
paternity 218, 223
path dependency of policy 41
pay equity 115, 250–1
payments for care 206. *See also* care work; Domestic Purposes Benefit; Parenting Allowance
Peck, Jamie 21
Pedersen, Susan 48
Phipps, Shelly 130
physical punishment of children 242. *See also* children: abuse of
Pierson, Paul 41, 62
political: discourse 6, 49, 249; left/right 61, 199, 249, 250
politics of choice 38, 106, 111, 122, 200, 239
'politics matter' 40, 236
population aging 33, 40, 85, 86
pornography 73, 161
'post-divorce family' 214, 233
post-Fordism 253
poverty: and children 46, 55, 61, 76, 155, 169, 171–2, 177, 197, 204, 211, 214, 218, 223, 240; 'deserving poor' 44; reducing 169; of time 122, 140
power-resource theory 43
preschools 239
primary caregiver 219
private/public responsibility 49, 61
privatization 79, 90, 110
protection plans 243
Pryor and Rodgers 214, 216
public discourse. *See* political: discourse

Quebec 47, 147–8, 193, 195–6, 203, 217

rape 92–3
refugees 71
remarriage 216
re-partnering 215–16
reproductive health and services 84, 247
replacement rate 29, 237
'resident parent' 219, 220. *See also* children: custody and access
'restructuring,' definition of 16
retrenchment 62, 253
rights: human 39; reproductive 39, 88, 89; father's 95, 218, 220, 230, 243; of foetus 93, 95
Rudd, Elisabeth 55

Sainsbury, Diane 54
same-sex couples 4, 14, 26–8, 73, 211, 243, 251
Scandinavian countries 33, 126, 147, 149, 179, 207, 239
'second shift' 117, 120
sex: education 91, 247; separation of marriage and 37
sexuality 87; double standard for 86

sexually transmitted diseases 90
Shaver, Sheila 54, 55
Shaver and Bradshaw 55
shelter movement 50
shift work 68
Social Charter (European) 76, 77, 78, 105, 121, 129
social: conservatives 249–50; exclusion 174; housing 180; insurance 44–5, 237–8; reproduction 54; rights 253 (*see also* rights: human); spending 46, 180, 253
Social Union Framework Agreement (Canada) 195
'soft politicking' 3, 76, 80
Sole Parent Pension (Australia) 197, 200. *See also* Parenting Allowance
'special needs' children 150–1, 200
sperm donation 109
state: intervention, principles of 159; support for families 56 (*see also* family support); support for women 54
stepfamilies 216
subsidiarity 94
subsidies: for childcare 145, 239–40; for housing 183
substance abuse 86
support, spousal 217. *See also* family: support
Sweden 46, 92, 99, 178, 205

Taylor-Gooby 118
taxation 46, 60, 145, 181, 184, 191, 196, 221, 240–3, 249, 254
Te Kohanga Reo 150
technological change 35, 37–8
teenage: birth rate 32; pregnancy 32, 86, 246
telework 35, 120

terrorism 74
Thatcher, Margaret 44, 182
time-budget surveys 136
time poverty 122, 140
Townsend, Peter 75
trade unions 44, 63, 118, 203, 244, 248
transition houses 243, 247
transnational: organizations 12, 74, 75; citizens 38
tuition fees 246
Turkey 209
two-earner family 51, 122, 250

underclass 206
'undertakings' 225
unemployment 68–9
UNICEF 76, 104, 162, 170
Uniform Child Custody Jurisdiction and Enforcement Act (US) 227–8
United Kingdom 216; and child benefits 241; and Hague Convention 226, 231. *See also* England and Wales
United Nations 5, 35, 76, 84, 87, 104, 110
United States: and Caesarean births 101; and child support 223; Constitution and gay marriage 27; Constitution and parental benefits 134; and Hague Convention 227; and home births 98; and lone parenthood 216; and parental benefits 130, 134, 237; and sex education 90; and welfare 56, 241, 245
universality 207

Vanier Institute of the Family 14
Vienna Declaration 88
violence against women 51, 224–32, 243, 247

'visible minorities' 71; and birth rates 32

Walby, Sylvia 78
welfare: fraud 14; programs 46; wage-earner's welfare state 47; 'welfare laggards' 59, 81; 'welfare mothers' 178, 241, 252 (*see also* lone parents); welfare-to-work programs 190, 204, 239, 246
welfare regimes 42–54, 63, 235; conservative 44; corporatist 44; feminist critiques of 48; gender and 48–51, 54; liberal 43; residual 43; social democratic 45, 251, 252
well-being: of family 180, 255; health and 85
Wennemo, Irene 56
Weston and Parker 29
'wifely labour' 55
widows 49
Winterton Report 98
women's groups/movements 54, 63. *See also* feminism: advocacy groups

'women's liberation' 114
Woodward, Ferguson and Belsky 215
work: balancing work and life 35, 138; cycle, two-phase 119; incentives 204, 205; and gender 68, 116–17, 136, 210, 238; low paid 70; male model of 238; non-standard 35, 113; part-time 66–8, 121, 122, 174, 203, 244; patterns 34–5 (*see also* gender: and work); shift 68; standard 78, telework 35, 120; welfare-to-work programs 190, 204, 239, 246; 'workless' households 52 (*see also* lone parents)
workplace, flexible 34, 120
World Bank 75
World Health Organisation 76, 84, 90, 99, 104, 110, 112
World Trade Organization 75, 79
Wu, Zheng 25

Yeates, Nicola 19, 21

zero population growth 35